B POSITIVE!

A Memoir by Dai Henley

en Press

© Dai Henley 2010

All rights reserved

No part of this publication may be reproduced, stored in a retrieval system, or transmitted in any form or by any means, without the prior permission in writing of the publisher, nor be otherwise circulated in any form of binding or cover other than that in which it is published and without a similar condition including this condition being imposed on the subsequent purchaser.

First published in Great Britain by Pen Press

All paper used in the printing of this book has been made from wood grown in managed, sustainable forests.

ISBN13: 978-1-907499-18-0

Printed and bound in the UK
Pen Press is an imprint of Indepenpress Publishing Limited
25 Eastern Place
Brighton
BN2 1GJ

A catalogue record of this book is available from
the British Library

Cover design by Dai Henley and Zip Imagesetters,
Romsey, Hants, UK

Acknowledgements

When I joined a writing class three years ago, I had no idea of the amount of work required to get my story written and published. I therefore owe a great deal of gratitude to all those who've helped me realise my ambition.

So thanks to:

Brendan McCusker, my brilliant, kind and patient tutor, and fellow members of my class whose critiques helped me be a better writer

The production team and editors at Indepenpress

Susan Swalwell, my friend who helped by proof-reading and offering editorial advice

And most of all to my wife, Lorraine, who apart from reading my story several times, correcting errors and improving my memory, had to put up with my unbridled enthusiasm for the project which has given me such immense joy.

Wessex Heartbeat is a charity whose mission statement reads;

"That everyone affected by heart conditions receives the best possible support."

I had cause to test it and am grateful to the charity for providing such a high level of care which is why I'm delighted to be able to pass on to them a proportion of the proceeds from the sale of this memoir.

Contents

CHAPTER 1
Early Nuturing — 1

CHAPTER 2
"What do you mean, we're moving?" — 17

CHAPTER 3
Adolescence in Eaton Road — 29

CHAPTER 4
The best days of your life? — 36

CHAPTER 5
It all happens at once — 54

CHAPTER 6
Turbulent times in work and play — 67

CHAPTER 7
Confessions, decisions, a birth and a death — 82

CHAPTER 8
Juggling sport, career and married life — 92

CHAPTER 9
Cars for life! — 105

CHAPTER 10
My new rugby club — 122

CHAPTER 11
Tourist, thespian and barrister — 132

CHAPTER 12
Career fast track – with problems! — 140

CHAPTER 13
A fresh business challenge! 155

CHAPTER 14
Guilt, family upheaval and a change of relationship 165

CHAPTER 15
Vet's rugby and touring – again! 182

CHAPTER 16
Thrilling business opportunities 193

CHAPTER 17
Software developments – South African connections 201

CHAPTER 18
Rugby coaching – dream cottage – health shock 212

CHAPTER 19
Golf – a four letter word ending in F! 224

CHAPTER 20
The rugby club presidency 239

CHAPTER 21
Another house move, another health scare 244

CHAPTER 22
Happy families – business and pleasure! 253

CHAPTER 23
The travel bug 267

CHAPTER 24
Retirement and round-the-world trips 280

CHAPTER 25
Epilogue 293

"At times our own light goes out and is rekindled by a spark from another person. Each of us has cause to think with deep gratitude of those who have lighted the flame within us."

Albert Schweitzer

CHAPTER 1
Early Nuturing

"You're a persistent little so and so, aren't you Henley?" The sound was totally familiar to me. It was spoken in the distinctive South Wales dialect I knew so well and yet was strangely out of place in the school gym of the St Albans Grammar School for Boys I'd just joined. I hadn't really thought of myself as anything other than just another 12-year-old trying to impress his gym teacher.

But this was no ordinary gym teacher. This was Bryn Meredith, the Wales and British Lions rugby hooker in the 1950s. He was built as you'd expect an ex-coalminer to be built. His unbelievably broad shoulders and narrow waist suggested immense power, something I experienced first-hand when I was caught talking during his demonstration of rope climbing – his favourite punishment was a vicious swish of the rope against the back of your legs. To say he was a cult figure in the school would be the greatest of understatements. So, for the great Bryn Meredith to call me persistent, I regarded as a compliment. It's only in later years I realised that this is probably my greatest gift. It's been a vital ingredient in determining my life. You can't learn it – it's just a result of a lucky dip into your gene pool.

The accent was so familiar because I was born in 1942 in Galon Uchaf, a council estate on the outskirts of Merthyr Tydfil. I lived there for those first 11 highly impressionable years of my life and developed the broadest of Welsh accents. This was surprising because my parents, Sid and Ruby, were as English as roast beef. My mother was born in Walthamstow and my father was born in Bailey's Lane, Tottenham, close to the Spurs football ground that became his Mecca – he was a life-long supporter. They'd both been married before.

Mum was having a particularly difficult time. She'd left an abusive husband and lived in a squalid little flat with two children,

Les aged 11 and Ivy aged 14, whilst trying to make a living doing needlework for wealthy families. It was so bad that at the time they met, my mother had, a year earlier, sent Les to a children's home, something she always regretted. She kept Ivy though, which has never been satisfactorily explained within the family. Maybe she thought that although Les was younger, as a boy he could handle the situation better than Ivy. When I grew to an age where I understood such matters, I realised it did have a profound effect on Les. He was sensitive, shy and introverted.

My father had just separated from his first wife who'd run off with someone called Alexander. Until it was explained to me several years later, I could never understand why every time the song written by Irving Berlin, and sung by Al Jolson, *Alexander's Ragtime Band* came on the radio, my father would, very uncharacteristically, lose his temper, shouting for someone to "turn that flippin' radio off!" The band was very popular in the 1940s and 50s, so this charade was a regular occurrence!

Sid, then aged about 40, fell in love with Ruby who was three years younger. Within a very short period, he made up his mind to do two things: get Les out of the children's home and move somewhere new with Ruby, Les and Ivy where they could restart their lives as a "married couple" with a family. Being known to be "living in sin" was a serious blight on your family in the 1940s.

It must have been an enormous step for them to decide to leave London and move to Merthyr Tydfil. Although the blitz in London was horrific (like many Londoners, they never knew whether they would survive the next night's bombings) they left behind many friends and family, although my widowed grandmother on my mother's side, Lily (Nan to me), joined us in Wales in 1952.

Insisting that Les be taken out of the children's home to join the new family was so typical of my dad. He was caring, polite and unassuming, a true gentleman, but his greatest attribute was his unfailing sense of fairness, which, fortunately, I've inherited. I regard this as another gift nature, or my dad, bestowed upon me. Had my business life not taken the direction it did, I would have almost certainly studied Law. Even now I sometimes visit the Criminal Courts of Justice at the Old Bailey and dream at the prospect of being a barrister! Any injustice makes me angry!

On November 2nd, 1942, a true love child was brought into the world, courtesy of the midwives at Merthyr General Hospital. Christened David, I was regarded as "the ultimate gift" by my mother and father as it was unusual to have babies at their advanced ages. My new half-brother and half-sister were delighted too! Although I was christened David, my brother always called me "Dave". Outside the family, especially in Wales, I was known as Dai, Welsh for David.

I never really knew what the term "spoilt" meant. It's generally a derogatory term but if "spoilt" means being nurtured and cared for and loved by everyone around you, then I was "spoilt".

Growing up in Galon Uchaf was idyllic. However, the surroundings could never be described as such! The council estate consisted of 14 avenues, unoriginally numbered from one to 14! I was born in First Avenue, but in the first 11 years of my life we moved to Fifth Avenue and then to Third Avenue. I think it was to do with the neighbours.

Lily Trailer was a good example. She was a tubby, stooped, ginger-haired woman who dressed scruffily and stank of a mixture of body odour and whiskey. She always pushed an old dilapidated pram that was used for shopping or for transporting anything she found on the streets or in dustbins that may prove useful.

She was the first eccentric I'd known. Although I never went into her house, my mother told me she'd used a wooden toilet seat as a picture frame! She was also the scourge of the local Co-op, asking for any cracked eggs or broken biscuits for free. On one occasion when the shopkeeper said he hadn't any broken biscuits, she replied, "I don't suppose you could break me a few?"

In the middle 1800s, Merthyr was a prosperous town – its wealth generated mainly from the iron and steel industries and coalmines that fuelled the Industrial Revolution. Its location too, at the head of the Rhondda Valley, was a major advantage. However, since the 1930s, recession had taken a very heavy toll on the town and unemployment reached epidemic proportions, from which it has never fully recovered. The coalmines around Merthyr, too, began to yield less of the black stuff.

Galon Uchaf was built to house the neediest people of the town and the estate was really just one notch up from being a slum. The houses were clad in the same dirty grey, pebble-dashed concrete, which seemed to reflect both the mood, which was sombre, and the climate, which was invariably damp. We were surrounded by houses with boarded-up windows where either the tenants or the local council couldn't afford to replace the broken glass. They all had outside toilets which were dark and dank, a place you didn't linger too long. Toilet paper consisted of newspapers cut into squares and rammed onto a spike or large nail hammered onto the inside of the wooden door. Some houses were in a state of disrepair with gardens overflowing with weeds. I remember a few homeless dogs roaming the streets. Washing lines running the length of the gardens always seemed full of grey washing. Many of the kids I grew up with wore dirty and ill-fitting clothes.

I'm sure my parents didn't know any of this when they decided to move from London. I remember, aged nine or ten, thinking our surroundings shouldn't be like this. I don't know why I had this thought because I hadn't experienced any other kind of location, except when we occasionally visited relatives and friends back in London. Perhaps it was because the contrast was so great.

I don't remember them having too many friends although socialising was hardly a major priority for the residents of Galon Uchaf! The side effects of the war had an impact, too. Although bombs never fell on Merthyr, the food shortages and other deprivations made life difficult. I never saw a real banana until my brother, who'd joined the Merchant Navy for a year, brought home several green bunches from the West Indies when I was nine years old. We placed them in the airing cupboard for a few days until they miraculously turned yellow. Such an odd shape, yet the taste and texture was unlike anything I'd experienced before. I still adore them!

One thing we never went short of was coal. There were dozens of slag heaps surrounding our town. I would be sent out about once a week with two buckets, usually joined by several other children and adults to pick through the latest offerings. One bucket I filled with coke – a by-product of coal used for smelting in the steel works – and one with slabs of brittle coal pieces. The coal was used for starting the fires and coke, which was slower burning, used for topping up. It was dirty work and my fingernails looked like I'd painted them jet-black!

My brother had left school at 14 and managed to obtain an apprenticeship as a stocking machine fitter, which meant setting up and minding the huge machinery at the famous Kayser Bonder factory in Dowlais, just outside Merthyr. This proved to be a sound decision as he was rarely out of work and once qualified, the job paid well.

My sister apparently found Wales so dull that after 12 months and now aged 18, she joined the Women's Army and was promptly billeted back to London, which, as it was still wartime, she found very exciting. Ivy was a lively, fun-loving girl, always laughing and game for anything, a trait she carried throughout her life. Within a further 12 months, she'd met and married a fellow soldier, Bob, also 18, who came from the East End of London. He shared Ivy's *joie de vie* and passion for "jitterbugging", a manic dance craze performed to music that was a forerunner of rock 'n' roll.

Bob had seen some action during the war in Burma and I remember quizzing him when I was at that curious age of about 12 and wanted to know if he'd killed anyone. He had to be pressed about anything to do with the war but he admitted that he *had* killed a man. This was so uncharacteristic of him, that on further badgering, he explained that he once found himself unexpectedly face to face with an armed Japanese soldier and it was simply a case of kill or be killed. This left a lasting impression on me but I suspect nothing as deep as on Bob. Neither he nor I mentioned it again.

My father landed a job straight away as a foreman at a button factory, also in Dowlais, and he often shared a bus to work with Les. He didn't appear to have any particular qualifications for this job. He'd previously worked as a clerk in Dents glove factory in London, but because so many of the younger men were fighting Hitler, there were plenty of vacancies in British factories.

When I was older, probably about six or seven, he often took me to the factory on Saturday mornings when he would catch up on paperwork and give me the task of counting out the buttons for stocktaking. The smell of the paint used for the buttons was very distinctive and even now, when I sniff the odour of cellulose used to thin the paints, it evokes warm memories.

Mr Adler who owned the factory was a plump Jewish man who was very demanding. Dad must have got on well with him though, since he invited the whole family to watch the Coronation in 1953 on probably the only television set in Merthyr – what a treat!

Like many housewives of that era, my mother's role was to ensure there was always a meal waiting when Dad and Les returned from work, to nurture me and to make the household budget stretch to match the wages Dad and Les brought home each week. Not only did she do a great job on all counts, she found time to indulge in her greatest passions: gardening, cooking and playing the piano. She was expert at all three and although in later years I inherited the gardening bug, I can't cook and still don't know the difference between the black and white keys on a piano!

I have very few regrets in my life but this is one of them. It's entirely my fault. Often she'd ask me to come and sit with her whilst she taught me how to play. But by that time I was deeply involved in my own passion – playing football with my pals. I'd give anything now to be able to walk up to a piano in a pub and pump out the kind of tunes my mother was famous for. She played in the style of Charley Kunz and Winifred Atwell, both renowned for playing jolly, happy numbers.

I've since thought a lot about the philosophy of parenting – when do you *insist* on something being done and when do you give free rein to your kids allowing them to express themselves? I so wish Mum had insisted.

My earliest sporting memories began when I started at Penydarren Junior mixed school aged five and discovered playground football. The school was two miles away from home and unless the weather was awful I'd walk with several other children across a couple of roads and through a field almost always full of sheep or cattle. Ken Adams Morgan was the head teacher who seemed to take *all* the lessons. He was a large, grey-haired, grey-bearded, fearsome-looking man but despite this appearance was patient and kind. His features reminded me in later years of a fire and brimstone preacher you'd see in the Western movies.

We never had a proper school football team until I was ten, but those playground matches every break-time had me hooked. We were only allowed to use a tennis ball and it required considerable skill to control. Teams of 20-a-side were common and we played in the clothes we went to school in – no uniforms for primary schools in those days! The goals were hand-painted onto the walls at both ends of the playground. My mother continually complained about having to buy new shoes every few months, not because the soles had worn through but because the toes had disintegrated through playing football on concrete!

After the two-mile walk home, I'd have tea, usually something wonderful my mother had cooked that day, then listen to *Dick Barton – Special Agent*, a wonderfully exciting children's radio programme that always left you in suspense at the end of each 15-minute episode. This show was incredibly popular with a record 15 million listeners, almost a third of the population, tuning in. It began in 1946 and was taken off the air in 1951 because the government were concerned about the potential bad influence it could have on adolescent boys! This was despite the scriptwriters' strict adherence to 13 codes of conduct, such as: no sex, no booze, no bad language and all violence must be limited to "clean socks to the jaw!" Such a programme wouldn't get off the ground today!

The second the programme ended, I'd be out again to play football either down the "Dell", a flat field just behind Fourth Avenue or, if it was too wet, or too dark, outside my house in Third Avenue. In both locations, someone's jacket was put down for goalposts, causing many arguments whether it was a goal or not. My pals turned up at different times and joined the game, which went on all evening or, if we were playing outside my house, until my mother called out from the front door, "David, it's about time you came in to go to bed!"

There were certain protocols that *had* to be followed. As each boy arrived they'd join the team alternately. They'd also have to spend the first ten minutes in goal or until there was a goal scored against them, which was hardly a great incentive to make saves! You couldn't choose which position to play except that the younger boys, my best pal George Mackinney and I starting in that category, were always stuck out on the wing. The most exciting games were usually under the gas streetlights in Third Avenue and I remember once playing with a tin can when we punctured our one and only ball!

George was a very good footballer. His parents were Scottish and his father worked at the local ICI gas works. As we progressed up the pecking order of street football, he became a star player and as his best mate I enjoyed some reflected glory.

Another pal George and I got on well with was Alun Jones, who lived near George in Fifth Avenue. He was four years older than us and saw to it that we weren't bullied or intimidated by the older boys on the estate. Alun was an outstanding goalkeeper. He was tall and very athletic. When he was 14 he was offered a trial for Wales Schoolboys in Cardiff, 25 miles south of Merthyr Tydfil. His father couldn't take him so my dad took me, George and Alun by bus one Saturday morning. We were really excited for Alun, but he only had one save to make in the entire match whilst the opposing goalkeeper had plenty to do and played a blinder. Alun didn't progress. This struck me as grossly unfair but he went on to play some seriously good football although never quite made the big time — a great disappointment to the Galon Uchaf boys.

My obsession with football was fuelled at home too. My brother played for his works team, Kayser Bonder FC and my dad, much to Mum's mild annoyance, was the team manager. This entailed, amongst other duties, Mum having to wash and dry by hand the team's kit at home each week! Dad took me to some of the matches, which were played on a pitch affectionately known as "the Bont". The playing surface was simply coal, coke and ash rolled flat into a semi-hard surface that just about took a stud. Very often after a match, my mother prepared an iodine concoction and applied it to Les's inevitable cuts and sores that were full of the colliery waste from the pitch.

In summer, we played cricket with the same group of boys from the council estate, although there was always a football match being played as well. I was quite keen on cricket at first and as a left-arm bowler, I had some limited success. For me though, it lacks the dynamism of football and rugby, which were more aligned to my impatient nature! Although I tried to get into cricket seriously later in life, another factor that put me off the game was that weekend matches were almost invariably being cancelled because of inclement weather. I'd look forward to a game all week and then be so let down, I'd become quite depressed!

When Ken Adams Morgan announced one morning at assembly, that Penydarren Junior mixed school were to start a football team,

I was ecstatic with joy and so sure to be picked. Then came the very first setback of my ten-year-old life. I wasn't selected! I was devastated. My parents and brother Les were very supportive but no amount of sympathy could console me. On the Saturday morning of the first match, ironically played at "the Bont", I watched from the sidelines with my kitbag at my side just in case someone didn't turn up; no substitutes were allowed in those days. My emotions were in turmoil; I didn't want us to lose or not play well, yet on the other hand how would I get a game if all went successfully? Fatefully, the team didn't play well and we lost.

The very next Saturday, I *was* selected! I had an overwhelming feeling of wanting to prove that I should have been picked in the first place. I literally ached with a desire to do well. We met at the Penydarren school gate at 9.30 am and were taken by bus to the Heolgerrig school grounds, five miles further up the valley. The pitch was level and the grass lush and there was a much larger attendance than in the first match. Unfortunately, my father couldn't attend because he had to work on Saturdays, which was a great disappointment to me.

There are certain events in anyone's sporting life, which can only be described as *ethereal.* You're elevated to a higher level from everyone else or indeed from anything you'd achieved before. No matter what you attempt, it comes off. Everything you do feels effortless. Golfers call it being "in the zone". I've experienced this feeling only about five or six times in a sporting career spanning nearly 60 years.

My performance at Heolgerrig School that Saturday morning was one such event. We won three goals to nil and I scored a hat trick! I glided over the turf covering almost every inch of the pitch. Every time I had the ball I did something useful with it and I began to hear some of the crowd murmuring compliments about "this kid on the wing". After the match I tried not to look too smug but inside, I was elated. I couldn't wait to get home and tell Dad who, although delighted, warned me I'd now set a standard I'd be expected to maintain. How right he was. Although I played for the school team in every match after that I never played as well.

Our winter weekends fell into a distinctive pattern. Friday nights were reserved for preparing for Saturdays' matches. We'd ensure my brother's team kit was packed up in a large kitbag, first checking that all the shirts, which had lace-up ties around the neck, were clean, any rips or tears having been repaired by Mum. Les and I cleaned our boots with dubbin, a greasy leather preserver, until they were immaculate. Football boots were large, cumbersome slabs of leather with the sides high enough to protect your ankles. The soles, before studs were introduced in the mid-1950s, had leather bars nailed across them. Often, during a match on hard grounds, the nails would pierce the sole through to your feet. From somewhere, Dad managed to obtain a cobbler's last, so it was an important job on Friday evenings to ensure any offending nails were hammered back into place! Shin pads were made of split bamboo cane enclosed within a slim plastic covering. Very often the bamboo shoots would penetrate the covering at the bottom and dig into your instep so you had to apply sticky tape to hold them in place.

Saturdays were the highlight of the week, especially for the men and the boy of the household. My game was always in the morning and Les played in the afternoon. Saturday evening, we'd spend listening to Sports Report on the radio and Dad carefully wrote down the results in the paper so that he could check the pools coupon later. Woe betide anyone making a noise during this exercise!

The Spurs result, of course, was always the most eagerly awaited. Dad's enjoyment of the rest of the weekend would depend on it. Immediately after the results were checked against Dad's pools selection, bringing the invariable sigh of failure to predict eight draws, we'd have tea of baked beans on toast, always followed by home-made, delicious fruit cake or my particular favourite, pancakes with lemon juice and sugar, both lovingly made by Mum. Occasionally, she'd buy some cakes – one type in particular went down well – forever known in our family as "four penny ha'pennies". She had no idea what the shop called them so she christened them after the price! They were huge, shaped like a small loaf of bread and made of a soft, sweet, baked dough, filled with cream that oozed out when you bit into them. They were delicious! It's little wonder I grew up with a sweet tooth. Later in life, if I went to a pub for lunch, consisting of a pint of bitter and a pork pie, I'd *have* to eat a Mars bar to finish!

If playing football was *my* passion, supporting Tottenham Hotspur (the Spurs) was my dad's. He was overjoyed when Cardiff City won promotion to the First Division in 1953. He took me to Ninian Park in Cardiff to see them play the Spurs three times whist we were in Wales. This was my first experience of being in a ground holding 36,000 people, the majority all standing. I'd been brought up a Spurs supporter so I knew all the players' names and could recite the team in my sleep. They had such wonderful players. Alf Ramsey, who went on to become Sir Alf after managing England to World Cup glory in 1966, Ted Ditchburn, the goalkeeper, who still holds the record for the most consecutive appearances, 247 – he missed just two games in eight seasons – and Bill Nicholson, who went on to manage Spurs in their best ever seasons in the 1960s and 70s when they won practically everything!

We always went into the ground early so we could watch the brass bands parade up and down the pitch and the stands fill up. The anticipation was palpable and the supporters of both sides affable and good-natured. When the whistle finally blew to start the match, I'm sure the roar could be heard in Merthyr! The most disconcerting part though, was the surge of the crowd whenever they wanted a better view of an exciting period of the game. In retrospect, it was really quite dangerous, yet to me it was thrilling! If the adults thought it was too perilous, they'd pass the smaller children over the heads of the spectators down to the pitch-side out of harm's way; unfortunately, it never happened to me! Leaving the ground as soon as the match was over was another hazard to be avoided. We tried it once and my feet never touched the ground for about 30 yards as everybody swarmed to the exits!

Sundays were an eclectic mix of washing and drying the football kit, roast dinner, Sunday school in the afternoon and sometimes chapel in the evenings. After breakfast, Mum placed the dirty kit into a bath full of water and suds and then rubbed it against a steel washboard to get rid of the dirt. (Ten years later, I'd be using this piece of corrugated iron as a musical instrument in my skiffle group!) Then the kit was taken out and placed in the sink whilst the bath was re-filled with clean water. The shirts, shorts and socks were thrown in and rinsed out. In our back yard we had a huge mangle and it was my job to help Mum feed the heavy, sodden kit through the rubber rollers before it was hung out to dry. She warned me a hundred times, "Don't get your fingers too close to the rollers, David, how many more times do I have to tell you!" She was paranoid about anything untoward happening to her "Darling David" or her "Little London Welshman" as she often called me!

The Sunday roast dinner was the highlight of the weekend for Dad, Les and I. Meat and many types of vegetables were still scarce but Mum always found ingenious ways to put a wholesome meal on the table. She was particularly adept at puddings and cakes. She seemed to be cooking all week so that on Sundays we had a feast. Chocolate éclairs made with choux pastry were her speciality and because they never tasted as fresh the next day and we didn't have a refrigerator, a dozen of them *had* to be consumed either after the roast or at teatime! I don't know where she got her supply of chocolate from – it was still rationed for a good few years after the war but these culinary delights appeared quite regularly! I'm sure this wasn't the usual diet on Sundays in Galon Uchaf!

I really enjoyed Sunday school, which was held in a corrugated iron building at the bottom of Second Avenue and doubled as a social centre. My parents were not religious, and it was never discussed at home. However, they clearly wanted me to have some exposure to the Scriptures so that I could make up my own mind. Sometimes they took me to the chapel for the six o'clock evening service. Despite this exposure I never became hooked on religion but my most abiding memory is of the singing. There is nothing quite like the sound of a Welsh male voice choir. Whatever the hymn, they summed up the euphoria, passion or pathos of emotions in such a moving way. Even today, when the choir and the spectators sing the Welsh National Anthem at rugby internationals, like many Welshmen, I admit to feeling a huge lump in my throat and sometimes I'm close to tears.

My parents, Dad in particular, set a fine example of how to live a "Christian" life without believing in God. They always looked for the best in everyone and were always the first to help out in any emergency. Throughout their lives they genuinely reached out the hand of friendship. I encountered many examples of this admirable characteristic over the years. They were taken advantage of a few times but they reasoned that life-enhancing fellowship was returned on many more occasions.

My parents were fanatical about my education, possibly because they weren't educated particularly well and neither were Les or Ivy. They regarded this obsession as a major contribution they could make as parents.

Strangely, this drive to get me educated only went as far as passing the 11+ exam and so get to a grammar school. I assumed they reasoned that once I got there, the rest was up to me. So up to the age of 11, homework simply *had* to be done ahead of playing football. There was a major incentive too. If I passed, a brand new top-of-the-range Raleigh bike with 3-speed Sturmey Archer gears was the much-coveted prize. I was suitably motivated! My parents sacrificed a great deal to provide this lure.

As well as playing football and doing my homework, another competitor for my time was *table* football. Subbuteo launched the game in the mid-1940s and it became an outstanding international success. The inventor, Peter Adolph, placed an advertisement in *The Boy's Own Paper*, a must-read comic if you were aged between eight and 15, purely to gauge the level of interest in a new game of table football.

He received postal orders to the value of £7,500 (equivalent to £200,000 today), from all over the country and went on to make a considerable fortune. The game was played on a green baize cloth marked out as a football pitch that was laid onto a table and complete with goals with nets, corner flags and, if you could afford them, battery-operated floodlights. The players were cut-out silhouettes, made of celluloid, and mounted on a half-inch-wide plastic, saucer-shaped base. They were propelled by the index finger and skilful exponents could engineer a way around the opposing celluloid players to strike the ball. I think I was the first to receive this game as a Christmas present but before long, about ten of us could claim to be reasonable players. Subbuteo encouraged the setting up of leagues and you could choose your favourite team's kit. Unsurprisingly, the Galon Uchaf league was up and running within weeks. Naturally, I was Tottenham Hotspur, and George Mackinney was Glasgow Rangers! This game became a national obsession with kids of all ages and some adults even started their own leagues. Subbuteo also supported a national competition with substantial prizes.

My brother Les often joined in and despite our 14 years difference in age, we became very close. He was my hero right up until he died in 2001, aged 73, and I often think of him. He got on really well with my father − his stepfather − and was, in many ways, like him. Les, too, was kind and gentle. He, literally, would not hurt a fly. I saw him on many occasions catch one that had been annoying him by covering it with a glass tumbler and sliding a thin piece of card between the rim and the base, trapping the fly and throwing it out of the back door!

He was also incredibly handsome and when he went out on a date, he was always dressed immaculately. He'd stand in front of the mirror in the sitting room for ages picking off imaginary pieces of cotton or fluff from his jacket and trousers. We'd tease him by pointing out some non-existent offending particles usually in a place he couldn't reach. Off would come the jacket and he'd examine it minutely like a forensic scientist!

He was petrified about losing his hair and he had dozens of bottles of fancy-coloured lotions he conscientiously applied morning and night. Although these lotions were "guaranteed to promote healthy growth" they didn't work!

He was once invited to a film premiere in London and he had his photograph taken with one of the lesser known, but outstandingly beautiful, female stars, whose name I never knew. This photo, resplendent in a silver frame, took pride of place for many years in my parents' various sitting rooms! Les looked every inch a film star too!

He also bought me some wonderful Christmas presents. I remember one in particular which was a wind-up model plastic army tank. I'd fill the gun barrel with white flour from Mum's pantry, and when I wound up the tank, it would miraculously fire with a loud "pop" and smoke emanated from the muzzle every few seconds! Very realistic! Every year he'd buy me the *Sunday Chronicle Football Annual* and the *Charles Buchan Football Annual* − essential reading, but not necessarily just for me − Dad and Les enjoyed reading them as much as I did!

Although football was the number one sport followed and played intensely in the Henley household, boxing was a close second. My brother had a particular interest having learnt how to box during his National Service between 1947 to 1950. He boxed as a middleweight, around 12 stone, and he was, according to my father, very good. He visited fairgrounds that had an all-comer's boxing booth. The resident boxer would take on anyone and if you beat him over three rounds you'd win £2. The bruisers were ex-pros who knew all the tricks and often boxed 20 rounds a night. I don't think Les ever won, but Dad told me he always gave them a good fight. I was never allowed to watch; Mum thought it too brutal for a young boy to witness, although it added further credence to hero-worshipping my big brother!

Wales is famous for producing world-class boxers and Merthyr in particular produced some of the best. Jimmy Wilde was probably the most famous boxer to come from our town. He was an ex-coalminer who was the world flyweight champion between 1916 and 1923. Johnny Owens, too, was a world champion and tragically died after being knocked out by Lupe Pintor from Mexico in the 12th round in Los Angeles in September 1980. Dai Dower, Tommy Farr – who fought the great Joe Louis for the world title in 1937 – and Howard Winstone also from Merthyr, were all wonderful boxers. Eddie Thomas, a British, Empire and European welterweight champion in 1951, was born in Merthyr and trained in the Sunday school/social centre I attended. Les once sparred with him and Eddie Thomas accidentally knocked him out, so he didn't return! It was Eddie who coined the famous quote, "Children born in the tough valleys of Wales were so angry, they were born with their fists clenched!"

Despite these distractions, I dutifully did my homework and revised hard for the 11+ exam. I really enjoyed Penydarren school and came fourth out of 30 in my last year. I was not especially good at any one subject but pretty average across the board. I didn't feel any exceptional anxiety about winning a place at the grammar school even though, as the exam approached, it seemed to be the sole subject of conversation in the Henley household.

However, my apprehension was diluted, because in the last year, I was selected to play the King in the school play. I don't even remember auditioning for the part. My mother made the most superb King's robe and crown. The robe was a deep red material, covered with hundreds of silver milk bottle-tops, hand-shaped as stars, lovingly sewn on. It flowed behind me like a crimson tide. I had a beard stuck onto my face, which, complete with a crown of red and silver cloth and a black ostrich feather, completed the transformation from a short-trousered, bespectacled, primary school pupil to His Royal Highness, the King of England!

I can't remember what the play was or who else appeared in it. I just remember wearing the robe and crown at home on many occasions to the delight and amusement of my mother and father! I loved dressing-up and almost getting high on the smell of the semi-congealed, sticky glue used for the beard. This was my first taste of thespian life and I loved it!

This joy was considerably superseded by the news of my passing the exam! My mother said, "Do you know, Sid, I think this boy will be Prime Minister one day!" She really meant it!

So I got the top-of-the range Raleigh bike with the 3-speed Sturmey Archer gears and was the envy of my mates. What made it even more special for my parents was that I was one of only three boys from Galon Uchaf to pass. The other two were my best mate, George Mackinney, and Brian Ellison who lived in Seventh Avenue.

Cyfarthfa Castle Grammar School could not have been more different to Galon Uchaf. It was a magnificent baronial mansion built in 1825 by the owner of the iron works in Merthyr, Richard Crawshay; he was once the 50th richest man in the country. The castle was surrounded by meticulously maintained lavish gardens. The Ironmaster, as he was known, bequeathed the castle and grounds to the town council on his death as way of repaying society for the contamination and desecration his filthy industry had infected on the town. It became a co-educational grammar school and a museum in 1913. My proud parents took George and I there before we started school. It took our breath away.

CHAPTER 2
"What do you mean, we're moving?"

The weeks before my first day of term at Cyfarthfa Grammar School were a flurry of excitement, particularly for my parents. Their overwhelming fear was that I'd be ill-equipped, not in the educational sense but in respect of my appearance. No expense was spared and many further sacrifices made so that I had the very best navy-blue blazer with the grammar school crest proudly displayed on the left-hand breast pocket, grey flannel short trousers (we weren't allowed to wear long trousers until the second form), long, grey woollen socks with two yellow stripes encircling the top of them and the shiniest of black shoes. The shirts *had* to be white and you *had* to wear the school tie with the school crest. The school cap was dark-blue with yellow piping.

The crest was *very* dramatic. It showed the head of a barking dog surrounded by flames. "Cyfarth" is Welsh for barking and "fa" means a place – hence Cyfarthfa. The flames represented the furnaces of the iron and steel works. No-one has ever satisfactorily explained the origin of the barking dog. Under the crest was the school motto, *"Cadarn Pob Cyfiawn"* meaning "The Just are Strong" – powerful stuff for an 11-year-old!

My gym kit, too, was of the highest standard and was packed in a white calico draw-string bag. Everything was brand new including a pair of black plimsolls known in Wales as "daps". I may not have been the brightest boy to start secondary school in September 1954, but I guarantee I was probably the smartest!

I don't think anybody can prepare someone so young for a change of school. Your life is transformed from having an intimate knowledge of the teachers, your peer group, the school rules and a feeling of security, to an alien, intimidating and sometimes frightening environment. On the very first day during break, I saw smoke wafting up from the outside toilets. I was puzzled, but on further inspection I discovered the older boys – aged about 14 plus – dragging away on cigarettes! I was told in no uncertain terms to "bugger off!" and rather more menacingly, "If you tell anyone, you're for it!"

As a first year, you have absolutely no status whatsoever. Although never bullied myself, simply because I was tall for my age, several of my contemporaries were, and nothing was ever done about it. I suspect the teachers regarded it as a ritualistic part of growing up.

I settled in very well and particularly enjoyed Welsh language and singing lessons. One of the biggest changes, though, was my introduction to rugby. The rugby teacher (the term "coach" was unheard of at this level) had an innovative way of introducing us to the laws of rugby football. At the first lesson, he picked two teams, threw the ball to one and told them, by any means they liked, to ensure that the ball was touched down over the other team's try line. The team without the ball was simply told to stop them! There ensued the most wonderful free-for-all with the ball being kicked, thrown forward, thrown backward, passed and carried with great enthusiasm, amidst a great deal of noise!

Several fights broke out when some players were tackled vigorously without the ball; if they could be "taken out" for a few moments they couldn't contribute to the team! Each week the teacher gradually introduced laws; you could only pass backwards, you had to tackle around the legs and not the neck and definitely no punching or gouging! After the first two months the matches really took shape so that by then, the teacher could concentrate on developing individual skills. I loved it but it still took a poor second place to my first passion, football. I had no idea this was to change in the years that followed.

"I've got some news for you, son. We're moving to St Albans". This was at the end of the first term I'd enjoyed so much.

"Dad, what do you mean, we're moving?" I said incredulously.

This was so unexpected; I'd had absolutely no idea. My entire world was Galon Uchaf, the grammar school, Sunday school and playing football with my mates.

"Is Les coming too?" I asked.

"Yes he is, and we're moving in time for you to transfer schools straight after Christmas," Dad said, so firmly, I instinctively knew there was no point in arguing.

I was desperately disappointed. I'd had a fantastic start to life full of enjoyable fun, warm love and loyal friendships and now I had to start again.

My parents made all this possible, so I couldn't really complain. I've never learnt the reason why we moved back to the London area although it may have been something to do with my nan dying in March 1953. She came to live with us in Galon Uchaf about nine months previously and was bed-ridden all that time. I do know why St Albans was selected though. The Ballito stocking factory was based there and Les, who by now was fully qualified, had managed to get a good job working on the new craze, "fully-fashioned" seamless stockings, whatever they were!

My life in Galon Uchaf was punctuated with some wonderful memories.

Mum was very protective of her "Little London Welshman". In 1947 the country endured the worst winter for two centuries. From late January to the middle of March, Britain, South Wales in particular, was crippled by huge snowfalls, raging blizzards and a numbingly freezing cold climate. In some parts of Wales, snow fell nearly every day and drifted to over 20 feet. I remember as a five-year-old waking up one morning and seeing that the snow had drifted right up to my bedroom window! How exciting! I was allowed to sit on a homemade sledge, hastily put together by Dad, and whoosh down to ground level into his arms. It was so unremittingly cold for so long that my mother knitted me a balaclava.

This was no ordinary balaclava. It was bright yellow; it was the only colour wool she could get in ration-blighted Britain. It didn't just cover my face; it had a deep yoke down to the shoulders and upper chest so that no draughts could permeate my delicate neck. It fitted tightly around my mouth; I ended up with chapped lips whenever I wore it!

I'd developed a "lazy eye" when I was about five years old. Although not quite in the Buster Keaton class (he was a cross-eyed comic actor from the silent movie era) it was nonetheless very noticeable. Although an operation was discussed by my parents, the less invasive remedy was to have a pink plastic eye-shield placed over my "good" eye together with a pair of thin wire glasses with thick, bottle-end lenses, all supplied courtesy of the burgeoning National Health Service, introduced in 1947. The combination of the balaclava, the pink patch and the glasses made me look very odd but no-one in the family or my mates ever commented about my appearance! At least they could see me coming from quite a distance!

I still have a lazy eye but it didn't concern me too much until I discovered, rather belatedly, the opposite sex at about the age of 14. When I discussed my "affliction" with my parents, Dad, ever supportive and positive, said he thought it was an engaging feature and that the girls would find it attractive!

Wales in winter, especially in the valleys, was a *very* cold place, and much to our delight, it always snowed. Many a moonlit winter's evening was spent flying down the ice-covered slag-heap on just about anything that would slide: tin trays, pieces of cardboard, corrugated iron, purpose-made, shop-bought sledges and in my case, the homemade, wooden contraption.

I don't know how many runs we made during the course of the evening, but sliding down and trudging back to the top pulling our sledges kept us warm! My protective balaclava caused my head and ears to sweat profusely!

There was nothing to protect me, though, when, one summer's day, I fell down what I thought was a mountain but was really a huge grass-covered slagheap! Aged nine, my pals and I went to an open-air swimming pool known as Pant baths. It was an hour's walk away mainly along country roads but partly over a high, wild and windy moor called the Bryn. When we were ready to leave, I said I knew a short-cut over the "mountain" that would save us at least half an hour. Nobody took up my offer so, to prove them all wrong, I went on my own – big mistake! After 20 minutes I reached the top of the "mountain", which was about 400 feet high, but I couldn't see a path down the other side to the road lined with miners' cottages I knew would take me home. I gingerly set off, half-walking, half-stumbling down, and considering I had my swimming trunks wrapped in a towel under my arm, I thought I was making good progress.

Suddenly, I lost my footing and fell, feet first, for about 200 feet with my arms held above my head still clinging to my towel. This is when I realised the "mountain" had only a slim covering of grass disguising the hard, unforgiving coke and clinker that was now tearing at my unprotected arms and knees! When I reached the bottom, I looked a sorry mess. My face was tear-stained through crying, I had coal and coke dust in my bloody wounds and I was in a state of shock. In desperation I knocked at the door of a cottage.

A delightfully friendly lady opened the door and with a horrified look on her face ushered me inside to the parlour. She bathed my wounds as I stood in a galvanised metal bath and applied some Germolene to my wounds. She was the epitome of kindness and I was so grateful.

I trudged the half-mile or so back home and told Mum what happened expecting her to berate me for not coming home with my mates. Instead, I think she realised that probably for the first time in my young life, I was really scared, and so she gave me lots of hugs and a piece of home-made fruitcake!

Every Christmas, we went to London by coach, which took all day, and stayed with good friends of my parents, known to me as Auntie Vera and Uncle Charlie. They lived in Berber Road in Battersea and hosted wonderful parties. Dozens of friends and relations turned up and had a lively, boozy, happy time. My mother played the piano, responding to the cry, "C'mon, Ruby, give us another tune!" She played all night until her fingers ached. She hated repeating songs so she built up a vast repertoire.

Although she played mainly by ear, she could read a little so she took a huge bundle of sheet music with her. Anything she couldn't understand, she'd make up! If she didn't recognise a tune she'd ask you to hum a few bars and she'd be able to pick it up and improvise − what a gift! Everyone joined in the singing, which got more and more raucous as the night wore on and the alcohol released their inhibitions!

There were several children my age, so we had a wonderful time too, opening presents, being allowed to stay up late and joining in all the games. One evening we discovered some gas masks under one of the beds and had great fun putting them on and spooking some of the younger children. I suspect these masks should have been returned to the authorities after the war finished, but many people kept them as souvenirs. We found them quite difficult to put on and the rubber smell made us nauseous. The entertainment value, though, was well worth it!

The parties were as *metaphorically* intoxicating to us as they were *actually* intoxicating to the adults! Many times, having all been sent to bed, we crept downstairs, found a good vantage point, sitting on the stairs just out of sight, and watched the adults partying.

Uncle Joe, no relation, was the "life and soul of the party". He once offered to carry some of Auntie Vera's crockery into the kitchen. He pretended to trip and wobble about in an exaggerated way.

"Joe, that's my best china, don't you dare mess about!"

"Don't worry, Vera, it'll be ok." Then, he really *did* trip and the china flew everywhere, smashing into bits and pieces onto the unforgiving linoleum-covered floor. There was a second's silence and everyone, except Vera, collapsed with laughter and so did we, blowing our cover!

One Boxing Day morning, Dad's team, Spurs, were playing at home, kicking off at 10.30 am and he was adamant he was going to see them play, especially as it was his birthday. Mum accused him of rudeness to our hosts.

"You can't go, Sid. Vera won't save you lunch."

"I don't care if I have bread and cheese," Dad said. I thought this was the ultimate sacrifice. Auntie Vera's Boxing Day lunch of cold meats, baked potatoes with pickles, followed by the remains of the trifles was a sumptuous feast in my mind! If it was anything to do with the Spurs, though, my dad became uncharacteristically stubborn, so he went. He returned at about two o'clock, just as we were finishing the meal. As Dad sat at the table, Auntie Vera brought in a plate with a silver salver covering the contents. I'm sure he thought Vera and Mum had forgiven him but as the salver was removed with a flourish by Vera, there was just a slab of mouldy cheddar, half a pickled onion, some crisps and a few half-eaten biscuits!

The children sniggered but Dad pretended it was perfectly alright with him – so what, the Spurs had won! Halfway through, Mum took pity on him and he was allowed to help himself to the remnants of the banquet and was presented with a huge birthday cake!

After Christmas and before we returned to Wales, I received my first experience of entrepreneurship and recycling! One of the sons of the friends attending the parties asked me to go out with him early one evening. "We're going to get some free chips!" he said. It sounded good to me. The venture involved visiting the houses in the road we were staying and asking the occupants to give us any clean newspapers they'd finished with. Within half an hour we had more than enough to carry so we headed straight down to the chip shop. For every load we handed over we were given two-pennyworth of chips! We repeated this exercise about four times each night until the chip-shop owner had enough wrapping paper to last a week – so told us to "clear off!" We repeated the process with another chip shop with exactly the same outcome! I love chips, but eight-pennyworth a night for three nights was quite enough, even for me!

In those first 11 years in Wales, I went on many trips to the seaside to either Mumbles Bay in Swansea or to Barry Island near Cardiff. Our annual Sunday school outing was a special highlight. We travelled by train, a hissing, sooty, smoke-blackened steam locomotive from Merthyr station, carrying our sandwiches in a tin box and our swimming trunks and towel in a cloth kitbag. Although the journey to the coast was less than an hour, we were mesmerised by this form of travel. We got to the station early and stood on the platform adjacent to the locomotive and talked to the driver.

They were cult figures and most of the boys I knew aspired to become a train driver when they grew up. The huge, steel wheels attached to giant pistons with smoke bellowing out from underneath the engine exuded power. We begged the driver to let one of us stand on the footplate, a place where he sometimes stood to check the track ahead, so we could see the furnace. I was never lucky enough to do so, but some of my pals did and never let me forget it! Once ensconced in the carriage, first the guard's whistle blew, then the far more piercing, reverberating whistle of the steam engine signalled the start of the journey – how exciting!

Although Mumbles Bay has the most dramatic beach on the Gower peninsular, Barry Island was my favourite. From Cardiff, the only way to reach it in those days was by a small-gauge railway track with tiny carriages. The sun always seemed to shine and the seawater glistened like a myriad of jewels. The first thing we did. though, was to visit the shop to buy our "pop" to take onto the beach.

The shop was amazing! It was shaped like a giant apple, painted green and red on the outside, but the area from which you were served was designed to look as if someone had taken a huge bite out of it! This was painted white to complete the illusion.

We rushed down to the beach and spent the rest of the day in and out of the water until it was time for lunch. My sandwich box was an old, battered, square, red Oxo cube tin I seemed to have forever, not that it worried me: I was more interested in the contents, greedily washed down with the bottle of "pop". We were all completely shattered on the way back home and always slept well that night!

Other treats were trips with my parents to the cinema; "the pictures" my parents called them, or to the Theatre Royal in Merthyr where I once saw Old Mother Reilly. I knew there was something a little odd about the act but it wasn't until many years later I discovered "she" was a man in drag. "She" was very funny though; we all enjoyed the slapstick humour.

Sometimes Mum and I would meet Dad at the pictures as he came straight from work. She always brought him jam sandwiches for his tea that he munched whilst watching the film! One thing she *never* brought was an apple. She was convinced that if you bit into it, there could be a maggot or two lurking inside which you couldn't see in the dark! This doctrine has been adopted and handed down to succeeding generations of our family. I'm sure my mother would be pleased to know that she has saved them all from a gastric tragedy!

We regularly went to my grandmother's house in Brighton Avenue, Walthamstow in South-East London. "Nan" (real name Lily) was born in 1876 in Camberley, Surrey, and in 1899 married James Pope, born in 1869 in Lambeth, East London, son of Charles James Pope, a fireman based in Walthamstow. They had three children: my mother Ruby in 1903, born in a room above the fire station, Pearl in 1908, and Leslie, born in 1913, who, but for a last-minute change of heart would have been christened Garnet!

Uncle Les was born in Brighton Avenue and lived there all his life. "Grandfather Jim" died of cancer of the tongue in 1925, aged 56, and so Uncle Les for most of his early adult life looked after Nan.

She had amazing looks; very dark and swarthy with exceptionally long, pitch-black, glossy hair invariably tied back in pigtails that reached down to her waist. I remember her hair showed only a few wispy grey strands when she died, aged 76. She looked as if she would be more at home in a Spanish *casa* than at 23 Brighton Avenue! She never enjoyed good health and when we visited her, she was usually lying in bed in a darkened room and said very little. She exuded a mysterious, almost spooky countenance, reminiscent of Miss Havisham in Dickens' *Great Expectations.*

When she came to live with us in Wales during the final year of her life, 1952 (she was a widow for 27 years), she perked up; my mother said it was down to the Welsh air that "smelt like wine!" I remember sitting at the bottom of Nan's bed when I got home from school and she insisted I tell her about my day. She was always interested in my sporting exploits!

My grandfather was a very brave man. He joined the Navy and became a deep-sea diver at the age of 18 when this was a very dangerous profession. Nan told me the Navy were only just beginning to understand the effects of decompression and for this reason the maximum depth divers could attain was 300 feet. They were brought up agonisingly slowly but despite this, she said there were many casualties. She was very proud of his diving heritage. On one visit she bought me a toy diver. I used to place it in a bucket of water and recreated the air bubbles by blowing through a tube attached to the diver's helmet and imagine it was Grandfather Jim!

Mum and Uncle Les inherited their mother's continental looks, although Aunt Pearl, less so. Uncle Les cut a very dashing figure with his dark, moody looks, enhanced by a thin black moustache, so typical of the RAF officer he became. After leaving the RAF, he was employed as a chauffeur and had the use of the most magnificent black Humber Super Snipe motor car which was always gleaming on the outside and had the striking smell of leather inside. Although my brother Les was 15 years younger than Uncle

Les – he was always *Uncle* Les to the family – they often went out together whenever my brother went to London. There are some photos showing them wearing dinner jackets, smiling confidently, huge cigars in hand, looking very dashing!

Uncle Les never married but had a series of long-term, glamorous girlfriends, the longest serving being a blonde, called Joyce. She was a vivacious, curvy beauty with a pretty, expertly made-up face and wore brightly-coloured, flowing summer dresses. They were deeply into ballroom dancing and won many trophies, proudly displayed in the living room at Brighton Avenue.

My mother was always urging him to marry Joyce, but it never happened. I overheard Mum telling Dad in hushed tones, "She's got fed up of waiting for a ring so she's run off with a black man who can't dance *and* doesn't have a car!" This became another of those incidents you didn't mention within earshot of the family!

Uncle Les lived a lonely, reclusive life for many years after this happened and died in Whipps Cross Hospital, a somewhat Dickensian establishment, in 1990, aged 77. My sister Ivy and I went to Brighton Avenue to sort out his effects and we found a thousand pounds in one-pound notes in a jar in a kitchen cupboard. This was accompanied by a note to say this money was to cover his funeral expenses.

It was a common trait of my parents' generation to be worried there wouldn't be enough money left to pay for a decent burial so they would salt some cash away for this purpose. The thought of being buried in a pauper's grave was too shocking for them to contemplate.

This scenario was an exact replica of the situation Les, Ivy and I discovered when our mother died in 1981.

Our visits to London were in stark contrast to our visits to see Auntie Pearl. She'd married a farmer, Uncle Jack, who farmed in Widford, near Ware in Hertfordshire. She had a daughter born in 1930, Pearl junior, who was always referred to as "Cousin Pearl". I suspect either my family loved their own names or they lacked imagination! Auntie Pearl was a large, jolly, woman, always laughing and saw the funny side of every event.

Uncle Jack was a typical farmer. Although quite slight in build, he was immensely strong and had a quiet, positive manner and a great sense of humour. The highlight of the summer visit was the cutting of the corn. Uncle Jack allowed me and Cousin Pearl to sit on the trailer behind the tractor. He'd start on the perimeter of the field and gradually work his way in circles towards the middle. One of the effects of this process was that we saw the rabbits, as they were disturbed, scampering further and further towards the ever-decreasing centre of the corn field. When this last tiny circle of corn was ready to be cut, there must have been at least 20 rabbits anxiously considering their fate. At this stage, Uncle Jack took us back home on the tractor. I never understood why. Either it was because the rabbits would finally disperse and he could go back the next day to cut the remaining corn or, more ominously, he would fetch his shotgun, return to the field, and live off rabbit stew for months without us witnessing the act!

It only occurred to me many years later that our trips to see relations were almost always to my mother's side of the family. My father was the youngest boy out of seven children, five boys and two girls. His father (my grandfather, who I never met and was never discussed in my presence) was a letter sorter with the Post Office for many years. Arthur Henry Henley was born in 1861 in Islington, North London and married Mary Ann Gregory, born in 1864 in Shoreditch, less than a mile away, in 1885. All the eldest boys apparently obtained a good education – I've never discovered how, I didn't think letter sorting paid particularly well – but for some reason, maybe because of the need for the family to have some income, my father left school aged 13. This coincided with the start of the First World War and it's possible the two events were connected.

The four elder brothers did very well for themselves: one became a city banker and another built up a flourishing business manufacturing baby clothes. Dad was closest to his sister, Alice, who was six years younger and whom we visited occasionally in Wood Green in North London. We also visited one of Dad's brothers, Uncle Bert, the banker, who lived in a flat near Big Ben, Westminster. Being woken up every 15 minutes by the chimes didn't put Mum and Dad in the best of moods the next day!

My father's lack of education and the events surrounding his affair with my mother, a married woman with two children, and then "living in sin" with her and having a bastard child when he was 42, cemented the feeling of being ostracised by his side of the family. I'm convinced this is one of the reasons they moved to Wales to make a fresh start.

My mother, understandably, didn't have much time for Dad's family. It's obvious to me now why my parents, Mum in particular, were so insistent about me passing the 11+ exam and going to the grammar school and why she became so proud of me when I had some success in my business life.

So, in December 1953, we said our goodbyes to 11 Third Avenue, Galon Uchaf, Merthyr Tydfil, South Wales. I was so pleased my English parents moved there. Wales gave me the best possible childhood in an environment that, although materially bereft, was spiritually and personally highly rewarding and laid the most secure foundation and groundwork for my life ahead. Although I don't possess "Welsh blood", I'm honoured to share the passion that all Welshmen have for their country, their kinship and their generosity of spirit.

My mother's favourite name for me as her "Little London Welshman" was apt!

CHAPTER 3
Adolescence in Eaton Road

Number 14 Eaton Road, St Albans in leafy Hertfordshire was to be my new home for the next 12 years. It was a very simple, terraced house built in 1890 with three bedrooms, an outside toilet and, most importantly for my parents, a reasonably-sized garden big enough for my dad's vegetables and Mum's perennials. It had linoleum-covered floors, a tiny scullery, a place just for washing dishes rather than a kitchen, and dark wood-stained panelled walls. It also had a very old fireplace, with a black metal grate. My parents always complained that the chimney never had a good "draught", so the only way to get the fire going was to balance a poker vertically in the middle and place a newspaper against the upright to create a down-draught. Sometimes the result was *too* effective and the whole newspaper occasionally caught alight with the resultant panic and bad language! The open fire was good for toasting bread, though, using a trident-shaped toasting fork although the bread sometimes endured the same fate as the newspaper when impatience overtook sensibility!

There was no central heating, just fireplaces in every room including the bedrooms and so the sitting room "blizzy", always lit in winter, was *the* focal point of the house. My mother sat so close to it she developed wonderfully marbled, bluish, purple legs that gave the appearance of a rare French cheese.

This was a common sight amongst older ladies of that generation who spent most of their winter evenings sitting by coal fires! Mum and Dad often argued about whose turn it was to go and make some tea because everywhere else in the house was freezing! And as for going outside to fill the coal scuttle from the bunker in the back yard (the coal now purchased from the local coalman as opposed to being scraped from the slag heaps of Merthyr for free), this was absolutely no job for a woman according to Mum! I often went to bed wearing a coat over my pyjamas when I couldn't see out of the window because it was covered with a translucent film of milky ice – on the inside!

But this was the first house they'd owned, so for my parents, it was paradise! They paid £1200 and took out a mortgage of £1100. Dad was obsessed with paying it off, often spending Sunday mornings assiduously examining a huge, yellow-lined accounts ledger where he had plotted every payment due for the next 25 years. He took great delight in ticking off each payment and recalculating the debt! Although we all pulled his leg about it, I found myself doing the exact same thing in later years! Gradually, they were able to afford improvements, such as bringing the outside toilet within the house and extending the scullery into a kitchen. Dad, with help from Les, was always decorating, Mum having spent hours and hours poring over large quantities of enormous wallpaper pattern books and endlessly debating with herself which one she preferred!

Dad built a shed in the garden, which was his domain and usually off-limits to everyone when he was in residence. I discovered the reason why some years later when I spotted him dragging heavily on a herbal cigarette – at least that's what he told me! I was aghast! *My* dad didn't smoke. He said nothing, but put an index finger to his pursed lips and shook his head to signify I shouldn't tell anyone – especially Mum – I never did!

He spent hours in the garden tending to his beloved vegetables, wearing his "uniform" of baggy trousers held up with wide braces, collarless shirts and his battered panama hat. Every summer evening I'd hear, "Sid! Sid! Your dinner's on the table." Sid would invariably turn up on about the fourth or fifth increasingly shrill rendition of the call to dinner with deepest apologies to Mum that she only gracefully accepted by the time dessert was served!

Most evenings were spent around the living-room fire with the radio on, listening to concerts, plays, especially Saturday Night Theatre which was often a spine-tingling thriller, and of course, sport. My mother was an accomplished knitter and she made numerous pullovers, cardigans and sweaters that Dad, Les and I *had* to wear. My role on many such evenings was to hold my arms out in front of me for what seemed like hours on end, upon which she'd place a skein of wool so she could make it into a ball before using the knitting needles. I often complained that I couldn't understand why the wool wasn't supplied in balls in the first place. All evening, we'd hear the click-click of the needles and sometimes "Knit one, pearl one ..." as she read out the pattern to herself! I still have no idea what this means!

On other evenings, we'd adjourn to the sacred front room, usually only used when we had visitors, where we kept Mum's pride and joy, a Steinway upright with a piano stool you could hardly sit on as it was always over-stuffed with sheet music. She'd play us some of the latest additions to her repertoire of popular music of the 1950s and ask for our opinion. I think Dad was as much in awe of her playing as I was – it was always sublime!

My mother also loved crime novels and she probably read just about all of Agatha Christie's novels. Whilst Mum was engrossed in tales of murder and intrigue, Dad loved making up crossword puzzles from scratch. Despite his lack of education, he had a surprisingly good command of the English language and wrote magnificent letters, usually to relations, which he'd read out to us with the usual, almost tearful response from Mum, "Oh! Sid, that's wonderful!" Truly, they belonged to a Mutual Admiration Society!

Both Mum and Dad had great senses of humour and the repartee between them was always smart and quick. They always saw the funny side of any situation. I could make them laugh easily and I developed one "party piece" that had them rocking with unbridled laughter. A popular musical work often played on the radio in the early 1950s when I was about 12 years old was *The Sabre Dance*, which I later discovered, was the music from the final act of an obscure Kurdish ballet by Aram Khachaturian called *Gayane*. This whirling, war-dance music is a very lively, manic, frenzied composition that lasts for seven minutes. Whenever it came on the air, I leapt about like a dervish, rolling on the floor, jumping up onto the sofa, waving my hands and legs about as if I were trying to set them loose from my body, spinning, turning, twisting and generally acting out of control. The more they laughed, the more boisterous I became. I've absolutely no idea why I did it or why to this particular music, but if I tried to stop halfway through, they implored me to carry on!

Our next-door neighbours were *quite* different from those in Merthyr! Mr Potter – we never ever discovered his Christian name – was a retired sergeant major in the Army who hadn't accepted that he *was* retired! He bossed about poor Mrs Potter and their daughter unmercifully with his typical sergeant major's "not-so-dulcet" tones. He wore to work a most impressive uniform, together with a peaked cap covered in gold braid; he was the commissioner or official greeter working in front of the Ballito stocking factory where my brother worked. As a family, we'd often gather at the window and chuckle to see him literally march to work down the long garden path, arms swinging vigorously as if still on the parade ground!

"Ashman" – another whose Christian name I never learnt – lived next-door-but-one, the other side of the Potters. When I heard he was a prefect at the grammar school I was about to attend, I thought I'd have some kudos amongst my peers if I got to know him. I really tried but was always completely ignored and I don't think he spoke to me ever, either in the street or at school.

My father got a job working as a clerk for DeHaviland Aircraft in Hatfield, a half-hour cycle ride away. He used a rickety, second-hand bike with his sandwiches safely secured in his saddle-bag. He was always working overtime or taking on additional part-time cleaning jobs so he could earn enough money to increase the tick rate on the mortgage chart!

My mother got a part-time job at the darts factory making flights and packing them into fancy boxes. The factory was at the end of our road and meant she could get home in time to prepare tea for the workers and the schoolboy!

However, an event of seismic proportions was about to overcome us! My brother Les had come to St Albans some months before our move to set up the house purchase. He lodged at Mrs Blight's guest-house. She happened to have two beautiful, blonde daughters, Pam and Peggy, still living at home! He fell in love with Peggy and wanted to marry her. My parents were overjoyed but I had mixed feelings; I'd had Les to myself for the best part of 12 years but I suppose as he was now aged 26, I had to let him go!

Mrs Blight was widowed for many years and her house was only a few minutes away from ours, opposite the grammar school I was to attend. She was a spiritualist and faith healer. Her influence on our family was significant. We'd never come across anyone remotely like her in our lives and her powers were considerable. When I was 13 I fell off my bike and had a severe gash on my ankle, caused when the steel pedal gored into it. It failed to heal, despite every type of ointment we'd tried, so Mum took me to see Mrs Blight, almost as a last resort.

She ushered me into her front room and told me to lie down on the settee and asked Mum to leave us. Mrs Blight drew the heavy velvet curtains and lit some sweet-smelling joss sticks, and began stroking all around the offending wound with her eyes closed, mumbling incoherently. I nervously stifled a yawn at this surreal setting, but within a few minutes the pain disappeared. Within the week the wound had healed. I was back playing football and cycling a few days later. I was impressed, and so, too, were my parents.

The Blight family's spiritualistic influence led my brother to believe strongly in the existence of the spirit world and for the rest of his life with Peggy, he attended séances and spiritual meetings. My parents were sceptical at first, but my mother had good reason to change her mind when my father died suddenly some ten years later. They'd had 24 wonderful years together and she was heartbroken with a grief that seemed would never end. Les persuaded her to go to a séance with him to see if she could find some comfort. I was strongly against it in case it caused her to become even *more* upset but instead she drew great solace from these meetings.

She asked me to go with her once when Les couldn't make it. Begrudgingly, and in a sullen mood, I did. Mum kept pointing out there must be something in it because she kept saying, "Just look at the educated people that are here, David – they can't all be foolish." I had to admit, the meeting I attended, held in a dimly-lit, first-floor apartment that was overpoweringly furnished in brightly- coloured, floral, chintz materials, had not only attracted some well-spoken, educated types of varying ages but also some large, overly made-up women who I thought would be more at home playing bingo! However, the common denominator that undeniably united this disparate group was their crushing grief. They were all desperate to make contact with their departed loved ones.

The medium, in whose apartment the séance was being held, was about 65 years old and dressed completely in black, including woollen leggings and a heavily brocaded black shawl over her shoulders. She was affable and friendly as we joined the group and after a few introductions she asked us to sit in a circle around her. We were asked not to speak to her unless she asked us a question and that it was especially important that when she was coming out of her trance we remained very quiet.

Each of the party was asked if they would give something belonging to the departed to the medium. Someone volunteered a man's gold signet ring which the medium held in her open palm. We sat very still whilst she "went over to the other side". After three or four minutes, she said in a quavering voice, "I can hear someone … they're very faint … is there a Margaret in the room?" She described the person who had "passed on" in great detail and Margaret was most impressed, almost fainting with joy.

"He's telling me to let Margaret know that everything is fine and that she shouldn't worry about him," the medium said in a shaky, tremulous voice. It went on like this for a few more minutes before she selected another item of a departed soul and this routine was repeated about six times until by now, quite exhausted, she began to emerge from her trance. Although on this occasion my mother wasn't involved, she was enthralled by the performance. I was less so. It was almost like a caricature of something I'd seen on TV. I *was* impressed though by how the medium was able to know so much about the departed. These experiences gave my mother great succour during her grief, which she never really got over right up to her death 17 years later.

Although I remained sceptical, I witnessed one event that was a "miracle". In her latter years, my mother became riddled with debilitating rheumatoid arthritis. She was often in excruciating pain and walked with great difficulty. She had tried every possible remedy prescribed by the doctor with little success. As almost a last resort, she decided to investigate faith healing. She'd discovered that Harry Edwards, one of the world's most famous faith healers, was holding a public session in Watford Town Hall one Sunday afternoon. I took Mum in my car and as we arrived, the hall was overflowing with several hundred people in wheelchairs, walking with sticks or clinging onto someone's arm. It was like a scene from the Bible and there was a curious feeling of cautious optimism in the air.

As we entered we were given a numbered ticket and we took our seats about halfway back in the centre of the hall. When Harry Edwards appeared, there was rapturous applause. Numbers were drawn from a drum and the lucky holder was asked up on to the stage. Harry then went through an identical ritual Mrs Blight had performed on me many years earlier. I was astounded to see some people who had been in wheelchairs *walk*, admittedly a little unsteadily, back to their seats!

When my mother's number was called, I could feel my heart thumping as I led her up on to the stage. Within five minutes or so of Harry Edwards laying his hands on my mother's head, uttering unintelligible mumbling addressed to an unseen figure in the rafters, she walked, unaided, off the stage. She didn't need words to convey her delight; her beaming, radiating face was evidence enough! She was ecstatic and told me she felt elated as if she'd taken a wonder drug. She was pain-free for the first time in years and almost weeping with delight.

This euphoric state only lasted into the evening and by the following morning, she was back to square one. So it *was* a miracle, but regrettably, short-lived. It put into perspective my thoughts about religion though, especially the miracles quoted in the scriptures. My experience with Mrs Blight, my mother's brief but exultant episode and stories I've since heard from other folk about the power of faith healing, have led me to believe there is something in it.

I lived at Eaton Road for 12 years until I left to get married. My entire adolescent life was spent in this cosy, happy environment. My mother lived there for a further five years before moving to a warden-controlled flat nearby. This modest little house witnessed an extraordinary range of emotions from utter joy to deep sadness in that time. My abiding memory of my parents is seeing them both wearing their trade-mark uniform – Mum in her flowery-patterned wrap-around pinafore, representing cosiness, warmth and motherhood, and Dad wearing his gardening clothes topped by a navy-blue felt trilby in winter and a straw panama hat in summer!

CHAPTER 4
The best days of your life?

"As long as you pay attention, work hard in class, do your homework diligently and most importantly, don't indulge in any hanky-panky with girls, you'll do well at this school!"

R F Bradshaw MA (Cantab), headmaster of St Albans County Grammar School for Boys, was the first misogynist I'd met and these words in front of my parents in his plush study were to be repeated for the next four and a half years. "Ron", as the head was known, was tall, gruff, and imposing with a grey-speckled beard. Like all the masters he always wore his billowing, black gown which accentuated his authority.

It was the first day at my new school and this was my initial interview to assess in which of the three streamed classes I should be placed. I also took an exam, which I found very difficult, and to my dismay I was to commence in the lowest grade – Form 1C. So from being a "high flyer" in previous schools, I was now at base camp. I assumed standards in this North London suburban school were much higher than those in South Wales. I spent my entire time at school in the C grade and up until the fourth form I was graded as a C student within the C grade – the lowest possible educational level in the school! I also spent an inordinate amount of time in detention and getting caned.

Some of my earliest reports included such comments as:
"He must try to do better than this."
"He is still weak on the whole."
"Inclined to waste his time in class."
"Behaviour is bad, with a consequent deterioration in his work. He must get down to some steady work."

This last comment was from Ron himself, so he wasn't a member of my fan club. I can't really explain why I was so bad – maybe I mixed with a group who weren't particularly academic – we just lived for sport and thought this was the most important thing in our lives. Rugby, cricket and athletics were a large part of the curriculum but the end-of-term report rarely included any comments about sporting achievements. I thought this was most unfair because it was something at which I excelled. My parents, too, seemed to shrug off these negative comments; "It must be the teachers' fault," was the common quote. This attitude was in stark contrast to their drive to get me to the grammar school. They seemed to think they'd done their bit and now it was down to me.

I thought it most inconsiderate that an entire term's work could be summed up by a single phrase. We never had parents' evenings, so they had to rely upon this sole assessment in judging their offspring!

However, something happened to me in the fourth form that dramatically changed my attitude and hence my grades. It was a combination of suddenly realising that within two or three years, I'd either have to go to university or get a job, both options requiring a certain level of academic achievement, and being properly mentored for the first time in my life by a wonderful English teacher, D A Hopkins BA.

He excited me by bringing alive the literary works of Shakespeare, Dickens, Conrad and Shaw. He saw something in me that he could develop and I responded. He was also Welsh, which in my mind, gave him a head start. He had a firm but fair teaching style and I'd do anything to make him praise me. I'd learn huge chunks of Henry V and spout them out in class.

Suddenly, I became a star pupil in English literature. It was the kick-start I needed and so began an upward spiral of thirsting for more knowledge. I'd impress him with my quotations, he'd praise me, so I'd want to do it again, and so on. This process clearly rubbed off onto other subjects and now my reports looked very different:

"He has made a great effort to improve work and behaviour."

"He has worked very well."

"Continues to make good progress."

And from Ron, "A pleasing result. He has maintained his fine effort. Well done!"

To get a "Well done!" from the great man himself was probably the highest accolade I could possibly have attained. Interestingly, I was now spending less time in detention and my rear-end wondered why it hadn't felt sore for a while!

D A Hopkins went on to become deputy head some years after I'd left school, a position fully justified in my opinion. I met him quite recently at an Old Boys' reunion and, to my immense joy, he remembered me although it had been almost 45 years since we'd seen each other. Amazingly, he recited the entire form register of my year! When I expressed my surprise, he explained that we were the first class he'd ever taught after coming down from university and that most newly-qualified teachers always remembered their maiden register. I was so glad of the opportunity to declare my admiration and sincere thanks for what he'd done to inspire me. I'm not sure how my life would have turned out had I not been so fortunate to have "D A" take such an interest in me.

Ron Bradshaw, too, played his part. Although he twice threatened to expel me and caned me on numerous occasions, his approach was noticeably less subtle than that of "D A". When I started playing rugby for the Old Boys after I'd left school, I got to know Ron quite well. He was president of the club and often came to watch our games. We'd share a few beers afterwards in the clubhouse and I was delighted to have a different relationship with him. When his wife died, I saw a softer, gentler Ron and he was much-respected in the club despite the fact that everybody there had "suffered" under him as a schoolboy. R F Bradshaw was the first headmaster when the school opened in 1938 and he remained until he retired in 1968. He produced the template for making boys take their education seriously, even if he had to beat them to get the message home. Not everyone agreed with this strategy, but it worked for me.

The school was built to accommodate 600 boys and although it couldn't compete with Cyfarthfa Castle aesthetically, it had a certain charm, despite having some temporary huts we used as classrooms. The approach to the school was through a huge pair of green iron gates and a long, straight drive, at the end of which was the main building with a clock-tower dominating an impressive green-tiled roof. Punctuality was never my strong point at school and I used to dread looking up at the clock as I invariably arrived late for morning assembly.

This took place in the school hall, which had a large stage and a mezzanine area. Each form sat in pre-ordained places, either on wooden, collapsible chairs in the main body of the hall or on the mezzanine area, which was a prime position to launch all kinds of missiles such as erasers, ink-splodged blotting paper pellets and paper clips to the sitting targets below, but it would cost you four "whacks" of the cane from the duty master if you were caught!

The masters, all "gowned-up" and the school captain, led by the headmaster, entered from the rear of the hall and on the audible click of the door opening, we all stood. The masters sat at the back of the stage, always in the same place and we all sang a hymn followed by prayers. After the Lord's Prayer the head made any announcements, delivered pompously from the lectern.

The hymns were accompanied by Willie Hunn on the piano, who, as our pathetic music teacher, made us rehearse them obsessively as part of our music lessons. Willie was the ageing organist and choirmaster at the local church and was as soft as marshmallow. We taunted him unmercifully, especially about his dress sense, which was non-existent. His suits were invariably scruffy tweeds of dubious colour and we knew he suffered from incontinence because of the tell-tale yellow patches surrounding his nether regions! He never taught us any worthwhile music so I was not destined to follow in my mother's footsteps.

There was no separate canteen or dining area, so lunch took place in the hall. This required a huge logistical effort to transform the assembly hall into a dining hall and back again. It was the unenviable duty master's job to co-ordinate the efforts of a designated form to achieve this immediately after assembly. The chairs were collapsed and placed at the back of the hall to be replaced by trestle tables and benches ready for the tablecloths and cutlery to be brought from the adjacent kitchen.

Lunch itself was another non-negotiable ritual. At the head of each table sat either a master or a prefect. Boys were seated down each side and if you didn't like the overseer, you'd wait until the last minute so that you sat as far away as you could. But you *had* to be in your seat before grace or you were in big trouble, so this was a dangerous tactic. If you did sit next to them, they simply ate their lunch in silence and rarely made any conversation except to reprimand an errant schoolboy!

After grace, the kitchen staff brought in the dishes of food and placed them at the head of the table. You never had a choice. The master or the prefect dished out the food, scrupulously ensuring that each portion was equal and the plates were passed down each side of the table. This was repeated for the second course. One of the least senior boys, usually a snotty-nosed first-former, was assigned the job of gathering the dirty plates and placing them back at the head of the table to be collected. You could only leave when the master or prefect stood to signify that eating had finished.

The next 20 minutes was spent restoring the dining hall back into the assembly hall which was achieved with a deafening babble caused by 20-odd schoolboys collapsing the wooden chairs in a completely unnecessarily exaggerated manner, yelling instructions to each other, and scraping benches across the just-swept wooden floor!

One shining light amongst this highly testosterone-charged atmosphere was the school secretary, Miss F Eagle, known affectionately as "Fanny". She was as round as she was tall, piled her hair into a greyish bun and was a bundle of well-meaning energy. She really made the school tick and had a marvellous knack of befriending any schoolboys who needed a quiet word, or to be told, always kindly, the error of their ways. She also ran the tuck-shop and sold school uniforms with a calm air of authority and at times, but only if she thought justified, she'd let you have a Mars bar on credit if you'd forgotten your pocket money. In many ways, she was the ideal antidote to the gruff, no-nonsense Ron Bradshaw. She was highly respected by the masters and prefects to whom she often lent cigarettes!

We had an astonishing ranger of masters – they insisted on being called "masters" and not "teachers". Some were eccentric and some we considered psychologically disturbed!

"Juicy" Bateman, a long-serving English master who taught me in the early years, was a good example. His nickname came from his obsessive use of the phrase "Do you see? Do you see?" together with the simultaneous adjustment of his glasses with the thumb and index finger of his right hand after making his point. He served as a magistrate in the Sudan after obtaining a degree in history at Oxford. This apparently qualified him to become the head of English at a grammar school teaching 12-16-year-olds. He had no idea how to instruct and would spend hour after hour discussing *exactly* how to use apostrophes, or in *precisely* what circumstances you should use semi-colons. This left us severely bored! Rumour had it that he was equally verbose in the staff common room, often arguing with other masters over the spelling of certain words, even *after* the Oxford Dictionary had proved him wrong!

He always wore a crumpled, silver-grey suit which perfectly matched his crumpled, pallid face and his mop of unruly, ashen hair. His only form of discipline was to throw a board rubber in your direction or to apply a plimsoll to hand or bottom, depending on the severity of the offence. As both penalties were reasonably benign, we'd continually goad him to see how many times we could get him to use his stock phrase in a single lesson by acting dumb and asking the same question over and over again.

Geoff Davies, who'd become my best friend and partner-in-crime in many adventures, once presented "Juicy" with a pear in class with the question, "Would sir like a nice *juicy* pear?" For the first time ever in my class, "Juicy" lost his temper and rushed at Davies only to trip over a well-placed satchel on the floor and fly head-first to the ground. The class erupted with laughter and I think we were the first class ever to be given one hour's Saturday morning detention en-bloc!

Mr Alexander, better known as "Bullet-head", mainly due to his extraordinary hairstyle which was hardly a style at all, but simply hair cut incredibly short on top but with the sides combed up sharply and stiffened with Brylcreem, taught us geography. He was a commando during the war and I don't think he ever *really* left the armed forces. His nickname came not just because of his hairstyle, but because, allegedly, he'd caught a bullet in his head during action in the Far East. I don't know if it was ever removed, but judging by his behaviour, I think not. He never, ever smiled and was incredibly strict. I could imagine him stealthily sneaking up behind a Japanese soldier in the jungle and silently slitting his throat! His classroom was Hut 22, another supposedly temporary location that, aptly, reminded me of the prisoner-of-war camps I'd seen at the cinema.

We sat on benches with trestle tables rather than desks and chairs and each lesson began by opening our exercise books to show that we'd done our homework. "Bullet-head" walked up and down behind each boy with an oversized geography book in both hands. If you hadn't done your homework to his exacting standards, he said, "Whilst in Saturday morning detention, you *will* do your homework properly." If you hadn't done it at all, this phrase was accompanied by a "thwack" to the head with the *Complete Maps of the World – Volume One*, or something equally voluminous! Under these circumstances, most of us diligently did our homework but there was *always* someone whose Saturday morning was spent in detention with a headache! Some of us even got a double dose when the attempted improvement, presented the following week, failed to impress him!

Occasionally, he watched the Old Boys play rugby and stand on the line well apart from the other spectators, even Ron, and never came into the clubhouse afterwards. It's a shame, because I'd liked to have discovered what made him tick; he was a cold fish though.

Mr Lewis, nicknamed "Gus", for a reason I never discovered, taught us French. He was a good teacher, but he *always* seemed to pick on me for the slightest misdemeanour. I don't recall upsetting him, but I must have unwittingly done something to make him act the way he did. This continued throughout my time at school.

An example of his attitude towards me happened when I was in the third year. Our school rugby pitches were about a mile or so from the school so on Wednesday afternoons, those picked to play had to make their own way there, carrying our kit. It was a school rule that you *had* to wear your cap outside the school during school time. This was never strictly enforced, so a crowd of us didn't bother as we made our way to the ground one beautifully sunny autumn afternoon.

Gus, the master in charge that day, rode by on his bike and shouted to me as he cycled past, "Henley, where's your cap?" in a thin, reedy voice that seemed to emanate from his nose rather than his mouth, probably as a result of trying to perfect his French accent.

He'd been nagging away at me all term. That's it, I thought, I'm not putting up with this any more. My birth sign is Scorpio and I'm a typical example; my threshold had just been breached.

"You're *always* picking on me! No-one else is wearing a cap but, no, you have to have a go at me and I'm bloody fed up with it!"

Gus cycled back towards me, got off his bike and sneered, "Now you're really for it, Henley! You'll be sorry you swore at me. You'll be dealt with tomorrow!"

As he remounted, I gave him the V-sign, I thought behind his back, but he turned just as I was doing it, and I could almost sense the rage boiling up inside him. I knew I was in big trouble. Of course, I was a hero to my rugby team-mates and Davies, my so-called best friend, was almost delirious with nervous excitement at the prospect of me being in hot water.

Next morning, I attended assembly as usual and after prayers and the hymn, Ron made some announcements, the last of which was, "I want Henley of Form 3C to attend my study immediately after assembly. He's been particularly *obstreperous* to Mr Lewis." An audible gasp seemed to choke the other 599 boys but mine must have been the largest. It was almost unprecedented for someone to be summoned to the great man's office in such a public fashion. I remember some of my classmates actually patting me on my back, and with this one statement, I became a *cause celebre* in the entire school.

Nervously, I waited outside Bradshaw's study trying to work out what to say. His secretary, the redoubtable Fanny Eagle, was her usual settling influence, and she smiled at me sympathetically. When I was called in, Ron's demeanour was even gruffer than usual and he gave me a real dressing down. I tried to defend myself as best I could, cataloguing all the times I'd been picked on by *Mr* Lewis, but despite this, I received six of his finest whacks on my bottom and was told, in no uncertain terms, that if this should happen again, I'd be expelled. At least there was no letter to my parents who'd have been utterly astonished that I was capable of such behaviour although no doubt accepting that I was provoked.

In my third year I had a respite from the Stalag 13 conditions of "Bullet-head's" class, and had "Tex" Bellis for geography instead. He was marginally less strict, although it was always a lottery where the cane landed if you misbehaved. This was partially explained by the glasses he wore – they had the thickest "bottle-ends" I've ever

43

seen. I once had six whacks from him for misbehaving in class and afterwards Davies and I went to the bogs (our term for toilets) to inspect the damage. "Christ, Dai, you've got six red stripes between the backs of your legs and just below your neck!"

Bellis did me one good favour though. At the end of the first term, he announced in class the end-of-term results.

"Henley, stand up! Now here's a boy who misbehaves in class, never does his homework, never listens to what he's told. I'm not surprised he is bottom of the class in 35th place. Sit down, boy." There was some cheering, guffawing and a few humiliating comments directed at me from my class-mates.

"Davies, stand up! Now here's a boy who diligently does his homework, is always attentive and is a model pupil in class. As a result, Davies, you are top of the class. Well done!"

Davies! Top of the class? It was inconceivable! He must have cheated surely! This is my best mate. My partner-in-crime. I never remember him doing homework! You can't do this to me!

If ever I needed a spur to avoid further public humiliation, this was it. I studied like never before. I stayed behind after school and went to the library (once I found out where it was) and swotted for an hour or two after school for the whole of the next two terms. I clawed my way to 12th position in the term following my crushing embarrassment but, best of all, I managed joint 4th place with Davies, of all people, by the end of the year! I'd just learnt a lesson in motivation – thanks to "Tex"!

If Bellis was inaccurate with his whacks, Collis, our maths teacher, must have used an in-built laser beam to home into his target. Not only accurate, but I swear he must have worked out in the gym every night given the power and timing of the strokes. I only misbehaved once and received four whacks, each hitting the spot with missile-like precision. Four from Collis was worth eight of anybody else's. On the customary inspection in the bogs, you could hardly get a cigarette paper's width between the ever-reddening wheals that glowed like a particularly vivid sunset. I couldn't sit down for days. I never crossed him again and my maths improved significantly.

I was absolutely hopeless at art and woodwork. My paintings and drawings were ridiculed by "Jack" Cannell, the art master and my classmates. I couldn't respond; I had no idea where to start or what to do. Our woodwork master, Mr Hill-Smith, was in despair. I was bottom of the class every year that woodwork was compulsory, except for one year when I came 23rd out of 35.

There was a very good reason for this apparent enhancement, of which I am not very proud. One of the practical tests that year was to produce a mortise and tenon joint. In theory it's simple enough. You take two pieces of rough wood about a foot long, plane them smooth, put each of them in a vice, and then using a chisel you prepare a rectangular hole in one of the pieces (the female part) and shape the other to fit snugly inside (the male part).

I chiselled away — just a bit here, just a bit there — no, not quite enough! I'll just chisel a little bit more off — and there — no — just a smidgen more — and so on for several weeks. When it came to put the two pieces together, the male part was too small, and the female part too large, so they simply fell apart!

We were told to write our name in pencil on all our work before starting a new project but many of us didn't until we finished. This was to be my saviour.

After a lesson had finished, I waited until everyone had gone, and rummaged around the desks until I found a piece that had no name on it and was a *reasonable* fit; no-one would believe me if it was *too* perfect. I wrote my name on it and transferred it to my desk, later passing it off as all my own work. I took my aberration home and threw it away.

Remarkably, no-one complained to Hill-Smith — I assume the unfortunate classmate was allowed to start again — so I got away with it. I had never done anything remotely like this before or even in the rest of my life since, and writing this now, I can't believe I did it. In my defence, I remember Davies, who I realise now, was generally a bad influence on me, putting the idea into my mind. His persuasiveness, which got me into trouble on many occasions, together with my desire not to be bottom of the class (again), was simply too powerful a combination to resist!

The best master of all was Bryn Meredith who took sports and gym. We got on like a row of Welsh miner's cottages on fire! I loved every aspect of his lessons and as one ended, I'd be looking forward to the next. He was a hard taskmaster though, especially in the gym. He was dark and swarthy and had the bushiest eyebrows I'd ever seen! He looked and sounded fierce but he had a genial, smiling personality that usually got the best out of people. He commanded great respect as one of the best rugby players Wales ever produced in the 1950s, a period of almost complete dominance of the British rugby scene by an outstanding Wales team. He played with great distinction for Newport and Wales and he was the first choice Test hooker on the British Lions tours of 1955 and 1962 to South Africa and also toured New Zealand and Australia in 1959 but injury kept him out of the Test side. It was therefore no surprise to learn that rugby was the school's most revered sport and played every games afternoon.

Coming from Wales and with a name like Dai, it was automatically assumed I'd be good at rugby. I was immediately selected for the junior house team and then the junior school XV despite being in the first year. The junior teams were selected from classes up to the third form, so this was very unusual. Considering I'd only been playing rugby for three months, I was delighted. I was very speedy, so I played on the wing and did sufficiently well to hold my place for each year and even played for the senior XVs whilst in the fourth form. But there was a problem. A big one!

The house matches were fine; these were played on schooldays but the school first XV matches against other schools were held on Saturday afternoons – *my* football afternoons! It was a real dilemma for me. My football obsession won the day, but at a cost. I'd be selected for the school team and then have to explain to Bryn that I was playing football instead. He insisted I play rugby and if I didn't, there'd be an automatic Saturday morning detention. I'd inherited my dad's stubbornness when it came to my sport, so winter Saturdays, whenever there was a school rugby match, fell into a pattern of an hour spent at school in the mornings writing the lines "I should be playing rugby and not football" 200 times, and playing football in the afternoons. I considered it a price worth paying. I wasn't the only one in detention. Draper and Powell were exceptionally good footballers. In our playground matches they could dribble, control and strike a tennis ball with great skill and both went on to play at semi-professional level.

I regret not accepting the situation and playing rugby for the school more regularly. I missed out on a uniquely wonderful opportunity to be coached by one of the game's legends and would almost certainly have been a better rugby player.

Many boys detested the compulsory annual cross-country runs. I loved it! On a usually dull, wet and wintry January afternoon, the junior (first to third forms) and senior races (fourth to sixth forms) were held in a large, muddy, wooded area around Marshalswick, a thick forest a mile or so from the school. Some of the boys "went sick" to get out of it, but usually ended up as shivering "marshals" under the strict control of the masters. Others would try to find a hiding place close to the entry point of the woods which was temptingly close to the exit point and wait until the leading groups snaked their way back and tried to infiltrate. At this stage of the race the "legal" runners were covered in mud so these pristine cheats in their all-white kit stood out like the "after" part of the "before and after" washing powder adverts we'd seen on the still new-fangled TV sets. They were easily discovered! I never saw the point of cheating. What pleasure did they derive from finishing high on the leader board without deserving it?

There were about 300 boys in each race, so there was much bumping and pushing going on at the start and throughout the race through the narrow, slimy paths. I had no idea I could run the two and a half miles across such a treacherous terrain so well; I finished in 27th place overall and was the third first-year home.

Running became another of my passions and I always incorporated it into my training sessions for rugby and football. I jogged in the streets before it became popular and got odd looks from people. I persuaded a couple of mates to join me so I wasn't too self-conscious! One evening, I ran up Eaton Road just as my father was returning from work. When I returned I heard him say to Mum, "I saw David out running earlier. Do you know, Ruby, that boy runs like the wind!" There was significant pride in his voice.

Fifty years on, I still jog twice a week. It's as natural to me as waking up in the morning although some people think I'm mad! The hardest part is always pulling on the shorts and vest. Once out in the fresh air and running, I'm fine and feel euphoric after I've returned, showered and dressed.

I find running is a great way to get life into perspective. I've often resolved really difficult problems on my runs, usually business-related, and so before an important meeting I always tried to run for at least an hour. I'd work out my strategy and at the end be bursting with energy and ideas − something to do with releasing chemical endorphins inside the body!

The annual sports day was the highlight of my schooldays. We trained hard for the events which in the first three years were limited to 100 and 220-yard sprints, a 440-yard race, long jump and high jump. I bought my first pair of second-hand running spikes, which were my prize possession. I attempted all these events but I struggled with the high jump.

This was Davies' best event and he won first place in successive years. He was also a very quick sprinter and we were friendly rivals, even in training. Once we got to the fourth form and above, the 880-yard and one-mile race was added to the track events and I usually did well without breaking any records. I was a strange combination; I could sprint well and I was good at longer events like the two-and-a-half-mile cross-country, yet I was only average over the distances in between.

The most memorable summer I spent at the school was when I'd taken my GCE O-levels in early June of 1959. Although there was no point in continuing lessons, we *had* to still attend school each day until the end of term in mid-July. We were given a choice. Either take part in various non-curricular events in the classrooms or report to the games master who would coach us in any sport we wanted – except football. This was marvellous news! For Davies and I, it was an easy decision. For six weeks in that gloriously sunny summer, we spent every day on the sports field taking part in just about any sporting event we wished.

I really improved at the field sports – javelin, shot putt and discus – and we went on unbelievably long cross-country runs. So when the exam results finally came through, I was incredibly fit, suntanned and ready to face whatever the examiners threw at me!

We were limited to taking six subjects only and I passed four: English language, English literature (of course – D A Hopkins would have killed me if I'd failed), geography (the penalty for not passing was death!) and history. I failed physics with chemistry, which I expected, but was very surprised to fail maths.

These results were just enough to be considered for the lower sixth form and possibly to get sufficient A-levels to go to university. In the 1950s only around ten percent of secondary school children made it so I was pleased to at least be considered, given my performance in the first three years at school!

"D A" was especially keen for me to stay on but I really wanted to get a job and earn some money, which I did. I often wonder if my career would have taken a vastly different course if I'd stayed on and gone to university. I'll never know.

Davies also achieved four passes but in different subjects. For as long as I'd known him, he'd always wanted to become an architect, so his strengths were drawing and the arts. He, too, left school and immediately joined a local architectural practice to undertake his seven years' training.

Throughout our school life, Davies and I were inseparable. We shared our innermost fears, dreams and fantasies. He was stocky and fair-skinned with a great sense of humour, which sometimes went too far − some comments were more hurtful than he intended. He shared my brother's obsession with his hair and his appearance; from a very early age, he'd coax and tease the front of his blonde mane into a pronounced quiff made stiff with Brylcreem. This got him into trouble with certain masters and he'd be forced to let his hair flop over his round, cherubic face. But once out of school, the quiff would return. His white school shirts were always pristine and the collars razor-sharp. His school tie was always perfectly fastened into a Windsor knot.

He was very persuasive and highly skilled in getting his own way. His father started work in the furnaces of the steel works in Ebbw Vale, just a few miles further up the Rhondda Valley from Merthyr Tydfil and was a staunch trade unionist and a devout member of the Labour Party. He rose through the ranks to become the president of the Iron and Steel Federation and was elected chairman of the Labour Party in the 1960s. He was knighted for his services and so Davies, as his son, became a Right Honourable − a title he jokingly insisted I should use whenever I spoke to him!

They moved to Redcar in Yorkshire when Davies was born, so he was the exact opposite to me; born in England but of Welsh parents. My mum and dad loved him and I think his parents loved me. We spent a lot of time in each other's house so were almost like brothers. The major difference though was that I was still hooked up to my football obsession whilst Davies was equally obsessed by rugby. This didn't stop us sharing some terrific adventures together, not all of them with happy endings!

The school held a fund-raising event one Saturday in the school fields when we were in the third form based in the adjacent Hut 29. One of the attractions was a donkey ride, so when we arrived on Monday morning the field was covered in their droppings. Shearman was the much-derided class creep; he allegedly reported any misdemeanour to the masters, so would never win a popularity contest in school.

He'd crossed Davies in the past and so retribution was in the air. During the morning break, Davies persuaded me to take Shearman's satchel and meet him in the field. He urged me to scoop some of the donkey dung into it using a ruler whilst he held the satchel open. We fastened the two buckles and restored it to Shearman's desk and told all the other boys in the class what we'd done, to considerable acclaim.

"What's the next lesson, chaps?" said Shearman, as he put his hand into the satchel to retrieve the appropriate books. As he withdrew his dung-covered hand, the whole class erupted with laughter, particularly Davies who was almost having convulsions, leaving Shearman in no doubt as to the main perpetrator. With his face contorted with hate, he threw the offending mass straight at Davies, hitting his immaculate, white shirt chest-high! Davies immediately stopped laughing, looked down at the green, putrid, runny mess, and ran at Shearman, grabbing him by the lapels and dragging him out of the hut. I joined in and we both rolled him in the donkey poo to the noisy delight of the rest of the class who were cheering us on. Shearman got up, collected his satchel and disappeared for the rest of the day.

Next morning we returned to Hut 29 for the first lesson after assembly. I saw Ron Bradshaw from the window, walking very purposely towards us, his gown billowing behind him like a black cloud. I sensed danger! He strode down the classroom between the desks, and we all stood as if we were in a court of law and the judge had arrived, which wasn't so far from the truth.

"All sit, except Shearman." Now, *I knew* we were in trouble.

"Shearman, I understand something despicable happened to you yesterday. Will you please name the perpetrators of this act?" It's not possible, I thought. He wouldn't, surely, not in front of the class; he'd be blackballed for the rest of his school life.

"It was Davies and Henley, sir." I couldn't believe it! I didn't have time to ponder.

"Davies, Henley, follow me to my study immediately," the "judge" scowled.

I don't think we'd ever been given such a *verbal* thrashing before in our lives. This was followed by a *literal* thrashing of six whacks each. We made our usual trip to the bogs to inspect each other's damage and must have been in shock because we both broke out into hysterical laugher despite our stinging rear ends. Ron also threatened us with expulsion, for the second time in my case; I assumed he'd forgotten about the first threat!

This event represented a turning point for me. It was the last time I ever got whacked. At last the message sank in. Misbehaviour *was* stupid *and* painful! Shearman, surely as he must have anticipated, became even more of a pariah and, like many of the class, we never spoke to him again. Although I felt sorry for him, I'd have had more respect if he hadn't snitched on us but sought a more imaginative way to balance the books!

Girls became an important part of our lives when we reached 14. We went to the Pioneer Youth Club three times a week. Youth clubs in the 50s and 60s were very popular and fitted neatly into that awkward, adolescent gap between childhood and being old enough to go into pubs. The club met in a large hall the size of an aircraft hangar and there were separate places you could do your homework, play snooker or relax and listen to music. You could play badminton or even five-a-side football but the real attraction was dancing to records with *girls*. Not that we actually danced with them at first. They were an unknown quantity to those of us from the boys' schools. They might as well be wild leopards, or tigers for all we knew about approaching them. Davies and I sat there sipping our cokes just watching the girls jiving together. We'd fantasise on the walk home about *actually* dancing with them or, even more preposterous, *talking* to them!

This went on for about a year until I could stand it no more. I'd developed a huge crush on Pauline, who was a superb dancer and I thought I'd never stand a chance with her. She danced mainly with the older boys. I watched her every move and used to practise my jiving technique in my bedroom using the door handle as my partner so that I felt I could do her justice, Davies having declined my invitation to be Pauline's stand-in!

One evening, with Davies egging me on, I finally plucked up courage to ask her for a dance. I was sweating and shaking but, to my utter amazement, she said yes! It went well and I floated home that night! By now, having fantasised about her for over a year, I was hooked and knew this was the girl for me. The next step was obviously a date, so I asked her to come to the cinema with me. She said yes and I was elated.

It was a disaster. She had about as much personality as a packet of frozen peas. She never said a word all evening and although not very experienced in matters of the heart, I used every possible way I knew to get her to converse. I was devastated! I didn't even get a goodnight kiss. The spell was broken and we never even danced together again.

We lived 40 minutes away from London by train and so to us, as we got older, a visit to Soho was not only possible but positively an essential part of growing into adolescence! We usually found a pub that wasn't too fussy about serving 16-year-old schoolboys. We both enjoyed a pint or two and I'm convinced that starting so young helped us develop a reasonable capacity for beer that stood us in good stead for the heavy-drinking rugby nights that followed!

Having built up some Dutch courage, we dared each other to approach the street-walkers in Berwick Street to ask how much they charged. We both agreed that we'd never go with one though; it would've been a blow to our manhood to think that we "seasoned Lotharios" had to *pay* for sex!

Davies, as usual, egged me to go first and so as I approached the prettiest one in the street, I felt my legs wobbling. I babbled out the question, "How much do you charge?"

"Ten shillings, love." This was equivalent to a night out. I mumbled something like "Er, no thanks", and began walking away. She yelled after me, "That's the trouble with you kids, you've got champagne taste and you've only got beer money! Now, p*** off!"

Davies had witnessed the whole thing and as we turned the corner, we both doubled over with laughter. This expression became another to add to our repertoire.

There were strip clubs on every street corner, and it was impossibly tempting to go in! In the late1950s, the models weren't allowed to move. They first appeared fully-clothed and sat on the stage for about 30 seconds. As the latest pop records were played the curtains were drawn and then opened again after about ten seconds to reveal the model in a sexy pose with one less article of clothing. This was repeated until she was fully naked but the final pose never revealed any pubic hair! Apparently, this was the law.

In one club we went to, we had sign a register. We were petrified someone would find out about our nocturnal habits so we signed it "Henlini" and "Davisimo". I've no idea why we adopted such wonderful Italian names but we thought this would make us fireproof.

Whenever Davies calls me, I know exactly who it is.

"Henlini, dear boy, how are you?"

CHAPTER 5
It all happens at once

For most people, life is pretty straightforward until the treacherous adolescent years, around 12 to 17 years of age. Most decisions are made for you. Relationships are confined to a fairly narrow band: parents, siblings, classmates, and the opposite sex are objects of curiosity rather than anyone you have feelings about. All your clothes are chosen for you, you eat what you're given and you're generally happy to do as you are told. You don't expect a lot of yourself and the future represents the next day.

Then; wham! What a difference! Now *you* want to choose what to do and when to do it. Almost imperceptibly, you get excited about a girl who shows you the tiniest amount of attention. You feel physically sick and nauseous at building up courage to ask her for a dance, let alone wondering what you have to do and say about getting to the next stage! You have to compete on how you dress; fashions suddenly gain your fervent attention to detail. You're worried about how you're going to afford the new clothes, shoes and ties that are essential to avoid ridicule. And what about getting a real job once the schooldays are over?

Competition for your time, too, is a major consideration. How long should you spend on homework rather than playing sport, listening to music, going to the youth club to chat up the girls, getting part-time jobs to finance your new clothes and going to the pub?

But never mind; *you* now know best. Your parents, the previous keepers of the key to all knowledge, lose it overnight and now know nothing – nothing important to you that is!

How does *anyone* cope with all this happening at once? I was not exempt. Every aspect of my life during this phase was affected: sport, football in particular, school and new relationships, especially with the opposite sex. There were monumental changes taking place within my mind, body and spirit – some mundane, some stimulating and thrilling and one, when I was 17, life-changing.

My stance on playing football and incurring detentions rather than playing rugby for the school was an early example of my growing assertiveness. I was addicted to football. Although I wasn't naturally gifted – the playground games with a tennis ball proved I wasn't in the same class as some of the other boys – I was tenacious, determined and dogged.

One example exemplifies these attributes. On one of my visits with my father to watch the Spurs play, he berated one of the players for only using his right foot. Had he been two-footed he would almost certainly have a scored a goal. This stuck in my mind like a limpet, so I spent hours after school, kicking a ball against a windowless school wall with my right foot, as I'm naturally left-footed. At first it was very difficult but after about six months I was equally proficient with both feet.

As well as pounding my right instep into submission, I cajoled my parents into buying me a Stanley Matthews correspondence course on all aspects of the game. This was sent in weekly instalments and I studied it religiously.

He was, arguably, one of the best players ever. I saw him play twice and the most memorable feature was the crowd's anticipatory roar whenever he received the ball. He was a magician with the ball at his feet and he'd add 5,000 spectators to the gate when he was in the team. He was never booked or sent off and was the perfect role model for any aspiring young footballer.

So, aged 12 and armed with these self-taught skills, and bucketfuls of determination, I embarked on my junior football career. It didn't start well. I joined St Stevens FC, founded and managed by the local vicar, the Reverend Charles Seymour, who was as nuts about the game as I was. Actually, I think he was just nuts! He was renowned for wearing his football boots and socks under his cassock during Saturday marriage ceremonies and christenings and would speed them up to ensure he could make a three o'clock kick-off on the pitch behind the church! Although he never played or refereed, he just liked to be part of the team.

I found it difficult to break into the team but always turned up with my kit to every match. There were no substitutes allowed then, so even if a player became injured, I still wouldn't get on the pitch. I attended 20-odd games before a player didn't turn up and I was thrown a shirt, with the words "Go on, Henley, just do your best" – as if I'd do anything less! Unfortunately, there was no repeat of my Heolgerrig exploits, and I had to wait a further ten matches before I got another game.

The following season, although just 13, I joined an under-16 side based largely on the players from the local secondary modern school, Townsend Rovers. They were a great bunch of lads, trained and managed by another football fanatic, "Spud" Murphy.

"Spud" was a very good referee but felt his talents were better spent in developing young players, rather than admonishing them. He was a great motivator. He was in his 50s, never married and the whole of his waking life was spent in and around football clubs. After training, he often took the team to "Jack's" café for a fry-up and gave us some money to play the juke-box!

I spent about three seasons with them and it was towards the end of this period that, one freezing, foggy night in February 1958, as we turned up for training, we heard the dreadful news about the Munich air crash involving the Manchester United team. We couldn't believe that so many young players – the "Busby Babes", named after their charismatic manager, Matt Busby – had perished and others were very badly injured, including Bobby Charlton. We all shed a tear that night and "Spud", although not overtly religious, suggested we prayed.

The best under-18 team in the area were Carlton FC, a feeder club to St Albans City FC who played in the Isthmian league, one of the top amateur competitions in the country. Carlton usually won everything and were regarded as providing a sound footing for any player who wished to progress to a higher standard of football. Two of my friends, Dai Rees, who was in my year at school, and Paul Jarvis, who I met at the Pioneer Youth Club, played for them at under-16 level and persuaded me to transfer to Carlton when I was 17. I was a permanent fixture for the next two seasons except for the very last game of my under-18 career.

In my last season, we reached two cup finals, both to be played within two days of each other at the St Albans City FC ground. In the first match, on a sunny, spring Monday night with the ground almost full to capacity, I had one of the worst games of my life – a real shocker. I played left-half and the inside-forward I was supposed to mark played irritatingly brilliantly and scored two goals within the first ten minutes, both my fault. We got back into the game though and finally emerged as 3-2 winners after extra time.

Although the others celebrated as if we'd won the FA Cup, I couldn't share their joy. Before I left the clubhouse I tentatively asked about the team selection for the second cup final and our very last match as under 18 year olds on the following Wednesday. The manager said, "Don't worry, son, it'll be the same team."

I was determined to put up a better show so I spent most of Tuesday evening practising my skills. When I got to the ground, I thought it odd that nobody spoke to me as I began to get changed. Then the manager sheepishly broke the dreaded news.

"Sorry son, you've been dropped." I'd have taken the news better if I'd known on the Monday evening, or even on Tuesday, but it was cruel to leave it until I was about to pull on the kit.

I couldn't help what happened next. I put on a brave face but simply couldn't bear to stay to watch the game, so I got dressed and walked home. As I tried to explain what had happened to my father, I broke down and blubbed in his arms. It seemed a pathetic thing to do as I look back on it now, but I was obsessed with the game and desperate to do well. As ever, Dad sympathised with me but even his kind words couldn't console me. The team won 2–0.

A month later, Carlton held their end-of-season dinner and presentation evening to which I was invited. We all shook hands, had a few drinks and I was presented with a spare cup-winner's medal which I cherished.

During that last season, Watford FC, then in the third division of the Football League, invited three of us from the Carlton team to attend trials. When we arrived at the ground there were about 50 boys, all from local youth football clubs, and we were split up into teams. Each side were initially given a 30-minute match playing on the famed Vicarage Road pitch. We three had played there under the floodlights about two weeks previously in another cup match, which we lost 1-0 when our best player, Alan Edwards, scored a spectacular own goal!

I was selected to play in the first 30-minute session and did pretty well. So much so, that I was kept on the pitch whilst almost everybody else was replaced. This happened again after the next 30 minutes, so I thought I was in with a chance. I couldn't believe it when this happened twice more, so having played for the whole two hours, I was confident I was on my way. After we'd all showered and dressed we were called into the coach's office one by one and told our fate.

I was flabbergasted when he simply said, "Sorry Dai, you've not passed the trial." When I asked why he'd let me play for the entire period, he said, "Did you? Sorry, I didn't notice!" My heart not only sank, it was submerged in disappointment. The other two players didn't get past the first session so our mood on the bus on the way home was decidedly glum.

At least by now we'd discovered other activities to distract us from our sporting or academic failures. As well as girls, we added music, parties and a drinking culture that began benignly but rapidly grew to pulsating hangover proportions! The Pioneer Club was a good source of enjoyment for three of these hedonistic pursuits, but we had to go to the pubs and clubs to enjoy our libations.

St Albans once held the record for having the most pubs within a square half-mile in the UK. The standing joke amongst us dirty-minded schoolboys was that the High Street was like a man's body; it had the King's Head and Blacksmith's Arms at one end, the Cock in the middle and the Boot at the other end!

One of the big attractions in pubs was the juke box. We enjoyed being holed-up on a cold winter's evening in the Dive bar in the Bell hotel, the Blacksmith's or the Harrow, downing excellent pints of the local brew, Benskin's Best Bitter, and listening to the fabulous music of Paul Anka, Johnny Tillotson, Chuck Berry and Jerry Lee Lewis.

There was something on every night of the week. We limited ourselves to Wednesdays, Thursdays and Saturday nights, mainly due to finances, although before we left school we'd got some part-time jobs, but also we still had to find time for studying for our GCEs. It all happens at once!

Wednesdays was live jazz night at the Market Hall where we were lucky to see all the UK jazz greats: Humphrey Littleton,

Chris Barber, Acker Bilk and Kenny Ball. The place was invariably heaving and you could run a small town's electricity supply from the energy generated by 200 gyrating dancers sweating the night away!

Thursdays was a more sophisticated night spent at the Waterend Barn; a beautifully restored medieval building with a springy dance floor and, a sure sign of a classy establishment, a dress code. A small orchestra often played romantic numbers designed for couples to meet and fall in love.

It was ideal for blind dates. But you didn't stand a chance if you couldn't waltz, foxtrot or quick-step so Davies and I took lessons from an Austrian couple who ran a dance studio above Burtons the tailors in the High Street. These took place on Friday evenings (yet another invasion into our time!) and apart from learning to dance, this was also a good place to meet girls, who out-numbered the boys by two to one.

We never discovered the name of the teacher but he quickly gained the nickname "Adolf", given his thick accent, diminutive stature and his propensity to bark at you. I'm sure I heard him snarl on many occasions, "You *vill* obey my orders if you *vant* to learn to dance!" This was usually after he'd walked up behind you, and thrust his hands heavily in a downward motion onto your shoulders to ensure they weren't hunched up as if you were trying to bury your ears!

So, armed with at least the basics, we were confident of not making too much of a fool of ourselves and were keen to test our rhythmic steps on the unsuspecting toes of the Waterend Barn lasses. The dancing, though, was really the bait to chat them up.

One night one of my mates set up a blind date with four girls from Watford. We arranged to meet them inside the "Barn" at 9:30pm. I went to football training with Carlton FC as usual – nothing got in the way of that – so I was late in arriving.

Suitably smothered in Old Spice aftershave, and my best Italian suit, I went to the bar, but I noticed that my three mates were already on the dance floor doing their stuff with some very pretty girls. At the far end of the bar, there sat a huge, Amazonian blonde girl whose biceps were almost the size of my thighs although, admittedly, not quite so hairy! She had huge breasts, but surprisingly good legs.

My first thought was: the bastards! I'm stuck with a "hulk" from Watford! I needed to be sure, so I skulked around trying not to be noticed to see if my mates and their new-found "birds" would return to the "hulk's" table. They did, so my worst fears were realised. I decided to slink off home, hopefully unnoticed but I was spotted by Davies who took great delight in waving and shouting at me to join them. Sulkily, I did. What happened in the next few hours taught me an important lesson.

Her name was Sue, and she was several years older than me and a superb dancer. She had a great smile and laughed at everything I said. She was animated, witty and her eyes sparkled when she spoke and we got on marvellously well! After the last waltz, she suggested we should go back to her place in Watford for some drinks.

Sue had a car – I hadn't even taken lessons then – and so Davies, who'd successfully won over his partner, and I were whisked off to an unknown abode in darkest Watford with a feeling of great anticipation. We were not disappointed. After a swift drink and some fumbling to a Frank Sinatra record, Davies went upstairs with his stunning brunette and Sue and I remained in the sitting room. Within minutes, I was flat on my back having the clothes ripped from me, and she was sitting astride my quivering body. She was like a dervish on steroids.

I responded the best I could. Fortunately, I'd lost my virginity at a party about a month earlier to a fiery redhead called "Tinny", so, by no means an expert, I had a good idea of what to do. After 20 minutes, I heard the sitting-room door open and saw Davies peering in. He'd had a similar experience and I think it had unnerved him!

Eventually, we got dressed and I felt slightly awkward. We couldn't stay the night; I suspected the "hulk" was married although it was never mentioned. She offered to run us home and we gratefully accepted – we had to go to school the next morning!

Davies told me later all he could see when he looked into the sitting room, were my legs and arms flailing about under an amorphous mound of unattractive flesh! The important lesson I'd learnt was that first impressions are unreliable!

Saturday nights were always eagerly anticipated, mainly because I could nurse my hangovers lying in bed on Sunday morning! The

"Spot" in London Colney, about four miles from home, was *the* place to be. It was even a step up from the Waterend Barn and usually had a sophisticated trio of piano, drums and bass playing cool, mood music. The Bull pub was next door so that's where the evening started. There was always someone playing a piano and an old-fashioned sing-song was compulsory including *Down at the old Bull and Bush* and *Goodnight Irene*! It reminded me of my Christmas holidays spent in London. "Last orders" was at 10.30 pm and so, suitably fuelled up, we'd stagger across to the "Spot" for a little sophistication until "carriages" – if you owned such a luxury – at midnight.

The trick was to get the last waltz with someone you fancied so that you had a number of options: ask them for a date; cadge a lift home if they had transport; take them home on the last bus, which left promptly at 12.05 am, or persuade one of your older friends who had a car, but had been unsuccessful in "pulling" a girl, to give you both a lift.

Although these options may appear comprehensive enough not to fail, many times Davies and I either caught the last bus, or walked home, alone and miserable, our dreams frustrated until the next Saturday!

In our last year at school, there was a musical revolution going on in Britain that just pre-dated rock 'n' roll – skiffle. It sounded like a cross between blues, hill-billy and country and western, usually with an exhilarating bass beat and memorable lyrics. Based on just three chords anyone could play it. DIY skiffle groups started up everywhere and Davies and I thought we'd give it a go. All we needed was for someone to learn the three chords and the lyrics to Lonnie Donnigan's songs (he was *the* skiffle supremo), someone who could play drums and washboard, and finally someone who could find a tea chest, a broom handle and some twine to make a bass!

Davies learnt the guitar, chords and lyrics, "Ginger" Robinson, a football-playing friend of mine, already had a drum set! I bought a tea chest from a local removal company for a shilling (five new pence) and together with my mother's washboard and an old broom handle I found in the cupboard at home, my investment in the group was minimal.

We practised in Davies's garage for ages and became, we thought, very proficient. Davies had a good voice and could belt out many numbers before becoming hoarse. Some of the most popular hits at the time were: *My Old Man's a Dustman* and *Does Your Chewing Gum Lose It's Flavour On The Bedpost Overnight*, so it wasn't exactly a challenging repertoire.

We called ourselves the *Jail-birds* for no particular reason I can remember, and I painted the tea chest dark blue with the name in bright red with paint "borrowed" from Dad's shed. We touted the local pubs with the offer of playing for free − "Just supply us with beer for the evening" was our negotiating strategy. We were taken on by the Camp pub less than a mile from where we lived.

Just as well, because although I thought I was smart in not having the expense of a guitar or drum set, the logistics of getting my beautified tea chest to the pub was a nightmare! I eventually got Dad to make a wooden trailer I attached to my bike. We had great fun and the pub nights went really well although I still have the scars on the index finger of my left hand caused by "twanging" the twine on my bass for hours on end.

Music was never a big deal at school, so this was my first meaningful experience of playing an instrument, albeit an improvised one! The school was so disinterested that Colin Bluntstone, a friend and schoolmate a year below me, who'd set up a group whilst still at school, was famously told by Bradshaw, the headmaster, "I don't know why you're messing around with this rubbish music, Bluntstone, it's a complete waste of time!"

Colin's group, formed with another friend, Rod Argent, became the "Zombies", who went on to have massive number one hits in both the UK and US charts and made a great deal of money! Colin was also a useful wing three-quarter and he and I played together for the Old Boys rugby team for a season just before his breakthrough. He was a good-looking lad and so he gave up rugby to protect his features for his audience of screaming female fans!

Our nightlife had to be financed, beer was ten old pence a pint (about four new pence in today's money), and a shilling (five new pence) for the good stuff! I tried newspaper rounds but I was hopeless at getting up in the mornings, still am. I eventually got a part-time job as a delivery boy for the local corner shop grocer. I worked for two hours straight after school on three afternoons a week and, if I wasn't in detention, I worked on Saturday mornings too, all for the munificent sum of two shillings an hour.

The tools of my trade were an aged black bike with a huge metal basket in the front and a slightly smaller one at the rear, a pair of cycle clips and a faded brown coat with the name "Brookers" prominent on the breast pocket.

Mr Brooker, proprietor of "Brookers – Purveyors of Excellent Foodstuffs", was a strict disciplinarian and proud of looking after his customers. He always wore an immaculate white coat, rather like a consultant physician, and spoke to his customers as if he were one.

Once loaded up with cardboard boxes, front and rear, and a list of the addresses, I'd be on my way; easier said than done! Balancing an aerodynamically-challenged bike and trying to get up enough speed to defy the laws of gravity was like trying to steer a lump of jelly across an ice-rink!

On many occasions I failed to master this feat, especially on corners or where I failed to detect that the camber of the road had changed. The bike would veer over on its side with the resultant smashing of eggs and breaking of biscuits! I'd carry on if the damage wasn't too bad and explain what had happened to the customer who'd call Mr Brooker and demand a replacement of the broken bits. On return to base I'd incur his wrath and he'd send me out with a replacement order without paying me for the extra time involved.

Amazingly, although this happened a number of times, this wasn't the cause of my getting the sack; it was pure greed and my sweet tooth. I finally mastered steering the loaded bike and so was confident enough to inspect the contents of the basket in front of me as I rode. Biscuits were sold loosely and by the pound. They were placed in white or brown paper bags, which were twisted at each of the top corners and, due to their propensity to break or crumble, were always placed on top of the cardboard box. I'd gingerly untwist the corners and open the packet as if handling an unexploded bomb to see what was on offer.

Usually they were custard creams or digestives – fatally, both my favourites. Surely the customer wouldn't miss *one*, would they? *One* was consumed and the corners of the packet carefully re-twisted. Had I stopped there, I might have got away with it, but I simply couldn't resist repeating the process, sometimes three or four times. This biscuit larceny lasted about two weeks before customers began accusing the unimpeachable Mr Brooker of selling underweight produce and his response was to set a trap that I, blissfully unsuspectingly, fell into. He meticulously weighed the biscuits and had one of his assistants witness the event before sending me out on the round. He'd asked a couple of his customers to weigh the bags when they received them and to report any discrepancy. The *only* possibility remaining was that the biscuits had been consumed en route.

When I was confronted with this overwhelming evidence, I sheepishly confessed. I received a ferocious telling-off and told that my employment was terminated. I reluctantly handed back my faded brown coat and cycle clips and accepted that my time working for "Brookers – Purveyors of Excellent Foodstuffs" was over.

Within a few days I got another job working for "Spendwise", a fruit and vegetable retailer. *Mr* Spendwise – nobody knew his real name – I suspect he adopted it for commercial reasons – was a kind man, who, despite leaving home at 3.30 am every morning to buy his produce from Covent Garden, was invariably chirpy.

I upset him once, though, and he never let me forget it. My job was to ensure that the large containers in the shop for potatoes, brussels sprouts, beans and cooked beetroot were constantly topped up from the large shed at the rear of the premises containing sacks of the produce. My hours were similar to Brookers except that Saturday mornings were compulsory. This had a positive effect on me since I simply couldn't afford to get detentions – my financial priorities wouldn't allow it.

My usual routine when I arrived was to inspect the containers in the shop. Invariably, the cooked beetroot was always low so my first job was to fill up a decrepit boiler in the back yard, empty a sack of raw beets into it and light up. Usually, it took about 20 minutes for the beets to cook and a further ten minutes before they were cool enough to be drained and put into a basket for transportation to the shop. Whilst the beets were cooking, I hauled sacks of spuds and greens from the back yard, and filled up the containers in the shop.

One Saturday morning when the shop was particularly busy I totally forgot about the beets! It's a wonder the boiler didn't explode. There was an acrid smell like an especially pungent compost. The water had boiled away completely, the beets were the size of tennis balls and were as hard as stone. No sales of cooked beetroot were made that day and the usually kind Mr Spendwise showed the other side of his nature. He gave me a second chance, though, for which I was especially grateful because my mum was a regular shopper there!

Three months short of my 17th birthday, and despite the attempts by D A Hopkins to persuade me to stay on and consider university, I wanted to earn some serious money. I wanted to get a full-time job but had absolutely no idea what to do.

Dad came to the rescue. "Accountancy's the thing, mark my words. You never see a poor accountant do you?"

"But Dad, I haven't even got maths O-level."

"No, but you're good with figures. And you're persistent. It'll take you at least five years to qualify and you won't earn much, but after that, you're on your way and the sky's the limit. Do it, son!"

I took his advice, which was the best decision I ever made. It set me up for a fantastic career in business. He was more aware of my strengths and weaknesses than I was!

I studied the job ads and discovered that Marconi Instruments Ltd, a large employer about a mile away from where I lived, were offering commercial apprenticeships to anyone with four O-levels and a good reference from your school. I'd qualified on the first requirement but what about the second?

I still have a copy of the most awful, cringe-worthy letter I wrote to Ron Bradshaw imploring, or more accurately, begging for a favourable reference so that I could be "meaningfully employed". He must have responded well, since I was asked to attend an interview with the Personnel Director, Jeremy J Bliss.

I've never been subjected to a more rigorous, comprehensive interview before or since than that personally conducted by "J J" as I discovered he was known internally. It was like an oral GCE examination and lasted the best part of the day. I thought I'd already cleared the two conditions mentioned in the advertisement, so I was totally unprepared for the test but within a few days I received an offer of employment. The arrangement was that I should spend two years in the sales administration department before moving to the cost control department for the remaining three years of the five-year apprenticeship. I'd be allowed day-release for the entire period and study for the Ordinary National Certificate in business studies and then the Higher Diploma, which gave valuable exemptions for the Institute of Cost and Works Accountants' examinations.

The pay would be two pounds and ten shillings for the first year rising to three pounds and ten shillings for the next year, and then pay would be subject to a general review. The start date was Monday September 7th 1959.

I had no idea the effect of joining Marconi's would have on the rest of my life.

CHAPTER 6
Turbulent times in work and play

If I thought the previous five years was an exciting roller-coaster ride, the next five was equivalent to an atomic explosion! Every aspect of my life evolved at breath-taking pace.

I didn't know what hit me on the first day of work. I was shown how to clock in and clock off and told the penalties of doing it for other people (which was getting the sack), had the organisation structure explained to me and where I fitted in (bottom of the pile) and met so many new work colleagues that my head was dizzy by the time I clocked off at 5.30 pm. I had no concept of a working environment of over 500 factory employees, nobody had warned me. It took a month for me to really understand what was required of me as a lowly office worker.

After J J Bliss had carried out the induction process, I was taken over to meet my new boss, Derek Gurner, Sales Administration Manager. I liked him immediately. He reminded me of D A Hopkins, my teacher and mentor, and had the same motivational style and gentle persuasive manner.

My overwhelming memory from that very first day was that I couldn't keep my eyes off Derek Gurner's stunning secretary. Her name was Ann, a vivacious brunette with long, black, lustrous hair, dark eyes, a curvaceous figure and great legs. She was 26 and married, so although I fantasised about her a great deal after we met, she was off-limits to a gauche, callow and immature 17-year-old youth; or at least I thought she was!

My first jobs as the office junior were: taking orders from the rest of the office staff for the tea trolley that came round at 10.30 am and 3.30 pm every day; filing invoices and letters and punched cards from the computer room; delivering messages; checking on work-in-progress in the factory and acting as a general dogsbody to everyone else in the office.

Once the shock to my system had settled down, most days were deadly boring, so I made sure I always went the long way round the factory to carry out some of these duties.

The factory was enormous. Marconi manufactured and assembled hundreds of different types of electronic instruments and sold them world-wide. There was a huge machine shop with giant steel presses, capstans, and lathes – a noisy, dirty place, and an aircraft-hangar-sized assembly department where hundreds of women sat side-by-side in rows, soldering tiny components to circuit boards to the sound of *Workers' Playtime* played over the loud-speaker system. This was a BBC wireless programme designed to ease the boredom of the work and often all the women sang along to their favourite tunes.

The typing pool was in the main office building, quite close to our open-plan sales administration office and employed 40 shorthand-typists hammering away at Remington typewriters all day long. Miss Shipp, an elderly, formidable, school headmistress type, with greying hair swept up into a fierce bun, was in charge. She always wore long, dark skirts with clumpy court shoes and ran the department with military precision. Ann, who'd started her shorthand-typing training in her department, told me many stories about her strict, almost cruel way of inducting young girls into becoming proficient. A ruler brought down with some force on the back of a delinquent hand was one of the minor correctional aids.

The typing pool was not as noisy as the main computer room, cocooned within glass windows and air-conditioned (I'd never heard the term before) to ensure the huge processors didn't overheat. One of my least favourite jobs was boxing-up and filing thousands of processed punched cards every day. The cards contained the software programs, embedded on hard disks today, so it was vital to have them accurately labelled and stored.

The stores and despatch department was also one of my haunts. I helped produce the stock lists, confirmed despatches to important customers and reported back to my department. I was exposed to every aspect of factory and office life that would serve me well in the future.

I realised what it meant to be stuck at the same post for hours on end doing mind-numbingly simple tasks like the women in the assembly department or the chaps in the machine shops. I never complained about clocking in and out; I really appreciated that at least my jobs were varied and I had some freedom to wander when I got bored.

Starting a new job, it's luck or fate whether you meet fellow workers who are genuinely helpful and keen to set you on the right career path or whether they're disinterested and show you only the shortcuts and skives. You wanted to make an impression and get off to a good start so you did everything they said. I was incredibly fortunate that in Bob Davidson, a Geordie who knew everything there was to know about office procedures and Terry Milton, perfection personified, I had exceptional tutors who accelerated my learning curve.

My day release course for the Diploma in Business Studies and accountancy exams was held at Hatfield Polytechnic and was a welcome relief from the day-to-day monotony of being the office dogsbody. I made some great friends on the course and with only ten in the group, we became a very close-knit unit. Paul Jarvis was an excellent footballer – it was he who persuaded me to join Carlton FC. He gave me a lift to college in his ancient Ford Thames van in the early days before I'd sorted out my own transport and we'd swap notes on our economics homework just before handing it in – we both struggled with the subject.

Mike Kiff, too, became a very close friend and our lives have intertwined over the last 50 years! He was a brilliant grass-track cyclist and I often went to see him race at Clarence Park during summer evenings. It was exciting and quite dangerous, speeding round corners at over 30mph with about 20 other riders!

Derek Allen was an enigma. He never did any homework, often missed lessons, yet sailed through every exam and qualified as an accountant in record time. This was so frustrating because Paul, Mike and I really plodded through the course and in my case it took many more years than it should have done to qualify although I can plead some mitigating circumstances, shortly to be revealed.

By the time I left the course five years later, I'd only passed my Higher National Diploma in Business Studies and the intermediate level of the Institute of Cost and Works Accountants exams. It took me a further three years of studying at night school three evenings a week, getting up at 5.30 am to do some revision before going off to work, and two failed attempts at the final exams before I gained my full accountancy qualification.

After the first year at work, I'd made a lot of new friends, many of whom were three or four years older than me. They introduced me to a much wider social life and expanded my horizons dramatically. They included me in their visits to the Royal Festival Hall in London to see Ella Fitzgerald or the Modern Jazz Quartet. Thus began my love of smooth jazz.

We had wonderful holidays in a caravan in Cornwall spending the evenings drinking and dancing until four in the morning, having a fry-up at midday and then recuperating on the beach until it was time to repeat the process.

"Bounce" Meager, a friend of Terry Welling who worked in the technical drawing department, was an enormous man with a huge belly and always wore black, supposedly to make himself look slim. He was dark and swarthy, wore large gold signet rings, and although he was a gentle giant, he had the look of a man you wouldn't want to cross.

It was entirely appropriate that he drove a huge, 1930s left-hand drive black Dodge automobile with a running board, complete with a spare wheel carrier on the side and white-wall tyres. This car was right out of the Al Capone era. We went everywhere in this cavernous "limo".

We were able to expand our social world to the far-flung outposts of the California ballroom in Dunstable, the George hotel in Luton, the Cherry Tree Club in Welwyn Garden City and Burton's Record Hop in Hemel Hempstead. Occasionally, we went to the Lyceum in the Strand or the Hammersmith Palais, both in London.

These were heady days in the music scene. Rock 'n' roll was reaching its zenith followed shortly by Beatle mania. We jived and twisted for hours but the bands always played a slow tune you could waltz to as the last dance. This was the signal for many would-be Lotharios to cut in at the last moment having spent most of the time in the bar. This was especially frustrating if you'd been dancing with someone all evening only to be thwarted at the last moment by a drunken youth who your prospective "partner" preferred to you!

We once drew lots to decide who should be challenged to ask the ugliest girl in the dance hall, chosen by the others, for a dance. I was the unlucky loser, and my evening turned to disaster when upon making the request, the unfortunate female looked me up and down scornfully and sneeringly declined! I was never allowed to forget it.

"Bounce" wasn't too interested in girls but Terry Welling, and another of his friends, Mick Thornhill, a dental technician from the East End of London, were brilliant at chatting them up. Mick, in particular, although not the best-looking guy in the dance hall, had something about him that had the women falling at his feet. And these weren't just ordinary women. He became renowned for the beauties he bedded; after all, these *were* the swinging sixties.

I once dated one of Mick's cast-offs and took her for a drink in the Bell hotel in St Albans. She was a stunner with fabulous blonde hair and a pretty face to match, a bit like Audrey Hepburn. As we sat chatting, an elderly lady came up to us and said what a lovely couple we made, much to my delight. Trouble was, she was still in love with Mick who'd dumped her for another equally dazzling girl, so despite my best efforts, I got nowhere.

We only encountered trouble twice. On both occasions "Bounce" wasn't present, which is probably significant. On one of our trips to the California ballroom in Dunstable, we decided to have a drink in a pub on the way. I felt uncomfortable when I first went in; the clientele looked a bit rough. We had a few drinks and got chatting to some girls and everything seemed fine until we were about to leave.

As we made for the door, a heavily tattooed man, much older than us, appeared from nowhere and hit Mick full in the face and as he fell to the ground, began kicking him and yelling, "That's for trying to chat up my wife, you bastard!" Instinctively I piled in to defend Mick. "That's my mate, leave him alone!"

The next thing I remember is being propped up outside the pub, my misaligned jaw aching, my teeth feeling as if they'd been re-arranged and my numb, bloodied nose making it difficult to breathe. A policeman was shining his torch into my face.

"Are you alright, son?"

"What happened?" I mumbled, fearing that some of my teeth might escape.

"You were knocked unconscious, son. We're trying to find out who did it. Would you recognise him?" I shook my head.

The attack had come from nowhere. All I wanted to do was to inspect the damage so Mick, who, ironically, hadn't come off as badly as me, and Terry, supported me to the toilets. My nose was spread over my face, obviously broken, and my jaw wouldn't quite click into place. Fortunately, my teeth were all there, but felt loose. I went into the dance hall after cleaning myself up although my chances of getting off with a girl were now greatly diminished!

When I awoke on the Sunday morning, I had two black eyes, a crooked nose and a blinding headache. Even now, my jaw clicks if I open it wide, and my nose is still bent.

My biggest problem was explaining my appearance to my parents and to my work mates. I came up with a story about bumping into a lamp post whilst out jogging but I don't think anyone believed me. My mother was very upset when I surfaced late on the Sunday morning. She didn't like seeing her "Little London Welshman" looking as if he'd just gone ten rounds in a boxing ring. We never went to that pub again, though "Bounce", when he heard what had happened, threatened to go there with some of his mates from London to exact revenge!

The second occasion we encountered trouble was a little more serious because we ended up in a cell at the police station! Davies had joined us for a visit to the Cherry Tree Club one Sunday evening. We all had a good time, except towards the end, a fight broke out between two rival groups. It was really getting out of hand with chairs flying around and glasses shattering on the floor, but rather than leaving them to it, we decided to try and stop them. Bad mistake!

By the time the police arrived, they couldn't tell who was doing what to whom so they loaded all of us, about 12 youths, into two Black Marias and took us to the station for cross-examination and possible charging!

We were genuinely worried. This was something else altogether. What would our parents say? What about our jobs? We were interviewed and statements were taken well into the early hours of Monday morning. We sat in the cells, each group segregated, until, around 3.30 am, our group were told we could leave without charges being brought, but, we were warned, this was our last chance otherwise we'd have the book thrown at us.

What a relief! I'm convinced that our grammar school backgrounds and studying the professions of accountancy and architecture respectively, stood us in good stead. We weren't the typical yobs the police usually had to deal with. It was another important lesson we learned – if there's trouble, don't get involved. Thank goodness, the police got it right.

A typical weekend comprised: playing football on Saturday afternoon, going to the pub for drinks and a sing-song before hitting a dance hall on Saturday evening, lying in with a hangover on Sunday morning, meeting the boys for a drink at Sunday lunchtime (making sure I was home in time for Mum's wonderful Sunday roasts), going to the pictures for a 4.30 pm screening, and rounding off the weekend with a visit to Burton's Record Hop in Hemel Hempstead on Sunday night! No wonder Monday mornings were an unwelcome blast of common sense, level-headedness and sobriety!

As well as going through a musical revolution, the fashion industry really came alive too as if in support. The two were inextricably linked. The dance venues were the parade ground to strut the latest fashions so different from previous eras. The *pace* of sartorial change, too, was electrifying. We seemed to pass from drape jackets, string ties, luminous lime-green, orange or pink socks and thick-soled, beetle-crusher shoes in the late 50s, to sharp, neat, shiny Italian suits (the jackets became known as "bum-freezers" due to their shortness) and impossibly pointed "winkle-picker" shoes, in just a few years!

One of my most treasured outfits was a thick, navy-blue serge Italian suit with wide lapels, a cream shirt with button-down collar, a yellow polka-dot tie and mustard-coloured winkle pickers! I thought I was *the* embodiment of high fashion, despite my mother continuously warning me about the dangers of my toes curling into one another causing in-growing toenails later in life. What did she know? Fact is, as always, she was right! Probably along with most of my contemporaries I now have distorted feet with some of my toes hiding underneath the others!

The teenagers of this period fell into two main categories: Mods and Rockers. The Mods rode scooters, wore parkas (loose-fitting anoraks), smart suits and ties, sported short, sharp hairstyles and liked pop music and jazz. The Rockers rode big motorbikes, usually Harley-Davidsons, had tattoos generously displayed on their arms, chest and backs, wore their hair very long and straggly, and loved rock music.

There was a general disdain between the two factions that spilt over into violent clashes sometimes, although I never experienced any real trouble; I had friends in both camps.

I was a *moderate* Mod; I never went as far as wearing a parka, although I drove a Lambretta scooter for a while but hated it!

The legendary 24-hour Busy Bee café on the A1 near North Mimms in Hertfordshire became a renowned meeting place for the Rockers, although we usually ended up there when returning from a dance in the area. Between 1 am and 2 am on Sunday mornings were their busiest times, the whole place buzzing with the rock 'n' roll sounds of the juke box, somehow providing the perfect background to the smell of deep-fried food. The café seated hundreds and although there was always a queue for food, the proprietors prided themselves on the speed with which they could process the orders.

As you approached the counter, you weren't allowed to dither over the menu. You had to shout out your order over the considerable din and the order-takers, who reminded me of school bullies, yelled it out to the "chefs" behind them, followed by a number.

You were then bawled at to move along into a receiving area where you paid your money and waited for your appropriately-numbered food to arrive. The dialogue went something like this:

Me – "Can I have a cup of tea, please, milk and two sugars, double egg, baked beans, chips and bread 'n' butter?"

Order-taker, yelling at the top of his voice so that the "chefs" behind him could hear over the noise of the juke box – "One tea, milk, two sugars, double egg, baked beans, chips, bread 'n' butter, number 148, one shilling and sixpence, next please. Hurry up! Move along, move along!"

In no time, the order-taker would bark out "Number 148" and the plate of food and a mug would be simultaneously slammed down on the counter. Both were always piping hot, and the white bread already buttered. If he had to call out the number again, he'd get very cross.

"Do you want this, then, or not?"

It was *the* original fast food.

Once, a fight broke out between some rival Rockers and chairs, tables and cutlery were thrown about. A mug narrowly missed my head. We'd already learnt not to get involved and rode the storm. The next time we went there, all the tables and chairs were screwed to the floor, so we felt marginally safer.

The Busy Bee was renowned for its motorbike racing. Rival gangs challenged each other to "beat the juke box". This involved two opposing gang members, one of which (the loser in the call of heads or tails on the flip of a coin) placed their money in the machine and selected a track. They rushed out to their bikes, raced around the nearest roundabout a mile away and tried to get back before the record finished!

This competition was probably the cause of the fight; sometimes the bikers would cheat by having someone block their opponent's progress to their bikes. Very few of them wore crash helmets and there were some fatalities. The Hertfordshire Police even commissioned some souped-up Daimlers to try to catch them before they had an accident!

My parents were delighted I never got into motorbikes; like most, they were terrified about having a policeman turn up on the doorstep to inform them that their son had been killed in an accident.

It did happen. A school friend, Roger Deamer, a motorbike nutcase, suffered the ultimate fate when he crashed his BSA Regal bike one wet, winter's night, aged just 18.

Davies was one of the first in our group to get some transport, a 50cc, cream-coloured Puch scooter that had as much power as a pair of caterpillars! This was the best he could achieve with his parents' blessing. Although he hadn't passed his test, I once rode with him as a pillion passenger, which decreased the power to that of one caterpillar!

The film *Psycho*, directed by Alfred Hitchcock, was playing in Hemel Hempstead one bitterly cold February evening. It was the first film ever shown in the UK where you weren't allowed to go in once the film had started. This added to the excitement created by this superb movie.

Davies decided that we'd go on his new toy. It's 15 miles from St Albans to Hemel Hempstead and usually took about 20 minutes maximum by almost any other means of transport. Not on this contraption! I've never been as cold since that raw, chilling *hour's* journey there and the agonising *hour's* journey back! My teeth were still chattering 20 minutes after dismounting! We had the added tension of *having* to be there at 7.30 pm latest and we only just made it in time. *Psycho* remains my favourite movie and I always remember that intrepid journey whenever I watch it!

I never got on with the 125cc Lambretta I bought second-hand on HP. There was no real centre of gravity, and I couldn't control it going round corners, more often than not falling off. I scraped my elbows and knees and most of the paintwork too. Also, I hated getting wet in inclement weather so after a few months I embarked on a car-purchasing "career".

My first car, bought in 1961, was a black 1936 Austin Seven which I bought for 22 pounds and 10 shillings. I didn't have any lessons at this stage and rarely bothered with "L" plates. I just went out with a couple of my workmates who showed me the basics and then I drove up and down Eaton Road to perfect my skills.

The car was a disaster, always breaking down. I was offered exactly the same model, same year, car by Terry Welling for one pound! It was so cheap because it used almost as much oil as petrol!

I reasoned it could be used for spare parts for my original car, but I never got round to it and used the "One-Pound Special" as my mother called it, all the time. It finally collapsed in a heap whilst returning from a trip to see my cousin Pearl in Widford, near Ware in Hertfordshire with my mother in the passenger seat. We had to call a breakdown truck and it towed us back home. Mum thought it was a great adventure and really enjoyed going out in the car and knew no fear. "Can't you go faster, David?" was a common lament!

Next I bought a 1939, royal-blue Flying Standard 12 with a dodgy suspension and questionable steering. It cost £50, and was a beautiful car but its looks belied its performance. This car finally retired in the summer of 1962, when, as I was parking outside my house, the steering wheel came off in my hand! I often wondered what would have happened if I'd been on the road.

I became disenchanted with cars and couldn't really afford one anyway, so I gave them up for a while. I'd got the taste though so knew I couldn't resist them forever.

On the job front, things began to develop encouragingly in more ways than one! After a year spent in the sales administration department, I was transferred to the accounts department a year earlier than planned due to a vacancy. I regarded this as a small promotion although they still wanted me to carry on as the "tea boy". I'd done it for a year, so I refused. Remarkably, I gained some support from sections of the office for my stand, and so I felt that I was at least *one* rung up on the ladder!

It was just as well I moved departments when I did because my relationship with Ann was getting somewhat steamy. We flirted with each other outrageously and I became even more obsessed with her and used every method I could to maintain close contact. I'd follow her to the staff canteen and sit opposite her. We played "footsie" under the table and I teased her with sexual innuendos. I finally plucked up courage to ask her out, not thinking for one minute I stood a chance. She was married and nine years older than me. When she said yes, I was beside myself with excitement.

Our first assignation was a double date. Ann's best friend was the secretary to the Marketing Director and she was having an affair with John Dunkerley, a mate of mine who worked in the machine shop. We went to the cinema in Potters Bar, some miles away from where we lived, and snogged incessantly in the back row. So began a sequence of events that affected the rest of my life.

David Lucas was my new boss and he reported to Gordon Harding. They were both Old Boys of my school, about ten years ahead of me, so I started with an advantage. They played for the Old Boys' rugby team and it's largely through them that within a few years I began to play rugby too.

Once a month, they organised a departmental "meeting" for the men of the office at the "Queen's Head" pub in Sandridge, a small village just outside the city. Mostly, the evening consisted of playing drinking games and singing bawdy songs learned from the rugby club. This was a wonderful induction into rugby culture. They both had a great influence on my life in other ways too.

They were actively involved with the firm's amateur dramatic society. They encouraged me to join in and paint the scenery and help build the sets. Later, I read for some parts and, to my surprise, I was cast in a number of leading roles. I was the white sheep in Ian Hay's *White Sheep of the Family* and Lord Arthur Savile in *Lord Arthur Savile's Crime*, a play written by Constance Cox from a short story by Oscar Wilde. David Lucas was the producer for most of the productions and he became my Svengali. I really loved being on the stage and it taught me the importance of timing and not to be afraid of expressing myself.

After rehearsals, usually at least three nights a week a month before the production and *every* night in the final week before the curtain went up, I could never go straight home to bed. I was so psyched-up, I stayed up for hours or went for a walk. It was even worse after the four production nights, although at least I could let my hair down at the mandatory end-of-production party!

Then came the dreaded anti-climax. What do I do now? After the intensity of learning lines, rehearsing and performing – nothing! I now understood why so many stars in the entertainment business get into drugs and alcohol abuse; their lives must be incredibly difficult to manage with such extremes of emotions.

What interested me most about this amateur dramatic society was that membership covered the *entire* spectrum of the company's employees. J J Bliss, the Personnel Director, was an excellent actor, and I found myself, the most junior of juniors, now on level terms with him on the stage! Out of office hours he was "J J" rather than Mr Bliss. Management and staff mixed freely in this environment and it had a positive effect on company morale.

Under David Lucas's direction, we attained a commendable level and entered several festivals winning some prizes for our performances.

Tony Rogers, who was about my age and worked in the same department, was also roped into the society by David and Gordon. He was a blonde-haired, larger-than-life character, full of fun. He and I and two other chaps from the stores department impersonated the Beatles at a concert produced by David Lucas for the firm's 1964 annual Christmas party. We wore their tell tale, buttoned-up suits, made by the costume department, donned Beatle-fringe wigs and made wooden guitars that looked very realistic. We practised miming to their records for hours until we were mime-perfect and tried hard to imitate their stage presence. We kept the whole thing a secret, so as the curtain went up and the music began, the audience, just for a second, thought we *were* the Beatles!

It's hard to overstate how popular they had become; almost every other record played on the radio was one of their hits they seemed to roll out every month.

When the Rolling Stones began competing for the Beatles fans' adoration, the nation's youth were divided. The Stones were far more raunchier than the Beatles. There's no finer example than in the titles of each of their Number One hits. The Beatles' *I Want to Hold Your Hand* was at the opposite end of the sexual revolution scale to the Stones' *Let's Spend the Night Together!* As a lusty 20-year-old, the irony was not lost on me!

My sporting career during the early 1960s also flourished, although it took a few surprising turns before I reached my true Nivarna. I still managed to play football almost every day during the lunch hour (unless I had an assignation with Ann!), my new playground being a small grass pitch outside the Marconi staff canteen. A group of about 20 of us rushed out at 1.00 pm, and picked two teams. We played until five minutes before clocking in at 2.00pm, went to the canteen, grabbed a cheese roll and a bottle of water and had lunch at our desks. We played all year round and so in summer, the perspiration used to run down my shirt for at least an hour after we'd finished; not a pleasant sight or odour for my fellow workers!

After leaving Carlton FC under-18s, I had a trial for St Albans City FC, by now a semi-professional side, along with Paul Jarvis, my college mate. He made it and I didn't. The pace of the match was much faster than anything I'd experienced beforehand and I felt out of my depth. It was dawning on me that perhaps I wasn't good enough to play at this level. The coach kindly suggested I approach Colney Heath FC, a club based just outside St Albans. They played several divisions lower, in the amateur Hertfordshire County League. I spent three enjoyable seasons there. At first I was the youngest player in the team but the senior players, especially George Williams, a nuggety full-back and Ian Stuart, a skilful inside-forward, took time out to look after me. There was a good social side to the club too, camping in the Queen's Head pub just 100 yards from the ground after training and home matches.

I played left-half and was a regular member of the first team from day one, so felt I'd found my level. The only trophy we won whilst I was playing for them was the Hertfordshire County League Division Two title. We had to at least draw our last game of the season against Sandridge Rovers on their pitch to secure the title.

The match was played in pouring rain on a Wednesday evening in the middle of April and the build-up was incredibly intense. There was a great expectation from the rest of the club and a huge crowd gathered to see if we could pull it off.

I rarely got nervous before a match but some of the team were almost shaking in the dressing room. George Williams, our solid rock of a full-back, who was as tough as they come, was violently sick, complaining he had a virus but we all knew it was his nerves. He had a dreadful game but we just managed to hang on for a 2-2 draw amid much celebration.

When we got back to the Queen's Head, it was all decked out in our black and white colours and the party lasted well into the night.

Marconi held an annual inter-department soccer tournament where "bragging rights" were a prized possession that would last a whole year until you had a chance to bid for them again! The accounts department reached the final in 1961 and played against the machine shop, a team including my partner-in-romantic-crime, John Dunkerley, and my skiffle group drummer friend, Ginger Robinson! They'd won the tournament for the last two years and were keen to make it a hat-trick and so we were the underdogs by a distance.

I played left-back and had to mark Bill Turner, one of their best players who also played in the firm's first team and for the county. There was a great deal of winding-up taking place throughout the preceding week, both John and Ginger sending quite cruel messages to me via the inter-departmental memo system, constantly telling me that Bill would make me look a fool and we'd get thrashed.

But on that evening, in front of a huge crowd, including Ann, I had another of those rare episodes I'd experienced just once before, eight years earlier in the Heolgerrig school match. I played like a man possessed with extraordinary, almost extrasensory, powers and the great Bill Turner never got past me. I noticed early on, that although he was a brilliant dribbler, he *always* tried to pass *outside* me and never varied his tactics. I was able to stop him every time and if anything, I made *him* look a mug! This performance was all the sweeter because Ann watched as I proudly picked up my winner's medal!

CHAPTER 7
Confessions, decisions, a birth and a death

After our first date, I was hooked. I couldn't get enough of Ann. I saw her every day in the office, but now even this wasn't enough. I was so enamoured, I even gave up one of my football training nights to meet her at "The Lake", a well-known beauty spot in St Albans. This coincided with her husband Gerald's training night; he played for Hatfield Town FC.

We took unbelievable risks to be together. Some evenings I went to their house. We'd have a few drinks, play Frank Sinatra records and sit in front of the fire for a couple of hours before he returned.

After a year of these clandestine meetings when it became really serious between us, we were caught by Gerald when he found us cuddling in an alleyway between my home and the Marconi factory. He angrily shouted some expletives at me and attempted a punch but I moved out of range.

He physically pulled her away from me and dragged her towards his car. I yelled, "Tell me if he hits you, Ann, and I'll come round to sort him out!" The extent of my adrenaline-filled bravado shocked me.

I realised that this crystallized our situation and some decisions would now have to be made. I was really mixed up.

I knew it was wrong having such a torrid affair with a married woman and yet it seemed so right for us to be together. My predicament was aptly summarised in the words of a Frank Sinatra record, *I've got you under my skin,* which was on the album *Songs for Swingin' Lovers* I'd bought for Ann. We played it incessantly.

The highly-charged, apposite, lyrics, by Cole Porter, are:
I've got you under my skin,
I've got you deep in the heart of me,
So deep in my heart, that you're really a part of me,
I've got you under my skin.

I've tried so not to give in,
I've said to myself this affair will never go so well,
But why should I try to resist, when baby I know that well,
That I've got you under my skin.
I'd sacrifice anything come what might,
For the sake of having you near,
In spite of a warning voice that comes in the night,
And repeats, repeats in my ear,
Don't you know you fool, you never can win,
Use your mentality, wake up to reality,
But each time I do, just the thought of you,
Makes me stop before I begin,
'Cause, I've got you under my skin.

Ann had previously told me how she was desperately unhappy living with Gerald and had been thinking about leaving on many occasions, despite marrying him just two years earlier. She told me he was a bully, very strict and jealous. This explains why I didn't feel guilty about the affair. I grew to hate him. We discussed her leaving him but it was a hopeless situation. I had no money, lived at home with my parents and although I may have *some* prospects, they were a long way off. Also, I was still only 18 years old and this was my first proper relationship!

Ann was full of life, in her prime at 27, and loved sport, especially netball. She was smart, shrewd and worldly-wise. She never accepted people at face value.

She had a great sense of humour, and until our relationship became stressfully anxious, when all we could talk about was how we were going face up to the future, together or apart, we had a lot of fun.

The biggest problem I had was that I couldn't share my joy about this relationship with anyone! For over a year I kept the affair bottled up inside me. My mother often asked whether I had any girlfriends but I said I was still "playing the field".

She even said to me once, "I'm sure you've got someone and we'd love to meet her. Your father and I don't even care if she's black. It doesn't worry us at all." They were not at all racist, but it was an issue within many families following the high immigration levels in the early 1960s. She'd probably guessed that I *was* in a relationship. Some people at work, I'm sure, knew what was going on, but no-one mentioned it to my face.

Eventually, I simply had to tell somebody and so I broke the news to Davies. He'd had his own love affair bubbling along, although in a much more conventional manner. He'd fallen for Delia, a petite, pretty girl with large breasts, of which she was always very conscious. He met her at the Pioneer Youth Club and she was a great dancer. Many of us ogled her lasciviously but once Davies had "claimed" her, we respected that they'd become an "item". He was as obsessed with Delia as I was with Ann.

When I broke the news, Davies was very understanding; he was going though the same emotions but without my complications. We discussed the difference between lust and love with no particular conclusion. I said something like, "I wish I was ten years older and had a good job so that we could just take off somewhere and start anew." His response was remarkably profound.

"Don't wish your life away, for God's sake. Just do what you think is best." I knew he was right.

"I think I'm pregnant!" These were the last words I needed to hear about a month before we were discovered by Gerald. Now what do we do? I can't believe we took so few precautions.

There were so many issues we now had to confront. Although we discussed and researched the possibility of an abortion, neither of us wanted it. Not because of any strong religious beliefs – but somehow, it just didn't seem the right thing to do although it was probably the easiest option.

We discussed it over and over again until our brains hurt. There was no question in my mind at any time of abandoning Ann, although that, too, may have been the easy option for me, but certainly not for Ann. It really boiled down to Gerald's reaction. When he caught us in the alleyway she had to confess the whole affair to him, including the pregnancy.

I never really discovered whether Gerald threw her out, or whether Ann left of her own accord. When Ann told her parents they agreed to have her back to live with them, at least until the baby was born. We'd then have it adopted.

There was still some doubt about who was the father; DNA profiling hadn't been discovered and blood tests weren't conclusive enough proof although I instinctively felt responsible and paternal.

We told no-one at work until the seventh month of the pregnancy. She didn't "show" until then and she was still playing netball for the firm's team! Eventually, though, she left work whilst the rumour mill at the factory was working at fever pitch. I just kept my head down when the full story broke and really got stuck into my work and sport, although I still had this nagging feeling of how to break the news to my parents and friends.

When I told Davies of the latest developments, he was aghast. "You're ruining your life! You're missing out on having 'proper' relationships!" When I pointed out that *he'd* only had one "proper" relationship himself, he calmed down a bit but he never really understood why I didn't just walk away from the situation.

Eventually, after another of my mother's inquisitions about my love life, I finally broke the news.

"Actually, I have got a girlfriend, Mum, her name's Ann."

"That's wonderful news, David. When can we see her?"

"Oh, there are a few things you should know first – she's a few years older than me."

"That's not a problem. How much older?"

"Only about seven years," I underestimated, on the basis that Ann certainly didn't look much older.

"That's fine. I'm just glad that you've finally met someone."

"There's something else. She's married, but getting a divorce shortly."

"Oh, no! Not damaged goods! Surely there are plenty of *single* girls available? Why do you have to settle on this one?"

The "damaged goods" remark stung like a jellyfish.

"Because I love her and want to spend the rest of my life with her."

"Well, I'm not happy about it and certainly your father won't be. But if you're sure you really love her, then I suppose we have to go along with it."

I don't know how I summoned up the will and courage to break the final part of this life-shattering trilogy of facts. I was a much-loved son, upon whom a mother had pinned such high hopes, breaking some desperately unwelcome news.

"By the way, Ann's also pregnant and the baby's due in 12 weeks."

"Is it yours?"

"I think so."

I had never seen my mother affected so badly. She slumped down in the chair with her head in her hands and began sobbing uncontrollably, so much so, that my father came into the room to see what was going on.

She half-babbled, half-wept the news. Dad's reaction was more to show concern for Mum, rather than take in the enormity of my situation. I got very cross with both of them.

"The trouble with you is, you don't understand, do you? I just love her, and we'll get through this with or without your support!"

I stormed upstairs and flung myself on the bed and began crying. It was an enormous relief shedding a secret I'd kept from them for over a year. At the time, I couldn't understand why they were so upset. Many years later, when I told the story to my then new wife, Lorraine, she said, "Of course they were bloody upset! You were their golden boy, you could do no wrong – remember? You were going to be Prime Minister!" Lorraine also pointed out that as my parents were both in a second relationship with the added complications of Dad taking on two children and having another (me!) out of wedlock, they didn't want me to encounter the same prejudices they'd endured.

An example of their concern happened when I was 15 years old. Dad called me into the front room one Saturday morning and said, "I have some good news for you, son. You're no longer a bastard. I married your mother yesterday." I was astounded! I'd assumed they *were* married but it demonstrated their generation's belief that children born outside marriage were second-class citizens. In marrying my mother, there'd no longer be a stain on my character.

Between Ann leaving Gerald to live with her parents on the outskirts of St Albans, and having the baby, I lived in a twilight world. I was single, yet I had a girlfriend who was pregnant, living with her parents. I visited their home three or four times a week. We rarely went out together and we had no money. Ann had left work with a little maternity pay and I was still a commercial apprentice earning a pittance.

Most nights, were spent watching TV or playing cards with Ann's parents. I still went out with my mates but it felt strange going to pubs, listening to their tales of womanising and who was doing what to whom, and so after a while, I concentrated on my sport and studying for my exams.

My relationship with Ann's parents, too, was unusual. Ann's father, Harry, was a curmudgeonly, suspicious sceptic with few social skills. To be fair, I'm not sure what he made of this "jumped-up, smart arse" who, in his mind, had ruined his daughter's marriage and made her pregnant. At least, that's how I perceived his impression of me. Ann had always been *his* little girl, and as an only child, she was greatly indulged. Nothing had changed in the 27 years of Ann's life.

I found him difficult to engage in conversation. His attitude was so far removed from mine. He'd had a tough upbringing, receiving nothing like the parental nurturing I'd experienced. As a result, he appeared resentful of anyone who seemed to be making a good life for themselves.

However, we had a mutual interest in sport, football in particular. He'd taken Ann to watch Watford FC play when she was so small, they had to lift her over the turnstiles! They were lifelong supporters, so at least we had something in common as I had the same commitment to the Spurs.

Ann's mother, Elsie, was the exact opposite of Harry. How they ever came to be together, I will never understand! She was very kind to me during this difficult time, despite being at the beck and call of her husband. For example, she'd rush out in the pouring rain to open the garage door upon hearing the honk of Harry's car horn when he returned from work and rush back in to ensure the dinner was on the table, piping hot as he walked in the house. She was also a great source of strength to Ann, especially in the latter stages of her pregnancy.

On Sunday, 7th October 1962, just after lunch, Ann was rushed to Nightingales Nursing Home in Latimore Road, St Albans. I usually spent Sundays with the family, but for some reason, I didn't get there until later in the afternoon. A neighbour told me Ann and her parents had gone to the nursing home. I furiously cycled the two miles there, but by the time I breathlessly arrived, I was greeted by a radiant Ann, sitting up in bed as if nothing had happened, Ann's mother grinning like a Cheshire cat and the most beautiful baby girl lying asleep in a cot. Ann's first words as I entered the room were, "We can't possibly let her go for adoption, can we, she's so beautiful!"

What was I supposed to say? Although adoption papers had been signed beforehand, I was never really happy at the prospect. Reading my mind, Ann said, tearfully, "Mum and Dad have said the baby and I can stay with them for as long as we want."

"That's great, thanks," I mumbled. I *was* truly grateful. It was a great weight off my shoulders, but what I *really* wanted was for the *three* of us to be able to live together. This is what I should have aimed for. But although I'm sure we'd have found the money from somewhere, in the 1960s there was a stigma attached to living with someone who was married to another man, *and* having a baby out of wedlock.

Both sets of parents would have been very unhappy with this arrangement, so we existed in this surreal relationship for a further four years until the divorce came through. I've no idea why it took so long except that I suspect Gerald still thought there was a chance he and Ann would get back together.

We finally married on September 3rd 1966, and at last became a family unit, moving into a rented maisonette in Marshalswick, St Albans. I was desperate to normalise matters, and now at last I'd achieved my aim.

The four-year period between the birth and the marriage was a difficult time for me. I continued visiting the family and my gorgeous daughter three or four times a week but I missed out on the day-to-day intimate bonding necessary to establish a truly fulfilling relationship. I had no say on how she was brought up.

Ann's father applied himself as unstintingly to Stephanie, the name we'd hurriedly given her, as he had to Ann, and during this period, he developed a deep bond with her. Ann and her mother doted on Stephanie too. With her long, blonde curly hair, rosy, chubby cheeks and infectious giggle, it was difficult to refuse Stephanie anything she wanted but I was powerless to interfere. I felt like an outsider.

For example, her bedtime was whenever Stephanie wanted it to be. There was no real routine, and so even when were finally together, getting her to go to sleep was always a major issue.

For the first three years of Stephanie's life, we all went on holiday to St Ives in Cornwall, funded mainly by Ann's parents, although Ann earned some money having got a job working part-time in the Anglia Building Society in Chequer Street whilst her mother looked after Stephanie. These holidays at least gave me a chance to spend some fatherly time with Stephanie, carrying her on my shoulders, making sand-castles and paddling in the sea!

Although Ann and Stephanie came to tea with my parents occasionally, my mother never really got over the situation. I remember her accusing Ann of being a "gold digger" but this was before she'd met her. "She knows when she's on to a good thing," she said to me.

"Don't be daft, I'm still studying. I won't be qualified for ages and there's no guarantee that I'll make some serious money even then, so what kind of a gold digger is that?" I replied.

But she wouldn't have it and so relations were always a little "frosty". Ann tried very hard to charm my mother into accepting her. She had more success in winning my dad over! He had a particularly soft spot for Stephanie, but I had no idea this flourishing relationship would be so short-lived.

I was lying in bed on the morning of December 19th 1964, and awoke to the uncharacteristic sound of my mother shrieking out at the top of her voice, "Sid! Sid!" I ignored it to begin with but I heard her repeat over and over, "Sid, Sid! Wake up! Wake up!" even more piercingly. I pulled on my dressing gown and went to their bedroom.

I was totally unprepared for what I saw. I'd only ever seen one corpse before, that of my nan when she died in Wales about ten years earlier. There was the unmistakeable pallor, coldness and utter stillness of Dad's striped pyjama-clad body lying in bed. It was obvious he'd died in his sleep just a week before his 64th birthday on Boxing Day.

"David, David, I ... I just can't get your father to wake up. I've been shouting and shouting at him for ages," Mum said, by now very close to becoming hysterical. I took her out of the room and we went downstairs and I tried as gently as I could, although trembling with my own feelings, to explain that I *thought* he *might* have passed over, although I knew perfectly well that he had.

I reluctantly left her for a few minutes whilst I dressed quickly and ran down to the phone box at the end of the street to call the doctor, who came swiftly and pronounced Dad dead with a suspected heart attack. He told me, in a matter-of-fact manner, what I had to do regarding funeral arrangements and suggested I sort it out right away bearing in mind that Christmas was less than a week away. Although his bedside manner was very matter-of-fact, he stayed with my mother whilst I went once again to the phone box.

My first two calls were to my brother, Les, who lived about five minutes away and to my sister, Ivy, who lived in Kent. It was only during these calls that I became overwhelmed with what had happened. They could hardly understand me through my sobbing. I had to repeat over and over that Dad was dead.

The funeral was held just five days later on a cold, crisp Christmas Eve and Dad's ashes were spread onto the rose garden at Garston crematorium, just outside Watford. Dozens of wreaths were laid in the grounds and for many years afterwards, I hated Christmas; it always reminded me of the worst moment of my life to date and I would never have a wreath in the house. I still don't, 46 years later.

Between Dad's death and Christmas Eve, we received all his birthday cards for Boxing Day. They'd been posted before anybody knew what had happened so I had the macabre duty of opening each one, all wishing him a wonderful day.

Mum took Dad's sudden death very badly. I hated hearing her sobbing and repeating his name deep into the night for many months afterwards. I dreaded going to bed as much as she did. She became very dependent on me too. She needed a lot of support to see her through those early winter months. She didn't like to be left alone. Apart from work, I rarely went out.

Ann was very understanding, but it meant I saw even less of two-year-old Stephanie during this period, so as well as having to deal with my own grief, I felt under a great deal of pressure. I was studying hard for my accountancy exams and took a part-time job to save enough money to ultimately support my family.

Mum gained some solace when Les took her to spiritualist meetings and had her at his home on the nights I was out. Les – always my hero! Until she died, 17 years later, she never ever got over the tragic events of that fateful December morning. It wasn't helped by a visit from the Department of Pensions. About two years after Dad died, I answered the door to two burly, officious men dressed in dark suits wishing to speak with my mother. I was glad I was at home when they called because they caused her a great deal of grief.

It appeared Dad's first wife was still alive and somehow had heard of his demise and had claimed the widow's benefit. So, too, did my mother, who was now being accused of defrauding the government.

Before Mum and Dad married, they approached the registrar in St Albans and explained that Dad had lost touch with his former wife 20 years previously, and Dad asked what he had to do to ensure he could divorce her and marry Mum.

"If you place advertisements in the papers locally to where you believed she last lived, asking her to get in touch to discuss a divorce petition, and you don't hear anything for a month, then I'll marry you!" was, apparently, the advice they received.

According to my mother, they placed the adverts in the relevant papers and as no contact was made, Dad was granted his divorce and they married in 1957 and had a certificate to prove it.

Despite explaining this to the two "goons", they suggested that my father was a bigamist! Our protestations and appeals were turned down and they immediately demanded repayment of the two years' pension my mother had received and stopped any further payments.

She paid the money out of her savings, which left her considerably worse off but, ironically, she was able to claim welfare payments almost exactly equivalent to the widow's pension she'd just been refused!

The net result was that although not financially worse off, emotionally it set her back a great deal and I was a bastard child after all. It was so unnecessary.

CHAPTER 8
Juggling sport, career and married life

In January 1962, I was becoming disillusioned with my soccer career at Colney Heath FC. I still enjoyed the social side, but I'd realised that, despite my dedication, I wasn't going to progress much further up the football pyramid. Davies, whom I saw regularly in between his romantic exploits with Delia and his rugby, played for the Old Boys of the school, and he persuaded me to come down for a game when we didn't have a soccer fixture. I loved it!

I enjoyed playing for the lowest side, the Extra B, but, more importantly, I was delighted to see so many of my old class-mates. We had a traditional rugby club evening, drinking, playing stupid games and, of course, singing our heads off to all the rudest songs we could remember.

"Is it always like this, Davies?" I said.

"Only on the home games. The away games are even wilder!" he replied with a grin.

Dave Lucas and Gordon Harding, my bosses and fellow thespians, played for the Old Boys, and they were delighted when I turned up. I made up my mind to play rugby on Saturdays and football on Sunday mornings.

I played football for the Blacksmith's Arms pub side and we won the Sunday League title in my first season. I played for a further four years and enjoyed every minute, probably because I could cope more satisfactorily with this lower standard of football.

I was becoming as obsessed with rugby as I had been with football and my enthusiasm and ability grew with each match I played. I was very rusty at first, but played with some older, wily characters in the lower sides, many of whom had played at first-team level in their youth.

Ken Hacker was about 15 years older than me and captained the Extra B. Although standing six feet three inches, he played fly-half and could throw one of the best dummies I'd seen at any level. He made all the breaks and fed me the ball so I could speed over for a try. We became quite a successful team.

I progressed through the sides and was soon playing for the second XV, the A side. Davies was captain and also a very useful fly-half with an astute rugby brain. The side contained many of my contemporaries so it was just like playing in a school match. Eventually, I broke into the first XV and played there until 1972. Those ten years were amongst the happiest of my life. I felt I'd "come home".

We played in an all-white strip. Getting it clean every week took hours of boiling and scrubbing. All the mothers, girlfriends and wives complained so much so that in 1963 we changed the club colours to royal blue with a wide yellow "V" across the front. It was my first experience of female emancipation in action! The "V" was appropriate, since the club was called The Old Verulamians, more commonly referred to as "The Old Vs". Verulamian is the Roman name for St Albans.

Rugby clubs are renowned for the extraordinary mixture of characters from all backgrounds and the Old Vs were no exception. Peter Wood was a prefect when I first started at the grammar school although our paths never crossed until I joined the club. He was a good-looking extrovert and became renowned in school for getting his childhood sweetheart, Anne, pregnant when she was 16. She attended the St Albans Girls' Grammar school and Pete was often seen carrying her books home. They married before the baby was born and they've already celebrated their golden wedding anniversary!

They had their fair share of ups and downs in life. One of their children, aged about ~~six or seven~~ *seventeen*, ~~burned to death when her nightdress caught alight whilst she was dancing in front of the fire when Pete and Anne were out of the room~~ *died in a road accident*. It was Christmas Eve. Ironically, a group called *The Crazy World of Arthur Brown* had just recorded a big hit in the UK called *Fire*. It was banned in the club and if I hear it on the radio today, I turn it off; I just can't bear to hear it. It must have been an unbelievably intolerable time for Pete and Anne.

Pete's party piece was the Egyptian sand-dance, made famous by Wilson, Keppel and Betty. He was extremely supple and he could

93

imitate them superbly, shuffling along on some imaginary sand, with a tea- cloth wrapped around his head, playing an imaginary flute. We'd all clap and hum the desert song. You could almost see the snakes being charmed from their baskets!

George North was a delightful, tubby, red-faced chap. He was the ultimate carefree bachelor and was usually game for anything, at least until he married very late in life and calmed down a bit! He was a leading light in the local operatic society and he'd often regale us with arias from his latest musical production. He had a wonderful tenor voice and his favourite piece was *Sing to me, Gypsy*, from which opera or musical I never discovered. It has a haunting chorus, and George would insist we all sit down on the floor whilst he strolled between us giving us the signal when to join in. Even after several pints, George always managed to put on a professional performance that was much appreciated, especially by the away teams who simply couldn't compete!

John Prime, or "Prime" (I never heard him called John) was a fantastic tennis and rugby player. He was a prefect too, when I was a first-former and like many of my contemporaries, I worshipped him. He won the school tennis championship for many years and his tough tackling on the rugby pitch became legend. Now, I was playing in the same team! He had a very dry sense of humour and revelled in his "hard man" persona. In truth, he was a shy person and found it difficult to make relationships although we always got on very well. When I was at school and working part-time for Brookers, delivering groceries on my "impossible to handle" grocer's bike, I made a delivery to a house in one of the better parts of St Albans. To my utter amazement, Prime opened the door. It was his parents' house, and I was so awestruck, I dropped the box as I was handing it over to him. Eggs, biscuits, cakes and cans of assorted vegetables went flying, much to my embarrassment. Prime helped me retrieve the offending articles to re-box them, almost crying with laughter, which only increased my sense of humiliation. I don't think a week went by when we were teammates that he didn't remind me of that incident and of course, by now, the whole club knew about it!

We did some crazy things that in today's environment would have almost certainly resulted in us being awarded ASBOs – antisocial behaviour orders. In the clubhouse there still exists a couple of authentic street signs bearing the names of two of our more illustrious members – Brookfield Avenue, for Geoff Brookfield and Wenden's Ambo, a small village in darkest Essex, for Geoff Wenden. These signs were "collected" whilst returning from away matches and we regarded them as our trophies! For some inexplicable reason, we also purloined an orange Belisha beacon globe!

We held some riotous "gentlemen's evenings" with comedians and strippers. Mike Read, who went on to become a famous actor in *EastEnders*, the popular TV soap opera, was usually the compere and told some brilliantly disgusting jokes in his coarse, cockney accent.

My 21st birthday party celebrations in the clubhouse were wild, not that I remembered much about it! My stag party on Thursday, September 1st 1966, just before my wedding on the 3rd, was even wilder! I had the foresight to allow a day to recover which proved to be a masterstroke! My drinks were being "spiked" from the moment I set foot in the club so that when I, literally, became helpless, my "mates" decided to debag me and apply luminous green paint to my private parts!

At least, this wasn't as bad as some of the things we did to other members of the club. Being chained to a street light in your underwear for an hour or so was a popular prank on many stag nights!

Davies eventually took me home, found my key, so he wouldn't have to wake Mum, helped me upstairs, undressed me and put me to bed. When I awoke with the worst hangover I've ever had, imagine my horror when I went to relieve myself and discovered what I'd inherited! I scrubbed the offending part with shampoo and soap for over an hour, ever-mindful that within the next 36 hours, I'd be deeply involved in consummating my marriage!

Although I managed to reduce the colour from a glowing luminous green to a less glimmering shade of pistachio, I would still have some explaining to do! I was sure that Davies, my best man, would have the answer!

So, over a gingerly-sipped pint on the eve of the wedding in The Boot public house, we discussed the best way to break the news to Ann. We should have been discussing the meaning of the vows and other such matters on my last night of freedom, but I was keen to hear his views. After all he was mainly responsible for what might be the shortest marriage in history! His advice was, as usual, succinct and to the point although not particularly helpful!

"Don't say anything – you might just get away with it." He stopped short of wanting to inspect the affected area when I said, "Don't be stupid! There's no bloody way it won't be noticed!"

The wedding took place in St Alban's Register Office and the reception was held in the Comet Hotel in Hatfield. I was glad that, at last, we were now a normal family. Stephanie, as a precocious soon-to-be four-year-old was probably more the centre of attention than Ann – not that she minded. My mother was understandably upset at losing her beloved youngest son and was still grieving for Dad who'd died two years earlier and would now be living alone. Although I felt incredibly guilty, I knew that unless I made the break now, it would prove even more difficult later on.

We honeymooned at the Isles hotel in Swanage, Dorset. On the drive down, I was agonising about whether to tell Ann about the paint job or to take Davies's advice. I decided to leave it until the very last moment, hoping that having had a few drinks in the bar and a bottle of champagne in the room, Ann's senses would be sufficiently dulled to lessen the impact. As I emerged from the bathroom wearing the Isles hotel dressing gown, I confessed, and opened it to reveal the result of my stag night. To my immense relief, she fell back on the bed laughing, pointing out that at least she'd have no problem finding the appropriate component for a successful honeymoon! It took a further week of assiduously scrubbing and scouring before any semblance of natural skin colour returned. Thanks chaps!

Two years prior to getting married, I realised I needed to earn more money. I'd have to find somewhere to live, get a reliable car and take my family responsibilities seriously. I found a part-time job at the Midland Arms, a scruffy, tobacco-stained pub opposite St Albans railway station. I'd never worked in a pub before, but quite fancied it having spent many hours on the other side of the bar.

I started at 6.15 pm, so I usually went straight from work. The landlord didn't allow us to eat behind the bar, so as I worked until closing time at 10.30 pm two nights week, I'd be starving at about 8 pm. The pub was exceptionally busy from the time I arrived to about 7.30 pm, commuters from the London trains rushing in for their "swift halves" before going to their homes.

After they'd gone, the evenings really dragged with very few customers troubling us. So the landlord would retire upstairs for *his* evening meal, leaving just two or three of us part-timers in charge. I was so hungry, I raided the scotch egg jar on the counter, taking a bite and then temporarily hiding the remainder if a customer came in. I meticulously paid the correct money into the till to cover the cost, but this wasn't enough to save my job when the landlord unexpectedly came downstairs and saw two of us bolting down the remains of a hard-boiled yolk.

"I made it quite clear that eating food of any description behind the bar when we have customers is very unprofessional and I therefore have no option but to sack you!" he sneered. He seemed almost glad he'd caught us. I thought he was under the impression we'd stolen the eggs, so I blurted out that if he checked the till, he'd find they'd been paid for.

"It's not the money. I run a professional establishment here, and I simply won't have this sort of thing going on when my back is turned!" God, I thought, it's hardly the Ritz, but I bit my tongue and left.

I told Ann and my mother that I just didn't like pub life and I'd get another job soon. Ann's father said they were short of part-time evening bottlers at his factory where they produced Rose's lime juice. He worked there as a maintenance man and he said he'd make some enquiries. I was very nervous about this developing into a job. I'd be too close to him and if I screwed up, he'd be the first to know. A week later he said he'd fixed it for me – no interview – just turn up on Mondays and Wednesdays for the 6 pm till 10 pm shift. The pay was a pittance, but how could I refuse?

The bottling plant was huge and ran continuously 16 hours a day in four, four-hour shifts. Most of the unskilled part-timers like me rotated through three job roles: stacking the filled bottles into cardboard boxes, checking to see that the adhesive labels were level on the bottles and feeding the giant sugar hopper. The foreman met me and several other first-nighters and explained each role in turn. We had to watch each operation for five minutes before being allocated our first job for the evening, which in my case, was filling each cardboard box with a dozen bottles of lime juice.

At the head of the line was a huge carousel where the bottles were filled via giant tubes emanating from the juice factory and screw-tops robotically turned tightly by machines. From here, there were two conveyor belts: one feeding the filled bottles down the line (they reminded me of upright lime-green soldiers) and the other carrying cardboard boxes designed to hold a dozen bottles. This conveyor belt ran in parallel but about a foot lower and was programmed to ensure that as bottles 11 and 12 were manually placed in the box, it would be shunted onto a pallet to be taken away by a fork-lift truck. Then, the next box would arrive like clockwork to accommodate the next platoon.

So for an hour before changing to one of the other tasks, I had to fully concentrate on making sure that I got into a rhythm of picking up a bottle in each hand, thrusting them into the cardboard box six times, and trust that immediately after bottles 11 and 12 were safely despatched, the next box would arrive to receive the same treatment. It always did.

After a few weeks, I developed extraordinarily strong wrists that to this date are the envy of my family when I'm required to undo a particularly difficult bottle of pickled onions or jar of marmalade! On one occasion, I accidentally smashed the two bottles together as I attempted to place them in the box – it was easily done. Sticky lime juice cascaded deep into the conveyor belt machinery. I was dismayed to hear a high-pitched whistle that signified that the conveyor belts had stopped. I was even more concerned when the foreman shouted down the line, "What the bloody hell's happened now?" as he walked towards me. I was so embarrassed, but then, behind his back, I saw a fellow-worker smile and give me the thumbs up. Other work-mates smiled a look of relief.

It always took at least ten minutes for the maintenance men to clear up the juice and broken bits of glass from the machinery, which meant the workers could enjoy a quick fag! Although it was a genuine accident on my part, I subsequently discovered it was sometimes done deliberately as a ploy to have a paid-for fag-break! If this was my *full-time* job, I think I'd have supported this low form of anarchy!

Staring at green bottles for an hour at a time as they careered down the conveyor belt to ensure the automatic label sticker machine had put the labels on straight was mind-numbingly boring. Only about one in a hundred needed pulling off to be returned so it was easy to become lethargic. It would win any "most boring job in the world" contest!

Filling the giant sugar hopper that stood ten feet high was altogether more exciting. It was physically demanding, but I used it as part of my rugby training programme. I had to empty huge bags of sugar onto a large wheelbarrow. The only way to get to the top of the hopper was via three narrow planks of wood that zigzagged to the top. I needed to get a good run at it so that the momentum would enable me to tip the sugar into the hopper. It took ten wheelbarrow loads before the hopper could be switched on and so begin the manufacturing process. By this time, I'd be sweating profusely, but I enjoyed the physical workout. Sometimes I almost lost control, my load becoming perilously close to tipping over the edge. I don't think this procedure would pass the Health and Safety rules today!

I stayed at Rose's for about a year, by which time I'd saved enough to pay the deposit on my first "real" car; a black 1960 Standard Eight with red leather seats, registration number RXO 382 which cost £160 financed by a £25 deposit and an HP loan. By now I'd passed my driving test with some help from Ann, who'd passed many years earlier.

During the years when she and Stephanie lived with her parents, we rarely ever had any time for just the two of us. So she picked me up every Sunday morning, ostensibly to give me driving lessons, but in truth, just to be together. We'd drive around for about half an hour, and then park up in a lover's lane …

Once I was married with a child to support, I needed to earn some more money. A part-time job was out of the question now that I was attending Watford Technical College two or three evenings a week to continue my accountancy studies. My five-year day-release course had just ended. So, I decided that if Marconi couldn't offer me a better job with more pay, I'd look around.

And so in September 1964, I joined Pratt (Watford) Ltd as an assistant to the Assistant Accountant – a title at last! Pratts was a very well-known builder's merchant in Hertfordshire and was an industry so different from electronics, which I reasoned would be good to experience.

Alan Tallent was an archetypal accountant. He was meticulous to the point of becoming obsessive and humourless. But he prided himself on being super-efficient. He'd deal with issues immediately they arose; his "in-box" was rarely full. At first, I didn't like him and didn't respect how efficient he was. But after sitting opposite him every day for a year, I really appreciated his work-rate and absolute dedication to his job. I adopted his attitude.

Within six months, I'd made a sufficiently good impression to become, in addition to my accountancy duties, personal assistant to the chairman of the board, Chas F Goulden. Although this was a general "dogsbody" job, sometimes serving Earl Grey tea and McVities digestives on white bone-china plates with the company motif proudly displayed in gold leaf trim, at least I was being noticed by the board. Trouble was, he was difficult to work for. He was a bully, with a very bluff, arrogant manner.

Despite his autocratic management style, I learnt a great deal from him: when to be diplomatic, when to speak and when to shut up. It was my first taste of what it was like to be powerful and in control, so in a sneaky kind of way, I envied him.

The Pratts job paid well so we lived in a spacious, rented maisonette in a good area. The rent was £100 per month and I had to find six months' deposit up-front and furnish it from the money saved from my part-time jobs. We even bought a dog, a beautiful golden retriever puppy with those sad, soft, appealing brown eyes we couldn't resist. Ella, named after Ella Fitzgerald, one of my favourite singers, brought us a great deal of joy. She had, as all retrievers have, a most benign nature. Five-year-old Stephanie could do anything to her (and usually did) without any negative reaction. I took Ella to obedience classes; she was brilliant! Very well behaved, yet with a mischievous edge to her. I felt like a proud parent every time she performed well! I really enjoyed taking her for walks. It's so impressive when a dog is obedient and walking to heel. I especially liked taking her out last thing before going to bed. I passed all the expensive houses nearby, which always looked more impressive at night, imagining what it must be like to live in one someday. I often had a conversation with Ella discussing the pros and cons of each house! I realised that I was becoming incredibly ambitious, and I felt again an imaginary clockwork motor inside my chest, ticking away, driving me on. I ached to be successful in my career.

I began working longer hours, and so our social life mainly consisted of taking Ann, Stephanie and Ella down to the rugby club on match days; my late-night Saturdays were a thing of the past but this was much better. I'd not discussed my somewhat turbulent love life at the club; men usually don't confer in such matters, especially in rugby clubs, but now I wanted to share my new family unit with everybody. Stephanie was still hopeless at going to bed each night. I tried to influence matters, but the pattern of the previous four years of her life was hard to break. Often when I came home late from work at about eight or nine o'clock, I'd find Ann still talking to her and reading her stories. Sometimes they'd both be asleep, Ann kneeling at the side of the bed with her head resting the pillow. This meant our evenings, even if I was at home, were usually dominated by a five-year-old. I did manage a minor breakthrough when we all discovered the wonderful Winnie the Pooh books. Stephanie was totally hooked and she'd cry with delight if I offered to read to her. I used all my thespian skills to bring out the best of the characters, exaggerating them greatly, so we both the enjoyed the experience and I could use it to lever some quality time for Ann and I! We thought it might all come good when she went to school, but if anything, she became even more lively and jolly.

She hadn't been at the school long when she volunteered to look after the school hamster during the Easter break. All went well for the first week or so until disaster struck. I'd been out to a business dinner one evening and opened the front door at about 11 pm to be greeted with a note in the hallway: "Don't open living room door – hamster up chimney!" Of course, I did open the door and was totally unimpressed with what I saw. When we furnished the maisonette, we bought a plain English mustard-coloured carpet we thought was the height of elegance. It was now covered in sooty hamster footprints! Ann, sleepily, came downstairs in her dressing gown and explained that after discovering he was missing, she'd cornered him in the living room and then he'd run up the chimney. He would then re-appear, run round the room several times, chased by Ann, and disappear up the chimney again! This happened several times throughout the evening. I moved the cage over to the fireplace and sealed off the sides so that if he appeared, all I had to do was to trip the door behind him. A frustrating hour later, he finally showed up and my plan worked! Problem was, his delightfully pink nose was now, literally, as black as soot! A very sheepish Ann and Stephanie had to explain what happened on the first day of the next term, but although the teachers saw the funny side of the hamster's adventures, we were never asked to look after him again!

In 1967, I saw a job advertised for an Assistant Cost Accountant for Ellams Duplicators Ltd in Bushey, a suburb of Watford. I'd had enough of the Pratt (Watford) Limited chairman's ill-mannered and boorish behaviour and also couldn't see any opportunities for promotion. Ellams was an extraordinary mix of businesses all related to office supplies. The main divisions were: duplicator machine production, carbon paper manufacturing and a cardboard-box-making department. Apart from the latter, all the other products have since been replaced by the photocopier and printers, but in the mid-1960s the company was flying.

Carbon paper manufacturing must be one of the dirtiest industrial processes. Huge, six-feet-high rolls of ink-absorbent paper wound round gigantic cogs are passed through a vat containing a mixture of carbon black, a sooty substance resulting from burning hydrocarbons, paraffin wax and mineral oil, all heated to a temperature approaching 80 degrees centigrade. It's like sheep being passed through a sheep dip! When the impregnated carbon-coated paper was dry, it was passed through a cutting machine, reducing the giant sheets to more manageable sizes, small enough to fit a standard A4-sized box. This process resulted in small particles of carbon permeating the atmosphere. When I first saw the men leaving the plant for the first time at the end of a shift, it reminded me of the Welsh coalminers I used to see in Merthyr Tydfil! One of my jobs was to carry out a detailed cost analysis of the carbon paper process. This involved visiting the plant every day for a week. I hated it. It was noisy, hot, sticky and with the air full of carbon particles, it wasn't a good place to be. It simply wouldn't be allowed to happen today. This was valuable experience, however, and mainly, I enjoyed my time at Ellams.

They had a useful Sunday morning football side and I was persuaded by some of my new workmates to transfer to them from The Blacksmith's Arms' team in St Albans. Ann seemed quite happy for me to play rugby on Saturday for the Old Vs *and* Sunday morning football. I think she liked me keeping fit and always having some tales to tell every weekend!

I'd now settled on playing left-back and although I felt I was playing well, I was astounded one Monday morning to be told by the coach that I'd been watched for a couple of weeks by a scout from Watford FC and they wanted me to spend a day training with them with a view to signing professional forms! I couldn't wait to tell Ann, but much more importantly, Ann's father.

Now, perhaps, he would have to grant me *some* respect. After all, I could be playing for a team he'd supported since he was boy. He never showed *any* emotion when Ann and I told him. I don't think he was capable of showing any, other than to Stephanie whom he idolised. How different if my dad was still alive! I could imagine *his* chest bursting outside his waistcoat with pride despite the fact it was Watford FC and not the Spurs!

Ellams kindly granted me a day off for the trial – I think they felt some reflected glory in an *Ellams* "boy" being considered for professional football. I was still studying for my accountancy finals and had set my heart on a career in business, but I'd already thought that *if* something came of it, I'd definitely give it a go. After all, this was my boyhood dream and I wouldn't miss the chance to turn it into reality.

When I reported to Vicarage Road, I was met by one of the coaches who ushered me onto a bus with the other players and then taken to the training grounds in Bushey, a Watford suburb, not far from the Ellams factory. I thought there might be several other trialists present but I was told I was the only one and we'd spend the morning going through some training routines and a special trial match would be held in the afternoon attended by the manager, Ken Furphy. I was, unusually for me, incredibly nervous. I'd be training and playing against full-time professionals and here was I, a Sunday-morning "kick-about" player!

I needn't have worried. I had another of those "Heolgerrig" moments. I trained and played as if in a dream! Once again, It all seemed so effortless and I didn't feel out of place at all. When the match ended, we all showered and I was excited.

"Bloody hell! What if I'm offered a contract? What should I say?" were just two of the questions buzzing around my head. When we returned to Vicarage Road, I was asked to wait outside the manager's office. I could hear some discussions going on with the coaches and suddenly the door opened and I was asked to take a seat.

"Son, you did very well today and you showed great promise." I almost blushed. "Trouble is, you're too old. At 24, by the time we've got you up to professional standard, you'll only have a short career left and it just wouldn't be a good investment on our behalf."

My balloon was pricked. Although bitterly disappointed, at least I'd been given my chance. I was treated very well by the club and I still look out for their results. I finally exorcised my football career obsession that day and now I could carry on enjoying my rugby, concentrate on building my business career and looking after my new family.

CHAPTER 9
Cars for life!

I loved my black 1960 Standard 10 car I'd purchased in 1964, but an unforeseen incident led me to replace it within a year. Cars of that era were very basic. Radios, heaters, wing mirrors and even floor mats were all optional extras. A radio was deemed a luxury. I was able to just afford a basic one from Halfords, but my budget wouldn't run to the cost of fitting it. Ann had a friend, Ken Foreman, whom she worked with at the Anglia Building Society and he kindly offered to fit it as a favour one Sunday morning.

I took up his offer, not realising that he had about as much knowledge as me, which was zero! I drove to his house for four consecutive Sunday mornings before he managed to get a reasonable reception but at least we could now motor along to the sounds of the 60s music which Ann and I both loved.

Shortly afterwards, we decided to take a trip down to the New Forest and left St Albans early in the morning just as dawn was breaking. It was a stunningly beautiful late summer's day and I remember feeling everything was right in the world – I had Ann sitting next to me with Stephanie, aged just two, sitting on her lap, the radio churning out the latest hits, albeit a little crackly, and I was driving my beloved car.

Entering the New Forest, we began to smell the acrid odour of burning wires emanating from under the dashboard. I ignored it at first, thinking it was coming from the car in front. Then flames began to emerge, licking at the plastic fascia. Although I was heading a line of cars, I slowed down to the sound of a few horns honking their drivers' impatience.

By now, Ann was screaming and Stephanie began to cry. Suddenly, Ann opened the passenger door and, clutching Stephanie close to her, she leapt from the still-moving car into a ditch! I eventually found a place to pull over 30 yards further on.

The whole car was filled with smoke and so, coughing and spluttering, I stumbled out onto the verge. I was embarrassed to be ogled by the slowing passing traffic, although one kind motorist stopped in front of my car and ran back with a fire extinguisher. Once the flames were put out, Ann and Stephanie, having survived the leap into the ditch, brushed themselves down, joined me and we had an argument in front of the good Samaritan.

"I'm never going out in that car again! It's a fire trap, you'd better sell it!" Ann, ever-protective of Stephanie, exploded.

"If your friend wasn't so incompetent, this would never have happened. And by the way, thanks for leaving *me* to sort out the problem, you're just bloody selfish!" I said.

We eventually drove on, radio-less, and had a great day out with a tale to tell. Ann was adamant, though, the car had to be replaced and so, in 1965, a 1958 pale-blue Morris Oxford with dark-blue leather upholstery and a *dealer-fitted* radio became my new obsession – for a while!

Two years later, driving home from work one evening, I was rammed in the passenger-side of the car with such force, the Morris Oxford went up on two wheels and only just avoided rolling over. A Jaguar had emerged from a side road travelling far too fast and a collision was inevitable. My car was a write-off, although, fortunately, I only suffered some bumps and bruises. As was usual for cars of that era, seat-belts were not fitted, so I was very fortunate.

I was totally reliant on having some transport to get to and from my office and also concerned about high running costs, so I decided I'd look for a job with a car. Within a week, I spotted an advertisement for a part-qualified accountant at Godfrey Davis (Welwyn) Ltd, a Ford main dealership. I attended an interview at the London HQ, and to my delight, I was offered the job by Les Tye, the Finance Director, and began a month later. My love affair with the motor trade was about to begin!

Although the salary was about the same as Ellams Duplicators, there was a company car included and "excellent prospects". My boss was a Scot, Tom Gibson, the General Manager. He'd started his working life cleaning cars for Godfrey Davis in Glasgow and worked his way through the organisation rapidly. I soon found out why. He was an outstanding businessman with a quick brain and high energy. He was also incredibly involved in the detail of *everything* involving his dealership. He was also very demanding and strict but also had a sense of humour. I couldn't have wished for a better tutor and we hit it off straight away.

On my first day, Tom introduced me to all the managers and I was surprised but delighted that the sales manager was Allan Brooke. He and I had played in the same football team once or twice over the years and we shared some common friends.

He was everything you'd expect a car sales manager to be: sharp, astute, witty, always impeccably dressed and a little crazy! After the tour, he came to see me in my new office – the first I'd had on my own – and told me about Tom.

"He's a good bloke, but whatever you do, don't cross him! He can give you a very hard time, but if you can gain his trust, he'll be great to work for." He also said, "You know, Dai, the motor industry is just one big club. Once you get the taste for it, you'll never leave. For a start, you'll have a car for life!" These words proved highly prophetic.

At the end of my first day at work, I went to Allan's office to pick up the keys to my new car. I was overjoyed! It was a brand new Cortina 1600 in Acquatic Jade – a fancy name for light green! There's a distinctive smell about a brand new car that arouses excitement and elation. So, driving home that night for the first time in a brand new car, absorbing its unique aroma, I felt I'd made a great decision in joining Godfrey Davis.

Trouble is, all of us in the motor trade, especially salesmen, became blasé, often driving as many as six or seven different new cars a year. These staff cars are used as demonstrators. So if a customer insisted on buying one because they liked the specification, then we'd sell it to them at a reduced price and replace it with the very latest model usually the same day! As this happened so often, we didn't always appreciate the excitement and emotions our customers felt when they parted with their hard-earned cash for a car they'd dreamt about owning for a long time. To us they became the tools of our trade.

Because Tom Gibson worked at the dealership all hours, I tended to do the same. I really threw myself into the job and positively sucked every bit of knowledge from him at every opportunity. On Friday nights, the managers and Tom visited the local pub to round off the week's work and to "bond" together. Sometimes, the "swift half" would extend until closing time and my protestation to Ann that it was all in the cause of building business relationships didn't go down too well!

In that first year at Welwyn, I had six different new cars covering almost the entire model range: Cortinas, Corsairs, Capris, and Mark 4 Zephyr/Zodiacs. As demonstrators, they were always immaculately maintained and cleaned every day. This was to be my way of life, car-wise, for the next 36 years, during which time I never paid for fuel, insurance, maintenance, cleaning or licensing – some perk!

My ambitious nature was now becoming rocket-fuelled and I was desperate to get qualified. In June 1968 I took my finals, for the third time, in Bethnal Green, North London. The results were due in August.

I'd known from previous ordeals that when the envelope containing the results dropped through the letterbox, you could tell if you'd passed or failed immediately by holding it up to the light. If you could see some boxes, you'd know you'd failed. The boxes contained the grades. No boxes meant a letter of congratulation – eureka!

When the post arrived early one August morning, I rushed downstairs and with trembling hands, I was almost afraid to offer the envelope up to the light. When I did so, I couldn't believe it!

"No boxes! No boxes!" I shouted upstairs to Ann who was lying in bed. She knew what I meant. This was one of the most important moments of my life. Now I was on my way. It had taken me almost nine years to qualify but people wouldn't know about that. I was now a *qualified* accountant with letters after my name and that's all that mattered! It was tough to qualify then because even if you failed in just one subject, say, economics, you had to take the complete exam again. By the time I qualified, I'd passed every subject twice! No one could say I'd scraped through! Qualifying had become another of my obsessions and my persistent nature simply wouldn't allow me to fail!

Now I had a reliable car that cost nothing to run, a decent wage as a result of qualifying, and a family keen to pursue what life had to offer, we began to venture further afield and had some wonderful holidays in the Isle of Wight and St Ives in Cornwall. We stayed in small hotels, which was a luxury beyond anything we'd previously experienced.

We really got the taste for holidays, so one summer, when a friend of mine offered us a week's free use of his crofter's cottage on the Isle of Tiree in the Hebrides, off the west coast of Scotland, we jumped at the chance. We left Ella with Ann's parents, so to keep seven-year-old Stephanie company, we took her cousin, Angela, who was the same age. She was brought up in Norfolk and had a very broad accent.

To make the 600-mile drive up to Oban where we would catch the ferry to Tiree, I swapped my Cortina for a berry-red Ford Zephyr, which was considerably larger and more comfortable. The kids got on really well although there was all the usual "Are we there yet?" and "We're bored!" comments about every 30 minutes. We lustily sang all the songs we could remember, and I made them laugh by changing the words to something ever so slightly risqué so they'd cringe with embarrassment, at the same time asking me to sing it again!

After an overnight stay close to the picturesque harbour of Oban that greatly restored our energy, we drove to the ferry port and looked out for the ramps that would take us onto the boat. The only ferries I'd seen before on TV were the huge vessels on the cross-channel routes to France, so I was somewhat concerned to see that only one car was allowed onto the deck! I had to drive onto a huge net laid flat on the ground by the side of the ferry. We left the car, and a crane lifted the net onto the deck of the ferry as if it were landing a huge fish!!

The ferry trip took an hour and a half, and as we entered the harbour at Tiree, I noticed quite a crowd assembled on the dockside. I assumed they were passengers waiting to go back to Oban, but I was told later, they'd come to see this enormous car being "netted" onto the island. There were so few cars there, and most of those were over 30 years old, so to see this brand new "monster" being driven around was quite something!

We felt like celebrities as we took our seats in the car and I almost felt like waving regally as we left the dockside to find the cottage. Everywhere we travelled, people would stop and stare, which was a little un-nerving to begin with, but the kids loved it!

Half an hour's drive later, we arrived at the remote cottage, set right on a magnificent beach that, surprisingly, looked like those we'd seen in Caribbean travel brochures. Admittedly, there were no palm trees, but the sand was a glistening white and the colour of the sea a mixture of turquoise and indigo. Our spirits rose even further when we cautiously opened the front door.

The cottage was delightful, and much more airy and bright than I imagined. It had a huge stone fireplace, and on some evenings when the temperature dropped alarmingly, I lit a fire with the driftwood the kids had enjoyed collecting during the day. The weather was fabulous, and the holiday was a great success despite two events that slightly impaired it.

As well as collecting driftwood, we decided to harvest some winkles from the nearby rocks. The kids had a great time seeking them out and putting them into their buckets. There was a giant cauldron suspended over the fire, and it was my idea to boil the winkles and have them for our supper – how adventurous!

I'm not a great lover of shellfish so I didn't take part, but Ann, and the kids in particular, tackled them with gusto. The next 24 hours were hell! Although Ann wasn't too badly affected, the kids spent all night groaning, vomiting and going to the primitive toilet every half-hour. If it wasn't one end, it was the other, and multiplied by two meant that, at any one time, the bathroom was occupied all night! They couldn't help having some "accidents" in bed so that by the morning the whole cottage smelt how I imagined a Third World refugee camp might!

We spent the next day washing all the bed linen and generally de-fumigating the cottage. Fortunately, the kids soon recovered, and although nervous about going to bed the next night, there was no repeat performance!

The second event concerned upsetting the locals. I saw advertised in the window of the only store on the island, that the annual Tiree Scottish Games was to be held whilst we were there. Entries were being taken inside the store and anyone was free to enter – at least that's what the notice said! There were all the usual Scottish sports like "tossing the caber" and "putting the shot" but I entered the

440-yard race, more for fun than anything else. On the day, which was sunny with a slight breeze, we turned up for the Games, as had *all* the 200-plus islanders. It seemed *we* were the only visitors.

My first impression was how seriously all the competitors were taking their respective events, stretching, deep-breathing and looking very determined – this was no fun day!

There were 20 competitors in the race and when the starter's gun fired, I was totally comfortable with the early pace. By the 220-yard mark, lying in third place, and knowing I had a fast finish, I thought I might just be able to win. As we rounded the last bend, I saw my chance, and flew past the two runners in front of me on the outside. One put up a strong finish, but I was able to breast the tape about a yard in front of him. The *only* cheers I heard were from my own family who were jumping up and down with excitement. I'm glad they were there because if not, I would have thought I'd suddenly gone deaf as I hit the tape!

The prize-giving was even worse – I'm sure I heard some booing – but at least I had the satisfaction of wearing the winner's medal around my neck.

It was only a few days later I discovered why they were so unhappy. Apparently, I'd beaten the Tiree 440-yard champion who'd held the title for the last three years and no-one could recall a time when an "outsider" had ever won. This, coupled with the celebrity status caused by driving the biggest car ever seen on the island, was just too much for some of these dour, insular Scots islanders!

"How do you feel about being promoted to the St Albans' dealership, Dai?" Tom almost reluctantly said one morning in September 1969.

"Great!" I said looking very pleased with myself. He didn't want me to leave him, but he'd been told by Les Tye, the Finance Director, that there was a vacancy at this much larger dealership, and he felt "young Henley" was right for a move to a bigger job. Tom's rule on personal relationships was that, initially, he distrusted people, and they had to *earn* his respect over time. I think I'd achieved that and so he was understandably nervous about replacing me. "Is there anyone you know who could do the job?"

"No-one comes immediately to mind, Tom. But I'll give it some thought." I had no intention of doing so, I was more interested in knowing the financial terms of the promotion.

A few days after this conversation, I was having a drink with Davies in the Tudor Tavern Inn in St Albans, when Mike Kiff, my college mate and his then girlfriend, Jacqui walked in. I hadn't seen Mike for a while, so we started chatting. When he said he was unhappy in his job, I almost hugged him! I explained to him the joys of working for Godfrey Davis, and within a month, Mike joined up with Tom who was, understandably, delighted. Mike's an outstanding accountant and when I left St Albans in 1972, he took over from me once again and enjoyed a great career in the company.

The Godfrey Davis dealership in St Albans was much larger than Welwyn, and I now found myself managing an accounts department of eight women and two men. I reported to Dennis Whythe who was very much the "old school" type of manager. A two or three-hour lunch was the norm, and his management style was laissez-faire to say the least! However, he was very generous and kind, and reminded me of my father in many ways.

Now that I was qualified, I thought I knew everything. Although I could handle the numbers, and developed a skill for interpreting the monthly management accounts, I had no idea how to manage staff. I'd received no personnel training whatsoever, despite being given the power to "hire and fire". When it came to motivating and encouraging the best out of people, I simply relied on my own enthusiasm and ambition. I hadn't even learnt that people's needs are different! I applied the same crude principles to everyone, which led to a few staff problems.

For example, I once sacked a couple of women whom I thought simply weren't up to the job. Looking back, this was a needless exercise; I'm now convinced they'd have improved significantly had I invested some time in training, counselling and getting to know them better.

One of the two men working for me was an urbane, upright, 51-year-old, Pat Fergusson. He was very quiet, almost sullen, and just got on with his job as an efficient bought ledger clerk. He rarely interacted with any other member of staff, and because he was very good at his job, I had little need to manage him. After about six months, Dennis Randall, the Sales Manager, with whom I had a friendly love-hate relationship (I'll explain later!) walked into my office one morning clutching a book about Colditz Castle, the German prisoner-of-war camp.

"You'll never believe this, Dai, you've got a bloody war hero working for you. Read this!" Dennis laid the book on my desk, opened about halfway through. The text I read made the hairs on the back of my head quiver. It was written by a Colditz prisoner-of-war who was sent there after escaping from other camps. He referred to he and another being discovered after one of their escapes by a German officer, armed with a rifle with a bayonet attached, amongst some piles of hay stored in a barn somewhere in deepest Germany. He described the scene vividly; the soldier ordering both of them to stand in front of him with their hands on their head; a loud noise outside the barn, and the soldier's attention being diverted momentarily. The text went something like this:

"In that split second, my fellow escapee, Pat Fergusson, lunged at the soldier, wrestled the rifle from his grasp and used the bayonet to pierce his heart. We quickly made our escape, scampering across the fields, not daring to look back!"

"No, it can't be the same Pat Fergusson. He's surely not capable of such a thing!" I said.

"Well, there's only one way to find out, ask him," Dennis responded.

I called Pat into the office and showed him the book. Although visibly surprised at this startling revelation, he barely responded to my probing, except to say that it was a part of his life he'd rather not discuss. He was so insistent, we finally respected his view.

He was a remarkable man in many ways. His obituary was published in The Times newspaper – he died in 2004, aged 86. He was taken prisoner as a subaltern with the remnants of the 1st Armoured Tank Division after Dunkirk in 1940. He escaped three times from German POW camps, was recaptured, and as a result, was incarcerated in Colditz Castle from 1943 to 1945.

The event described in the book was his last escape prior to being sent to Colditz, where he was a leading figure in helping to build the famous glider, in which it was hoped two men would fly to freedom. The war ended before it could be deployed.

After the war, he became a racing driver, once finishing 10th in the gruelling Le Mans 24-hour race. Now here he was, working as a clerk for someone almost half his age, with no real experience of life.

It set me wondering; how on earth do men, who did some unbelievably heroic things during the war, seem to be able to slip back into what must seem a very humdrum, civilian way of life when they returned? I think I'd have found it exceedingly difficult.

Dennis Randall usually struggled to make his car sales monthly target, which was a key ingredient to keeping his job! (Although we didn't apply it, it was common practice in the motor trade in the 1960s and 1970s that whichever salesman sold the least number of cars in any given month was immediately dismissed and replaced with a new recruit! This certainly made the last few days of the month interesting!) I liked Dennis immensely. He had a ready wit, and he didn't seem to take life too seriously and possessed some surprising gifts.

The Friday evening ritual of celebrating the end of the week was as important to the managers of St Albans as it was to those of Welwyn, so at 6.00 pm we'd all adjourn to the pub just a few steps away from the dealership.

My friendly love-hate relationship with Dennis began when on one such evening, having sunk quite a few pints, he casually strode up to the piano and began belting out some well-known pop songs. Damn! That's what *I* wanted to do! This made him very popular and so became a weekly event. He was a very good pianist, but I consoled myself that at least he'd studied music and must have practised for hours, and so deserved his success – unlike me, who'd declined such lessons from my mother, preferring to play football every night instead!

I was not a cricket fan, but Davies had persuaded me to join St Columbus cricket club. He was a very good wicket keeper, and as their ground was right next to the Old Vs rugby pitch, not far from home, it seemed a good way to spend summer Saturday or Sunday afternoons there. It was great for Ann and Stephanie too and they often helped to prepare the teas, assisting with the scoring and watching me play badly!

I was not very skilful. My highest-ever score was 14 runs. A career in first-class cricket was never an option!

I was discussing my dubious cricketing career with Dennis Randall one Monday morning, when he said he used to "play a bit" and would love a game. He told me he used to open for a well-known team in North London so I assumed he might be a useful player.

He was! I introduced him to the other players at our next match and we watched in awe at his debut innings. He had *all* the strokes, and was aggressive, too. He loved attacking the bowlers, fast or slow, often walking down the wicket to smash the ball over the boundary. I wished I could play like him.

Cricketers are probably the most social of all sporting animals, and the players' wives, girlfriends and children looked forward to getting together every weekend for a cricket tea or picnic. Dennis brought his family and Davies brought Delia, his childhood sweetheart whom he'd now married. After the match, we'd play records, drink beer and tell naughty jokes, sitting on the clubhouse verandah whilst the kids played hide and seek in the gathering dusk – life couldn't get any better on a balmy English summer's evening!

After two years at the St Albans dealership, I wasn't really making much progress at Godfrey Davis. I thoroughly enjoyed my job as the accountant, but I wanted to progress to becoming a general manager. There was no formal management development available in the company, and that motor in my chest was still feverishly whirring away, driving my ambition.

Lex Motor Company was one of the largest motor dealership groups in the UK and were renowned for their management training and development courses. I wrote a letter to Trevor Chinn, the charismatic Chief Executive, asking to join their General Management training programme. I was delighted to get an interview in London, and even more chuffed to be offered a job. Just one snag – they felt I wasn't yet ready to go through the induction phase for a general management job – I'd have to join them as an accountant and this would be reviewed in 12 months.

It wasn't what I wanted but I was deeply impressed by their commitment to training and development, once on the conveyor belt. There were no guarantees either, about where I'd end up working. Lex was a national group with dealerships as far apart as Newcastle and Southampton.

Ann and I discussed the change of job over and over again, but I was absolutely certain it was the right move even if it meant leaving St Albans and the rugby club.

So, in May 1971, I reported for duty at the London HQ to experience the exciting development into general management, except that it didn't seem that way at first! For the first three months, I was stuck on my own in a small office in Soho, close to the London School of Music, where, when the windows were open on hot summer's days, I could clearly hear less-than-harmonious renditions of classic compositions, played badly by the students. I was given a succession of tedious accountancy tasks that I could easily achieve.

I spoke to the Chief Accountant, who, whilst sympathetic, told me to bide my time. Occasionally, sensing my frustration, he'd take me on some visits to dealerships or to divisional offices that I greatly enjoyed. On one such visit to Maidenhead, I met Tony Axford, Divisional Manager for the south west, who'd play a major part in my development in months to come.

I was sent to attend a conference, held in a hotel in Weybridge, Surrey, on used car retailing, really just to give me something to do. It was led by Tony Axford and involved an overnight stay and some syndicate work in the evening. The next day, each syndicate had to present their proposals for improving sales.

Most people hate making presentations, but I'm sure a combination of my thespian activities together with my driving ambition, gave me the confidence to volunteer to do it. I also had some good ideas on the subject, developed from my time with Tom Gibson in Welwyn. The presentation went really well and so I reluctantly returned back to my lonely office the next day.

"You've made a bit of a name for yourself with your Weybridge jolly!" The Chief Accountant always thought that an overnight stay at an expensive hotel at the company's expense was just an excuse for a "jolly". In reality, together with the rest of the syndicate, I'd worked on my presentation after dinner, refining and honing it, getting to bed in the early hours of the next morning, not drinking alcohol for fear of a hangover.

"Really, what do you mean?"

"Tony Axford wants to see you. He thinks you're ready for the general manager's induction programme. Although he doesn't have any vacancies coming up, I think he just wants to get you into his team before anybody else grabs you!"

Within two weeks, I'd been interviewed by Tony and his team and been granted a six-month induction programme. This meant visiting over 20 dealerships all over the UK, preparing reports comparing and contrasting every aspect of the retail motor business. I spent many evenings in hotel rooms, which although exciting at first, became the least enjoyable part of the process. I also attended courses on inter-personal skills, marketing and financial management. I mopped up these activities like an absorbent cloth and came into contact with hugely experienced General Managers, who were happy to pass on their knowledge.

This broader education into the operation of car dealerships was invaluable and fundamental to my future career. On many occasions since, I've had cause to recall some of these experiences. It also made me supremely confident that I could now manage any size of operation.

This personal development didn't cease once I became a General Manager. Throughout my ten-year career with Lex, they organised some outstanding courses. They once flew over from the US a Professor of Marketing from Harvard University to share his knowledge and wisdom with some selected General Managers. I was delighted to be included. I also learnt so much from the inter-personal skills courses run by some remarkably talented tutors. These courses were run in four-weekly sessions spread throughout a 12-month period, each one designed to refine the essential skills necessary to get the best out of people.

I, along with nine other managers, attended the modular course at the same hotel – a week on the course then three months at the dealership, repeated four times. It was compulsory for *every* General

Manager to attend. The instructor, Les Garlick, was outstanding, just as well as a great deal rested on his shoulders.

The major thrust during the first two weeks was to break you down, to get to the raw bones of your personality. It was considered important that in order to truly understand other people, we had to gain an understanding of why we acted the way we did under certain circumstances.

The following two weeks was dedicated to rebuilding you, ensuring you were much more sensitive to the needs of others and being able to spot strengths and weaknesses.

As General Managers, we likened the trainer's job to a motor mechanic; he'd strip down a basic model to the bare engine and then rebuild it into a souped-up version, with new bits and pieces attached! We just hoped he had enough skill to carry out the modification effectively, otherwise you were destined for the breaker's yard! Fortunately, my engine became supercharged!

Les didn't always succeed.

The basis of the course was based on the answer to these questions: How do others see us? How do we *think* others see us? How would we *like* others to see us? The greater the gap between these perceptions, the greater you had to change.

The answers, almost exclusively, related back to childhood and concerned relationships with parents, siblings and partners. We also learnt that *everybody*, when you first meet them, puts on a front that is almost always not a true indicator of their true self. We were taught the skill of getting behind this façade so that you could relate to people far more effectively.

Early in the course, and as part of this process, we had to walk around with a piece of paper with a single word written on it taped to our back. The single word was chosen by the rest of the group. You had to guess what the word said. Some of this role-playing was quite cruel. Mine, to my surprise, said "selfish". Other managers wore the word "arrogant" or "untrustworthy".

You were encouraged to bare your soul on the basis that the more you gave out, the more you got back. Some managers just couldn't handle it – they found the process painful and would break down in tears. In a roomful of other men, this was not what they wanted to show. Some never got over it, a few even resigning from the course, which usually consigned them to managing smaller dealerships and dropping out of the Management Development Programme.

One example was an experienced General Manager who had never been exposed to this type of in-depth analysis and whose façade was bold, blustering and pompous. This disguised a complete lack of self-worth brought about by his early parenting. He *thought* he came across as a confident, likeable person and this was what he *wanted* others to think of him. When he was told, uncompromisingly, that he was *actually* seen by the rest of the group as someone full of his own self-importance, a bully and entirely unapproachable, he broke down, sobbing embarrassingly. The difference in perception was so vast, it must have seemed an impossible chasm to bridge. He never got over it and immediately walked out of the programme.

I couldn't get enough of it! I also learned a great deal about myself and my inter-personal skills were greatly improved. I worked hard to, literally, get the word "selfish" off my back. I didn't believe I was but it was the impression I gave so I was more considerate of others. My antennae became highly tuned into relationships with my other managers and staff and I learned how to get more out of them. I learned that not everybody responds to the same motivation. I learned not to pussy-foot around with certain people – they needed a good rollicking to get them going. Others, by far the majority I discovered, needed very gentle persuasion and thanks for a job well done.

Lex were so far ahead of all the other motor retailers and their vision in providing such fantastic training and development resulted in outstanding success for the group.

"How does being the group's youngest General Manager, reporting directly to me and working out of Basingstoke sound?" Tony Axford, my new mentor, was pleased he'd found a vacancy for me in a medium-sized Rover-Triumph dealership. I was delighted, but I'd have liked to have commenced my fledgling general management role in a more *sexy* town! All I knew about Basingstoke was that it was a boring, London overspill about a 45 minutes' train journey from the capital.

"Great! When do I start?" I said, as enthusiastically as I could.

"You've got about two weeks to brush up your product knowledge and to explore where you want to live. I'll introduce you to the staff and sort out your new company car. I'm relying on you to put some "oomph" into the dealership. Don't let me down!" He heavily emphasised this last sentence.

When I told Ann the news, especially about moving, she wasn't overjoyed. She raised a number of issues that would have to be resolved. I tried not to appear selfish, but this was my big chance and I was determined to sort out *any* problems. Some weren't easy.

One was my mum. She lived alone since Dad had died just seven years earlier and was still fragile. Les, my hero as ever, took on the responsibility of ensuring she wasn't lonely and promised to visit her frequently. I, too, promised to visit as often as I could.

It was a big step too, to leave all my schoolmates at the rugby club, especially Davies, with whom I'd shared so much of my adolescent years and life-changing decisions.

The biggest problem, though, was what to do with Ann's parents. They were such a close unit, especially during Stephanie's early childhood. Ann, Stephanie, Harry and Elsie seemed joined by an invisible umbilical cord. Harry and Elsie were understandably crestfallen at the idea of "losing" their daughter and grand-daughter to Hampshire. My solution, based on pragmatism and ambition rather than emotion, was to buy a house for us and an apartment for them out of the proceeds of the sale of our house in Queen's Crescent. We'd bought it just after my promotion to the St Albans dealership and it proved to be a sound investment. Their house was rented, so had no equity, whilst mine had risen in value by over 50% in 18 months from £4,000 to £6,000!

The final part of the jigsaw concerned Stephanie. She was now ten years old, so if we were going to make a move, this would be a good time before starting her secondary education.

All that remained was to find two abodes that would suit everybody's taste – not an easy task. On our first drive down to show Ann and Stephanie the dealership and the delights of Basingstoke, I asked Ann what she thought. She simply said, "Keep driving!"

The next major town was the city of Winchester which she found much more interesting and so, although it involved a half-hour drive each way to Basingstoke, I could see her point of view. We discovered a delightful three-bedroom semi in Harestock, an estate north of the city, and a two-bedroom apartment in Northlands Drive about a mile or so away. With my considerably enhanced salary as a General Manager, we were able to send Stephanie to an excellent private school, Princes Mead, so at least the family issues were dealt with surprisingly quickly.

My time away from home, training to become a General Manager, together with my unquenchable ambition, had a profound effect on my relationship with Ann, although this wasn't to crystallize until some years later. From my perspective, I felt we were drifting apart emotionally and I didn't feel particularly close to her. In retrospect, it's possible, too, that my increased awareness of relationships as a result of my inter-personal skills training, highlighted the paucity of my feelings for Ann. This is not a criticism of her, but more a result of my growing maturity.

On my first day at the Basingstoke dealership, I met the 80 or so staff and Tony Axford presented me with the keys to my new company car. It was a brand new green Rover 3.5 litre with luxurious tan leather trim. It was magnificent! I couldn't wait to get home and show Ann and Stephanie that *I'd arrived!*

So, not only was the "Cars for life" prophecy materialising, we were starting out on an exciting new adventure full of hope and good feelings about the future. Except I hadn't joined a new rugby club…yet!

CHAPTER 10
My new rugby club

Amidst all the issues surrounding the move to Winchester in June 1972 – taking on a new job, moving house, dealing with Ann's parents, leaving the Old Boy's team – the one that concerned me most was the change of rugby clubs. I knew nothing about Winchester Rugby Club, so, in keeping with tradition, I wrote a letter to the club secretary, Andrew Leadbetter, asking him to organise an introduction to the club. He wrote back informing me that he'd set up a meeting with the club's head coach and captain, Gordon Jones, together with three other members of the committee, Gerry Rowe, Eddie Warwick and John (Nosher) Eames at the Eclipse Inn in Winchester.

As soon as I walked into the pub, I knew exactly who they were – rugby was written all over them! We shook hands and I was asked if I'd like a drink. In those days, I'd developed a taste for a premium beer called *Tankard*, which also carried a premium price. "A pint of *Tankard* would go down well," I said.

"You'll have a pint of bloody ordinary bitter, or nothing at all," said Gerry, without a trace of a smile. "Oh! That'll be fine," I said, somewhat embarrassed. I subsequently tuned-in to Gerry's sense of humour and when I started to give him back the same treatment, we really hit it off. He's about five feet seven inches tall, with curly blonde hair and played scrum-half. He was an outstanding player, with an incredible side-step and we played together in the same team for many years.

Eddie Warwick had a dry, laid-back laconic sense of humour, which went down well with the ladies, although he was seriously attached to Kath, his American girlfriend whose stock response, when asked "How are you?" was always "Pretty good".

J G Gordon Jones, commonly known as "Jonesy", is one of the most charismatic men I have met. He's extremely intelligent and I've often wondered how far he'd have progressed in one of the professions or in business if he'd focussed upon them. Instead, he lived life vigorously, almost recklessly, involving females (he admits to three marriages but we believe there were more), drinking and rugby. He was fanatical about all three, but rugby was his real passion and he devoted himself wholeheartedly to Winchester Rugby Club. He was born in West Wales, spoke Welsh, and, before moving to Winchester, played for Glamorgan Wanderers, a first-class side in the 1960s.

He's a natural leader. When Jonesy was around, you knew you'd have a good time and as my captain and coach for many years at the club, I did anything he asked me to. He led by example on the pitch and you felt it was your *duty* to follow his example off the pitch too, especially in the drinking stakes.

His beer consumption capacity was phenomenal. In the 38 years I've known him, I've only seen him slightly the worse for wear about three times. He explained to me once, that no matter how many pints he'd consume in an evening, he never, ever got a hangover! *My* hangovers were a real deterrent, at least for a day or so!

He's a ready wit and his expressions could usually reduce us to gibbering wrecks. As a testament to his legacy of quotes, they're still used today in the club, despite the fact that Gordon moved back to Wales nearly 20 years ago!

John "Nosher" Eames, although younger than me, already had a receding hairline that within a very short time, disappeared forever. He'd grown a black moustache to compensate for the loss but this only accentuated his lack of locks. He got the name "Nosher" when he was once caught stuffing his face with, allegedly, the largest baguette ever seen in Winchester, just before a match. The sobriquet stuck, and to this day, his reputation as a man who enjoys his food has been carefully nurtured!

I felt completely at ease with these boys, and we had a great time in the Eclipse, which was the club's local pub, and we stayed on until well past closing time, discussing everything to do with rugby.

I was disappointed to learn that Winchester Rugby Club didn't have a clubhouse! I was used to a wonderful set up in St Albans and regarded a clubhouse in the same way a religious person would regard his cathedral. They played on a council pitch at King George V playing fields, which had a severe slope (worth at least ten points playing downhill) and changed in a small hut with a six-foot-deep communal bath, large enough to hold 15 players.

Unless you were the first in the bath after a particularly muddy match, it was a serious health hazard. The colour of the water resembled onion soup within minutes, and so any open wounds were subject to all kinds of infections! It reminded me of the scars my brother used to pick up after getting his wounds infected playing football on the "Bont", a pitch covered in coal dust from the slagheaps of Merthyr!

We had our teas and après-match beers at the local tennis club, about a ten-minute drive from the pitch. The tennis members were a snobby bunch, usually dressed in smart tennis gear and pastel tracksuits and hated us going there. We were somewhat scruffier and noisier. John, the bar steward, made a point of always serving the tennis members first.

We had to leave by 6.00 pm, and if we started singing, a fundamental part of any Saturday night in rugby clubs nationwide, we'd be asked to leave immediately! So the Eclipse was the place to go for the evening entertainment but this meant another drive back into the town.

When I expressed my disappointment to Jonesy about these arrangements, he told me the president of the club, John Broadway, a local councillor, had some plans for our own clubhouse and ground in North Walls, just half a mile or so east of Winchester town centre. My mood brightened considerably. He arranged for me to meet John so that he could show me the plans. He also told me that pre-season training would be taking place within the next week.

Thus began a 38-year love affair with the club that has considerably enriched my life. I've had many adventures with a great bunch of people that I strongly believe would only be possible within a rugby club. There's something about going into a physical "battle" with your comrades that brings out the best in people. It's war with a referee replacing weapons. You look after your own.

Afterwards, you have a beer with your mates and the opposition and look forward to seeing them next season – there's nothing quite like it!

Although aged 30, I was exceptionally fit and felt I was about to enter my prime as a player. During the first two or three training sessions, I overheard a few of the boys making very complimentary remarks about by ability and speed. I was being compared to their star player, Leroy Angel, who played as a wing three-quarter, my position. "Is he as quick as Leroy?" and "Leroy'll have to watch his place in the team!" were a couple of examples. I looked forward to the challenge.

He never started pre-season training as early as the rest of the team, not through arrogance, but, allegedly, never needed to! When he did, I was astounded! He was several classes above anyone I'd ever played with before. He had everything: blistering pace, a sidestep off either foot, and a good rugby brain. It was no contest. I may have been as fit, but that was about the only area I could match him. He's a delightful man, and we played together in the first XV on the wings, for a few seasons; I changed from left wing to right wing to accommodate him!

He went on to gain a record number of caps for the Hampshire County team and I strongly believe that had he moved on to a London club, he'd have played for England. He was exceptionally loyal to his club. Following his retirement in 1977 due to a serious knee injury, he began his rugby administration career, culminating in being elected the president of the Rugby Football Union. The club are very proud to have spawned such a VIP! We're still in touch and he remains a member of Winchester Rugby Club. I'm very proud to know him.

On one of the training nights, the club president, John Broadway, turned up to check on progress of the team and to discuss the new ground and clubhouse. He was a giant, around six foot eight inches tall, about 15 years older than me, very well spoken and heavily into local politics. As a councillor, he had considerable presence and not just because of his physique. He'd played for the club for many years and was as passionate about it as Jonesy.

"Dai wants to know all about our new ground and clubhouse, John, is it fact or fiction?" he said.

"We'll be playing rugby there within the year, mark my words! I'll take Dai up there next week if you want," John replied.

When he showed me the location of the ground, big enough to accommodate three pitches and a training area, I nearly wept. It was a massive rubbish tip with old cars, prams, washing machines and cardboard boxes filled with every imaginable type of waste as far as the eye could see. The clubhouse wasn't even started.

"John," I said, "there is no way in a million years that we'll be playing rugby here next season. In fact I doubt we'll ever play on it."

"Just have some faith. I have this vision in my mind. It'll be the envy of all the local clubs, wait and see!" John had considerable drive and enthusiasm and although I thought he was slightly mad, there was something encouraging in his demeanour that led me to believe that he may just achieve his ambition.

Being a city councillor helped. He packed a powerful punch on the local committees, getting all sorts of concessions, such as the free supply of 250 trees to surround three sides of the ground. OK, we had to plant the two-feet-high sprigs, but when I look at them now, 38 years later, they're magnificent!

John continued, "Don't worry about the clubhouse. Jack Mummery, a club member and local architect, has drawn up the plans and I'm sure planning permission won't be a problem, I'll see to that!" It wasn't, and incredibly, by the next summer, 1973, the clubhouse was built, the rubbish cleared and three pitches laid with grass. Now the really hard work began.

We had no idea about running such a club. There was beer to order, pitches to maintain, a clubhouse to be cleaned and rugby posts to be erected and painted. Working parties were set up, usually by Jonesy, to pick stones off the pitch. This was a problem for many years. Although it was hard work, the club developed a wonderful culture of "belonging" and we all look back on those days with a great deal of satisfaction.

Jonesy's training sessions and motivational methods became legendary within the club. Pre-season, June, July and August, was the hardest. He sent us out on seven or eight-mile runs deep into the Hampshire countryside *before* running a skills session. Sometimes a player would get lost and not return until 10.00 pm just as we were locking up! Another much-feared, sadistic test was the run up the steps at St Giles Hill, about a mile from the clubhouse. These are incredibly steep and there must be at least 150 of them! They *had* to be attacked five times in succession under his watchful gaze, whilst he sat on his bike with a loudhailer. You couldn't afford to slacken off, otherwise he'd release a torrent of abuse.

"You wretch! Put some bloody effort in, Henley!" was a typical comment.

His best quotes, however, were when we were training with the ball. If somebody dropped it, he'd yell at the poor unfortunate "You're useless! You're like a nun handling a navvy's cock!" or "You've got hands like feet!"

He related some amusing anecdotes from his job in the courts as a chief prosecuting solicitor's clerk. He told us once about a down-and-out alcoholic who was up before the judge for the umpteenth time for being drunk and disorderly. He was dressed like a tramp and had no fixed abode. The judge, after hearing all the evidence, said, in a superior, serious manner, "I'm going to give you just one more chance, otherwise you'll go to jail. I want you to promise me that you'll *never*, ever drink alcohol again, not even a small sherry before dinner!"

That summer of 1973 was spent training furiously, stone-picking the pitch, and helping to organise the grand new clubhouse opening set for September 9th. The first-ever match to be played at the new ground was supposed to be against a team of ex-internationals, but they let us down at short notice. One of our members used to play for Worthing and so he persuaded them to play us instead. It was all last-minute stuff. For example, we didn't get round to cutting the grass until the morning of the match! Then the gang mowers packed up! John Broadway sent out an SOS to the players asking them to bring their lawnmowers from home! It must have appeared a somewhat surreal sight, watching ten of us frantically pushing our machines up and down the pitch, so that it was in a pristine condition before 3.00 pm!

Competition for places in the team for this prestigious match was keen to say the least! So I was delighted to be picked on the wing in a match I'll never forget. It was a superb day; sunny, no wind and the pitch looked in great condition, thanks to everybody's efforts. There were several hundred spectators, including the mayor and several city councillors who'd all played a part in turning this rubbish tip into a wonderful sporting venue.

The opening ceremony took forever. There were several speeches and photographs, cutting of the ribbon at the clubhouse entrance and, of course, Jonesy's passionate team talk – an oration of Shakespearean quality delivered in his strong West Wales accent – colourfully describing what it meant to play for Winchester in general and in this match in particular.

I really looked forward to the match starting and had a couple of early runs which helped my confidence. After about 20 minutes, I received a pass just inside our own half with a bit of space ahead. I sped away, side-stepping and swerving and made a lot of ground. I could see the try line about 15 yards ahead, and really went for it. The next thing I was aware of was lying on the ground, my head spinning, stars appearing, and noticed that my right shoulder was in a place it shouldn't be! I was in a lot of pain but my overwhelming feeling was of annoyance that I hadn't seen the tackle coming. I'd been dumped heavily into the unforgiving turf.

This was an undoubted turning point in my rugby career. I'd never been tackled before without knowing it was about to happen. Up until this point, I could sense it happening and either avoided the tackler or at least braced myself for a fall. Not this time! The ground was rock-hard, and I now regretted mowing the grass so short, it gave me no protection.

I was rushed to hospital in someone's car, feeling sick and nauseous, taking the weight of my dislocated right shoulder by holding my elbow with my left hand, which gave some relief.

"Doc" Hill, an Australian, who'd become a club colleague the following season, was a no-nonsense, unsympathetic type, who simply said, "It's obviously dislocated – let's see if we can get it back in without too much pain or complication. Are you ready?" I nodded. With the help of a nurse, he carefully placed his hands over the offending shoulder and with one short, sharp push, he snapped it back in place. I yelped like a wounded dog.

"I'll give you some painkillers now. I suggest you don't drink tonight and you'll definitely not be able to play for a while. We'll just have to see how much damage we've done to the ligaments and tendons in a week or so when the swelling goes down! By the way, you can buy me a drink the next time we meet. I'm joining the club soon."

The party at the clubhouse was in full swing when Ann, who'd picked me up from the hospital, and I returned with my arm in a sling. My team-mates were anxious that I shouldn't miss out on the fun. They cut up my food, amid much hilarity, and then plied me with drinks "just to help you forget the pain, Dai".

Stupidly, I ignored the "Doc's" advice and downed a couple of pints and suddenly felt better! By the time I left the club, having downed many more, I thought the injury wasn't so serious after all. The combination of the drugs and alcohol had sent me into a twilight zone, where not only did I not feel any pain, I actually felt terrific − until the middle of the night! As the effects of the "comforters" wore off, not only did my shoulder hurt like hell, I also had a massive hangover!

The main problem with these types of injuries is that one can't sleep. Although propped up by several cushions, every time I dozed off, I involuntarily moved, which resulted in a sharp pain acutely reminding my body that I was not 100 percent fit. This lasted a week or so, but eventually, my shoulder began to settle down, and thankfully I was able to get some sleep.

When I went back to the hospital for check-ups, they seemed divided regarding my treatment. The debate concerned whether I should rest my shoulder or undertake some physiotherapy. I probably did too much of the former because I subsequently developed a "frozen" shoulder and I could only move it a small distance with some difficulty several months after the collision. I became so frustrated. I even wondered whether this was the end of my rugby-playing career. I realised how important it was to me to play rugby each week. I didn't even go down to the club. I couldn't bear to see all my mates enjoying themselves.

Four months later, having worked hard with the physio, my shoulder began to feel better and so I started turning up for the regular Tuesday and Thursday night training sessions. By February, I was ready for my comeback match in the fourth XV away at Havant.

Just getting back into the changing room, smelling the pungent, sporty odours of Wintergreen and Deep Heat liniment, hearing the good-natured banter between the players and pulling the Winchester club shirt on for the first time in six months made me feel very emotional. I actually remember a teardrop running down onto my cheek when, as we kicked off, the captain, Paul Tubb, winked and wished me good luck.

The match was quite uneventful but at least I got through it unscathed and revelled in the hot steamy showers afterwards, followed by a few drinks with my team-mates – my God, how I missed Saturdays in winter!

Although I never regained my regular first-team place, I had one more taste of glory when, in 1974, I was a member of the winning team at the Embley Park Sevens tournament. I really loved Sevens. The abbreviated game gave me some space to run, but there was always the downside that with just seven-a-side on a full-size pitch, you could be cruelly exposed by a speedier player.

I played for the second and third XVs until the club formed an over-35s veterans' side in 1985. I was honoured to play in the inaugural Vets match although I couldn't help but think back to that other inaugural match 13 years earlier! No injuries, though, this time!

We had some great parties at the club, and I hated the close season when I didn't see my mates. So in summer, a few of us would go for long jogs in the evenings, running the six or seven miles out to Easton or to Medstead. These runs would take about an hour and a half and there was some friendly rivalry about the time taken, usually discussed over a pint when we got back!

For ten years, I was Father Christmas at the rugby club's kids' Christmas party. It was held on the closest Sunday evening to Christmas Day. As the parents arrived with their little darlings, they'd drop a pre-wrapped present with their name on it into a sack, hopefully without them seeing. One of the players or parents would organise games of musical chairs or pass the parcel and then have them all sit down to tea of jellies, trifles and cream cakes.

Whilst this was happening, I dressed up in to my Father Christmas outfit and dragged the sack outside to the far end of the pitch, in darkness, about 100 yards away from the clubhouse. On a pre-arranged signal someone would dim the lights in the clubhouse and turn on the floodlights outside and tell the children that if they looked closely, Santa was on his way! Sometimes there was a smattering of snow on the ground, so it looked magical!

I have never seen children so excited! I could see them, noses pushed hard up against the windows, fighting to get a better view! I could hear them screaming and shouting and so by the time I entered the clubhouse, I was usually mobbed by this infant crowd!

Someone found me a seat and as I picked a present out of the sack, I called out a name. The recipient let out a yell and came forward to sit on Santa's lap and take their present. Once, one of the kids who'd been coming to the party for many years sat on my lap and immediately pulled down my white beard and moustache. She exclaimed, "I thought so! It's Dai Henley!" I just pushed her off my lap and re-adjusted my facial hair.

"No presents for those who are naughty!" I said. I think I got away with it!

CHAPTER 11
Tourist, thespian and barrister

Touring is a very important part of rugby life. When you travel away from home with a group of friends, you learn so much more about each other. You return to life as a schoolboy – game for anything and no responsibilities – just for a few days!

My first tour with Winchester Rugby Club was to Versailles in May 1977. The cities were twinned with each other, so it was a natural choice. John Broadway, our president and Winchester city councillor knew a great deal about the twinning arrangements, so he organised a fantastic trip.

We took two teams plus some reserves, so the party was about 40 strong. There's a rule amongst touring rugby teams that whatever happens on tour, stays on tour, so I'll have to be discreet. But that would be boring, so I've recalled a few incidents of note, changing the names, where necessary, to protect the not-so-innocent!

We set off from the club on a Friday evening, the coach packed with enough cans of beer and lager to sink the overnight ferry we caught from Portsmouth. We arrived in Le Havre at about 7.00 am, most of us hoarse with singing and bleary-eyed through lack of sleep and too much alcohol. (In future, I vowed to always check whether there was a rugby touring party travelling on the ferry whenever I wanted a quiet trip to France with my family!) Some of the boys had a drinking competition involving bottles of whiskey and so were particularly damaged. Mark Welch was so ill, he spent the first two days of the tour in bed!

We drove to the outskirts of Versailles arriving at about 9.30 am and found a bar open that was serving English breakfasts – no fancy croissants and pain de chocolate for us! I couldn't face another beer, although some did – litres of hot black coffee was my tipple for the next few hours!

We finally arrived at the Versailles Hotel de Ville, to be greeted by the mayor and other local dignitaries. They'd laid on a reception and magnificent buffet. John Broadway impressed us with his response to the welcome speech, a peculiar kind of Franglais – every *other* word was English. The French contingent found this highly amusing, sniggering over their canapés and glasses of champagne.

Two hours later, around 2.00 pm, the first match, a second XV encounter, including me at centre-three-quarter, took place in a superb stadium with half the town watching. We were minor celebrities!

One of my team-mates was Tony Routley, a huge, muscular man, around six foot five inches tall with broad shoulders and large hands. He looked fearsome and enjoyed a reputation as a "hard man" but in truth, he was a gentle leviathan. He revelled in his various jobs as an HGV driver, bouncer and minder.

After drinking all night and most of the day, he was in a belligerent mood, psyching himself up for the battle, banging his head against the changing-room door. A few of us said to the captain, Mike Cross, "Mike, there's no way Routley should play. He'll probably not survive."

"If you feel so strongly about it, you tell him. He'll probably hit me!" Mike, not unreasonably, responded.

We wisely declined. Routley went on to play the game of his life. He was a revelation! Tackling anything that moved, jumping higher than anyone else at the line-outs, and running hard and fast at the opposition. Despite his performance, we lost but at least we could now enjoy the rest of the tour.

We showered and came out to watch the first XV match, which kicked off at 4.00 pm, enjoying the bright spring sunshine. Just before half-time, Pete Langley got injured and Jonesy, the coach, signalled for me to get changed to replace him! One and a half games of rugby after the night we'd just had wasn't on my agenda. We lost this match too, but we were about to have a truly memorable time…

Versailles Rugby Club were sponsored by Guinness and Ricard, the Pernod producer, so there were ample supplies of both in the clubhouse. After this liquid buffet, we were taken into Paris and entertained in the Pernod club on the Champs Elysees. Standing out on the terrace, sipping Pernod, watching the sunset and waving at the crowds thronging one of the most famous boulevards in the world was a cherished moment.

Eventually, we split into groups, each being hosted by some Versailles players or officials. Phillipe Cappelle, their equivalent of our Jonesy, was the team leader and was assigned to chaperone about ten of us. He took us to a restaurant a few blocks down from the Pernod club. I don't know how it started but the highlight of the meal was explaining to the French how to play cricket! We couldn't make ourselves understood verbally, so we demonstrated on the table with the only materials available to us. A bread roll was the ball, a place mat (with two spoons on top to resemble the bails) was the wicket and a large baguette was the all-important cricket bat! It all became very animated and noisy. The other diners and the waiters were bemused at first, but then some of them joined in! Inevitably, a bun-fight ensued, though it was all good-natured.

It was now midnight, but the evening was far from over. Phillipe took us to the Crazy Horse Salon, famous for its sexy Crazy girl dancers and they did not disappoint! It was a fabulous revue, tastefully erotic. We drank champagne as if it were on tap and through my drunken haze I wondered how we were going to pay for it. I looked at the wine list at one point and gasped audibly at the prices.

I needn't have worried; the entire bill was picked up by one of the Versailles officials, much to our relief. We finally crashed into bed at about 4.00 am, declining the offer of a nightcap at Phillipe's flat where Nosher Eames and I were assigned.

Next morning, nursing a giant hangover, we breakfasted on black coffee and croissants before going back to the Versailles clubhouse. The night before, Phillipe had told us that we had another match arranged against a Versailles over-35 team on Sunday morning – this wasn't planned but we could hardly refuse.

Our team consisted of those still standing and a few who weren't! I was feeling distinctly queasy myself. Amazingly, we scored a try that the Versailles officials described as the best-ever seen at their stadium. It was, in many ways, similar to that scored by the Barbarians against New Zealand in 1973 at Twickenham, universally recognised as the greatest try ever scored. The spectators gave a generous ovation – it really was a special moment. We've returned to Versailles several times since, and *that* try is always discussed!

On Sunday night, we poured ourselves onto the 8.00 pm overnight ferry to Portsmouth, totally exhausted and yet, somehow, elated. Another night of drinking and very little sleep saw us arrive at 6.30 am looking and feeling shattered. Many of the boys had to go straight to work – I'd anticipated the effects of the tour (I'd been on a few before!) so had wisely arranged a day off to recover, which I badly needed!

It was customary back in the 1970s for the players' wives, girlfriends and sometimes mothers to prepare the club teas for the players after the match. You may have spent 80 minutes in a gladiatorial, physical, sometimes bloody battle with your opposite number, but the real appeal of rugby is respect for your opponent, shaking hands at the end of the match and sharing a beer and some tea after the game. The home-team players were expected to help with the washing-up so two or three of us would be assigned by the captain to do our bit.

Shortly after joining the club, I was up to my arms in soapsuds when one of the mums began talking about her amateur dramatic society. Trying to impress, I said that I'd acted in a few productions back in St Albans. Soon, I found myself agreeing to read for a part the following week in the Ropley Amateur Dramatic Society's production of Agatha Christie's whodunit, *Murder on the Nile!*

The part was one of the lead characters, and the mum, Babs Nielson, was my newly-married wife's French maid! The set was aboard a paddle-steamer in the 1950s upon which my wife and I were honeymooning. As with all Agatha Christie's novels or stage plays, there was an eclectic range of characters and during the course of the voyage, murder and mayhem ensue.

We rehearsed for three nights a week for three months, usually in a room over the Horse and Groom pub in Alresford or at Babs' house. She's a very good actress and the general standard was excellent. I never told anyone at the club. I thought they may have thought I was a show-off, and I was concerned they would tease me mercilessly. I don't think even Kit Neilson, Babs' son and one of my team-mates really took much notice.

The production took place over three nights: Thursday, Friday and Saturday in November at Ropley village hall. I played rugby on the Saturday – nothing got in the way of my rugby "fix". I didn't give a thought about suffering an injury that might hospitalise me!

I made the mistake of giving the reason for not staying on at the club after the game as, "Just off to appear in a play at Ropley village hall."

It was the third and final night and as I went on stage, I noticed Jonesy and several other rugby team-mates in the audience. I immediately realised they'd picked up on my throwaway comment and decided to watch me and Babs in action.

There was one moment in the play where Babs and I had a huge row on stage. I accused her of poisoning my wife. It got pretty serious. So serious, that I drew a revolver and shot her ... twice. The audience gasped; they weren't expecting the retorts of gunfire. As she dropped to the ground, dying, there was the most extraordinary silence, broken only by Jonesy's West-Walean accent. "Bloody hell! Who's doing the rugby teas next week?"

There was a peal of laughter from my team-mates. This is when I knew I had *some* acting ability. How I kept a straight face and carried on in the grave manner the part dictated, I'll never know.

After the play, we held the customary party and I wasn't totally unsurprised to learn that Jonesy and the boys had invited themselves at the last minute. I gave him a really hard time about his outburst but he just thought it was a great joke!

They came to watch a few more productions (on the strict understanding there would be no more comments during the performance), one of which was the Noel Coward play, *Present Laughter*. I played the narcissistic part of Gary Essendine, a typical Noel Coward role, that entailed me being on stage for almost the whole time. It also meant learning a colossal number of lines, one example being "You must be brave!" Since then, every time I got injured playing rugby, Jonesy or one of my team-mates would run up to me and repeat the phrase, to their obvious glee!

I found learning lines fairly easy, but I relied a great deal on the cues from the other actors. Provided they gave me their line, I could trot out mine. This worked well except for one occasion, when I was on stage right at the beginning of a play. As the curtains went back, Guy Ingram, an elderly, hardened thespian who'd performed Shakespeare, even playing King Lear at some time in his career, entered from stage left and delivered his opening line. Trouble was, it was at least eight pages into the script! Naturally, I responded – eight pages in, too!

We covered a couple of pages more when Guy realised his mistake. Being the seasoned veteran he was, he decided to exit the stage to check the script to see if any of the first eight pages were relevant and to somehow work the lines back into the play. This left me on stage on my own! For what seemed like an eternity, I fiddled with the ornaments on the mantle-piece and dusted some imaginary cobwebs, muttering and ad-libbing to keep the audience interested. Guy finally re-entered stage left, and this time delivered the correct opening lines. Now we had to remember *not* to repeat pages nine and ten! We just about managed it, but it caused a few sweaty moments on my part!

I thoroughly enjoyed acting despite it being very time-consuming and emotionally draining, especially after a difficult day at the office. During the build-up, I'd be out every night of the week, either rehearsing or rugby training. I only realised much later *why* I didn't spend much time at home. I wasn't *unhappy* living with Ann and Stephanie but somehow it wasn't stimulating enough. Ann didn't seem to mind either; she was pre-occupied with Stephanie and her parents, but it was the beginning of us growing apart.

My very good friend and team-mate, Peter Langley, had a father who was an Oxford Blue at rugby; he played in the 1949 varsity match. Because he could get tickets for the annual match easily, for about 15 years from 1974, a group of us from the club spent every second Tuesday in December at Twickenham to watch the match.

As I had access to the latest model cars as part of my job, I was always the driver. We met at the club at 10.00 am and stopped at three pubs on the way up. We always took some beer cans, wine and food, sandwiches at first but on later trips we graduated to barbeques.

This alfresco meal was hungrily wolfed down in the west car park at Twickenham before the match along with several thousand other supporters doing the same thing in a festival atmosphere. On many occasions the temperature was below zero with a smattering of snow, and I recall shivering a great deal. However, we learned to cope, taking some cardboard with us to act as an insulator between our feet and the frozen ground and wearing several layers of clothes and relying on the occasional swig of a "winter warmer" from someone's hip flask!

The match always kicked off at 2.00 pm (there were no floodlights at Twickenham then) and we were back in the west car park at 3.30 pm, finishing off the beer and wine in the gathering gloom! It didn't end there. We stopped at another three pubs on the way back and seldom got home before midnight! I shudder to think how many pints we sank. Although I was the driver, I stupidly drank my fair share but drove very carefully. In those days the drink-driving laws weren't so heavily policed – thank goodness! It's not something I'm proud of.

It was after one such trip that I realised how much Jonesy could drink. I woke up with such a bad hangover, I'm ashamed to say I called in sick on Wednesday. When I asked Jonesy how he'd felt when I saw him next, he calmly told me that as he was on his way to work at Southampton assizes court, which wasn't sitting until 11.30 am, he'd killed some time by going for a few drinks beforehand!

On another occasion, I was unable to make the trip due to a business appointment. My mates were very upset; it was the first time I'd missed the game for ten years. I heard a rumour that on the next visit they were going to hold a "court" to examine my evidence for missing the trip. There'd be a heinous penalty if I was found guilty. I wanted to put up a robust defence, so I hired some barrister's robes and wig and hid them in the boot of my car.

I suspected that the "trial" would be held in one of our favourite pubs on the way back. My plan was to smuggle the robes and wig into the pub and change in the toilet so that I could appear as my own "defence counsel". I'd prepared an eloquent script I was sure would lead to a "not guilty" verdict.

When we got to the pub, I frantically searched the boot whilst the others went in but I couldn't find my robes anywhere! Damn! I must have left them at home. What I didn't know was that Pete Langley had discovered them whilst we were in the west car park and guessed my plan. He'd told the others and now they'd have great fun in setting me up.

As I walked into the pub, I was greeted by the sight of Pete dressed in *my* robes and wig, and he presided over my "trial". One of our gang, Jeff Lee, a qualified solicitor, prosecuted very professionally. My eloquent defence statement was roundly jeered by the whole gathering and I was found guilty on two counts: letting my mates down and not supporting the varsity match. My sentence was, under the circumstances, not too bad, after I pleaded for leniency and "throwing myself at the mercy of the court". I argued this was a first offence and I'd been the official driver for the previous nine consecutive years.

Although this was reluctantly accepted by the "judge", he dramatically passed sentence by hitting the table with a makeshift gavel (actually a huge spoon) after the judgement … "A round of drinks on the house."

I considered this fair under the circumstances and decided, on the advice of the "judge", not to appeal. He advised me that the sentence could be doubled for wasting the "court's" valuable drinking time!

CHAPTER 12
Career fast track – with problems!

I threw myself into the Lex Basingstoke Rover/Triumph dealership job, determined to make my mark and repay Toy Axford, my Divisional Manager's faith in me.

The dealership had not performed particularly well. This was partly due to morale being very low when I arrived. The previous manager was a dour, introverted accountant – not at all like me! – and I soon learnt that the staff lacked motivation and leadership.

One of the first things I did was to ask every member of staff to come up with some ideas for the prestigious divisional Best Showroom Display award. In previous years, the dealership had never bothered to enter, but I thought this was a good way to get everyone to work together. It turned out to be a master-stroke.

Each department came up with some fantastic ideas before finalising on a "Sprint to the Dolomites" theme, based on the Triumph Dolomite Sprint model. The showroom was transformed into a winter wonderland of snow-capped mountains, ski runs and Swiss lodges. All the work was carried out by the staff with some initial help from a design company. I was amazed at the skill levels displayed – carpentry, painting and erecting the "set". We had a great reaction from customers, and an even better reaction from David Morgan, the Managing Director, who awarded us first prize!

This success provided the springboard for a major change in the company's fortunes. I've always adopted this rule of staff involvement in all my business ventures. It's really simple: most people want to be taken seriously and want to feel they've contributed to the success of the organisation.

OK, there are some who are just content to do their job and no more, but they soon find themselves ostracised by the rest of the staff and feel uncomfortable in a culture of participation. In recruiting staff, one of the key things I looked for was a personality that *wanted* to contribute. The power of *everyone* in the organisation *wanting* to be part of a venture and not just on the payroll cannot be overstated.

The pub across the road became a meeting place on Friday nights where every member of staff was invited – quite a few came. It was deliberately informal; some stayed for 30 minutes, some for several hours! It's amazing what you can learn after a pint or two! I didn't make any managerial changes although I was fully prepared to do so; instead, I worked hard on getting them to buy into my ideas and plans and I was proud that the company began to prosper with the existing management team in place.

After a year, I was summoned to the division office in Maidenhead for a meeting with David Ruskin, the new Divisional Manager. He'd replaced Tony Axford who'd been promoted to start up a Lex business in the USA. I was naturally sorry to see Tony go, but in David, I discovered an equally good ally and firm friend who had an excellent grasp of the business.

"I'm delighted with your progress, David. You've done well. How do you fancy running a Rolls-Royce and Bentley dealership?"

"Are you serious?" was all I could manage in reply.

"I think you're ready. I've got someone to run Basingstoke who'll be available in about three weeks. You'll have to either move to Maidenhead or commute – I'll leave that to you."

We agreed contractual terms, which were greatly improved. They included the free use of a Rolls-Royce or Bentley demonstrator which had the distinctive cherished number plate RR11, together with a driver if I required one!

Although sorry to leave Basingstoke, this was a serious promotion. I discussed with Ann the option of moving, but neither of us wanted to. We'd settled well in Winchester, as had Ann's parents, and so I elected to drive the hour and a quarter each way every day.

I often took RR11 to Twickenham for the varsity matches and other internationals. I quickly learned that I could drive straight to the front of any queue and the attendant would always find a parking spot, expecting a good tip on the basis of being famous or very rich!

I remember once arriving late for a show at a theatre in Bournemouth. I was waiting in the queue behind five other cars, and the parking attendant pointed at the Rolls and indicated that I should pass through to the front! He parked me right outside the stage door and held out his hand for the expected tip. I didn't disappoint!

Lex Maidenhead was a *very* different business from Lex Basingstoke. The new car business took care of itself. We had a four-year waiting list, so with an annual contract of 50 cars, we had 200 customers who'd paid a hefty deposit. We also had a flourishing used-car business too, which, under these circumstances, was not surprising – customers didn't have to wait for a used model. The main objective was to source and purchase at the right price as many of these used cars as we could.

Tony Gosnell was my New and Used-Car Sales Manager. He was, like all the salesmen at Maidenhead, public-school educated, very bright, with a wealth of knowledge about this business. He had an exceptional understanding about used car values and was extremely well connected. It was rumoured that Robert Lloyd, Tony's assistant, was a distant cousin of the Queen and always took his holidays from August 12th, the start of the grouse-shooting season "somewhere in Scotland". He'd attended Gordonstoun, the well-known public school, famous for educating royalty.

At first, I was apprehensive and felt very slightly in awe of these two. But I was confident in my ability to manage them although I sensed I would have to prove it. I would soon have the opportunity!

I learned that in the prestige car business, one should never judge a potential customer by his or her status or appearance. For example, many of our better-known celebrity clients asked their chauffeur to select the specification of each hand-built car so they'd visit us and spend a day going through each and every aspect of the factory-built bespoke programme. They were very important to us and so we treated them as if they were the customer. The occasional rock star would sometimes stroll into the showroom dressed in jeans, open-toed sandals and a psychedelic T-shirt. But, it was rare to see any of the big stars. It would have been a treat for the staff to see Tom Jones, Englebert Humperdink, Ernie Wise or Terry Wogan appear over our threshold! All we saw were their chaffeurs!

However, on one occasion, we all became very excited when a client walked into the showroom, spoke to Robert and finally ordered a used Rolls-Royce Silver Shadow, Mark I model. He made out a cheque for the deposit and said he'd call back in a couple of days and bring the balance. On the way out, he stopped at another model, same type but a different colour.

"Oh! That looks great! I can't make up my mind now which one to have."

After about a five-minute delay he said, "OK, I'm going to have both!" He wrote out another cheque for the deposit. Robert was ecstatic! Selling one car in a day was memorable, but to sell two was exceptional! His commission cheque would probably enable him to buy a new pair of Purdy shotguns to terrorise the grouse in Scotland!

About three days later, a uniformed police officer entered the showroom. I met him and asked if I could help.

"Have you had someone of this description buying up some stock recently?"

After I looked at the photograph, I said, "He looks familiar. I think Robert dealt with him. Shall I call him in?"

"It might help."

"Robert, this police officer wants you to identify someone who was recently in the showroom. Do you remember him?"

"Oh, yes. That's Mr Spencer. I've got an order for two Shadows. They're being prepared for delivery right now. Is anything wrong, Officer?"

The policeman could hardly keep a straight face when he said, "I shouldn't bother. Mr Spencer isn't Mr Spencer. He's a patient at the local mental institution and has a thing about Rolls-Royce cars. He stole the cheque book from his carer and he's bought six cars already and they're just the ones we know about!"

Robert's face turned ashen. I just burst out laughing. He had his leg pulled mercilessly for weeks once the story broke.

Both the Basingstoke and Maidenhead businesses had prospered in 1972 and 1973 despite some turbulence in the economy. The

1972 miner's strike, the first since 1926, created a lot of problems but this was nothing to what was about to hit the country in 1974.

As a result of the 1973 Arab/Israeli war, the Arabs quadrupled the price of oil to the West in December. The most militant of all the unions, the miners and power workers, brought in an overtime ban immediately, seizing the opportunity, not for the first time, of effectively "holding the country to ransom". The twin effect of these actions on the country was catastrophic. The Ted Heath Conservative government announced a State of Emergency and from December 31st, commercial and industrial premises were limited in the use of electricity to three specific days a week. More than 18 million petrol ration books were printed and distributed to post offices and motorists throughout the country.

Matters became even worse when, on 9th February 1974, the miners came out on strike, seeking a significant wage increase. The strike was finally called off on March 4th when they settled for a 35 per cent rise, but not before the Heath government, who'd called a General Election on February 28th to seek a vote of confidence, were out-voted by Labour supporters. Normal working re-commenced on March 8$^{th.}$

What a time to be in the luxury car market! On two days a week, for nine weeks, during the shortest, coldest days of the year, we couldn't operate our workshops and from around 3.30 pm the showroom was candlelit! The office staff kept their overcoats on during the day and couldn't even make hot drinks until someone brought in a Primus stove, which we set up in the accounts department! Fortunately, petrol rationing was never introduced, but it was always a constant threat.

Our market simply disappeared overnight! No-one wanted their gas-guzzling Rolls-Royce or Bentley when it was delivered and our four-year order bank melted like the snow that fell in January. I had a showroom filled to bursting point, containing shiny metal worth well over a million pounds, losses in the workshop and spare parts department and freezing staff huddled around candles. It resembled a scene from a Dickens novel but without the poverty!

So what did I do? I devised, rather cleverly I thought, a marketing plan that involved selling these once highly-prized vehicles to people who wouldn't usually be able to afford them. We all knew we couldn't make a profit – this was a damage limitation exercise. I agreed with my boss, David Ruskin, how much we could afford to lose and re-priced the cars at considerable discounts. I produced a lavish brochure and mounted a direct mail campaign to hit just about every household in the southern counties at great expense. The result? Absolutely nothing!

The plan was totally unrealistic but everything else I had attempted in my business career to that date had worked, so why not this? It was a chastening experience that stood me in good stead the next time we hit a recession. The fact was, there *was* no market – at any price. I'd wasted a great deal of money on promotion when what I should have done was to cut our costs. The problem we faced was that no-one knew how long the State of Emergency would last or whether petrol would be rationed.

My boss was not entirely pleased with my efforts; he was under a great deal of pressure too. He was ultimately responsible for three other Rolls-Royce dealerships.

During the following months, things very gradually got back to normal although it was a real scare for the country. There was also a real feeling of antagonism against people who drove these cars. For the first time, our clients were very aware of the effect their fuel-hungry transport was having on the economy. Our Body Repair Centre dealt with quite a few cases of brake fluid being thrown over the bonnets, or graphic graffiti generously applied to the customised paintwork of our customers' cars.

Working at Maidenhead in the early 1970s was an excellent experience. It broadened my knowledge and I felt that if I could deal with this recession, I could deal with anything.

In September 1974, after about 18 months in the job, I was asked by David Ruskin if I fancied running Lex Southampton, a Rover/Triumph dealership about twice the size of Basingstoke. He wanted to promote the existing manager, Peter Johnson, and felt he could more easily find someone for the Maidenhead job. I was delighted. I was getting tired of the two and a half hours' travelling each day, and felt more comfortable with the Rover/Triumph franchise.

As soon as I stopped commuting, I instantly felt stronger, more alert and sharper. I didn't realise how much the travelling was affecting my performance at work.

When I walked into the Southampton dealership for the first time I was met by Ed Oakley, Sales Manager, little knowing I was to share the next 30 years in several business relationships with him. We got on superbly well. He was the most complete manager I ever encountered; brilliant at motivating his sales team and shared my values and ideas. My secretary/pa was Phyllis Heather, who, although older than all my previous secretaries by some margin, was undoubtedly the best. She also possessed more energy than any of them and was superbly efficient. She was brought up in the "old school" of secretaries where discipline, typing speeds and accurate shorthand were paramount. She was a real asset to the business. So much so, that we persuaded her to join us when we left Lex and started our own business some years later.

Rover was still a car manufacturer with products very much in demand, and many customers aspired to own one as a mark of "having made it!" So imagine the excitement when Rover announced the launch in June 1976 of a new model, the SD1 3500 V8. This was the last car launched without anybody, apart from the manufacturers and dealers, knowing what it looked like! These days, the latest models' details and photos are "leaked" to all the car magazines months and sometimes years before production.

Simultaneously, with all the other Rover dealers in the country, we launched the car in the showroom packed with prospective customers. We had licence to launch the car in as dramatic a way as possible, so we teased them all night with the car covered in a shroud.

As we played *The Fanfare for the Common Man*, the evocative, haunting, trumpet-led music composed by Aaron Copeland, the lights were dimmed, the shroud was lifted tantalizingly slowly, dry ice was released under the shroud and a single spotlight highlighted the car. There was an audible gasp from the crowd. They all rushed forward and just wanted to touch it before placing their orders. We took about 30, which was one of the highest in the country, so we felt all the hard work in setting up the "tease" had paid off.

Regrettably, the car failed to live up to expectations. It drove superbly, but was dogged by many technical problems. Something similar had happened to the Triumph Stag sports car launched in 1973 and so two of the brightest stars in the British Leyland firmament began the steady fall in market share and ultimate demise.

It was incredible to witness a car manufacturer (which became the fifth largest in the world as a result of the merger between Austin/Morris, Rover/Triumph and Jaguar in 1968) with a UK market share of over 40% becoming extinct by 2005. This, despite considerable government financial support, import restrictions and powerful brand images. A combination of appalling trade union relations, poor decisions on distribution, diabolical quality and excellent Japanese and German models literally drove the business into the ground. Many dealers who were axed because of "non-performance" or "geographical rationalisation" were greedily snapped up to distribute these imports and this simply accelerated the process. The British Leyland factories were the catalyst for the worst industrial relations the country had seen. It was close to a workers' revolution. Such a shame.

I spent four memorable years at Lex Southampton, which gave me an excellent experience in running a larger dealership. I developed a great relationship with Ed Oakley and with his help we became one of the best performing dealers in our division. However, one incident during this period almost changed my life.

As well as developing our management skills, Lex also arranged a comprehensive annual medical inspection with a Dr Rogal in Harley Street. It was compulsory for all general managers to attend and I had done so every year since joining the company in 1972, usually receiving a glowing report on my level of fitness.

Dr Rogal, aged around 60, was almost Dickensian in appearance – tall, slightly stooped, wearing pince-nez spectacles, a black, pin-striped suit with a waistcoat to match and thinning hair. He had a very genial nature that seemed at odds with his businesslike appearance. The examination lasted most of the day and was *very* thorough and invasive!

Usually late in the day, probably to save you from embarrassment, he'd ask you to drop your trousers and pants and to bend over his desk, rather like preparing for the cane. Almost without warning he'd place his gloved finger deep into your rectum and perform a figure-of-eight manoeuvre checking for any unusual growths.

This became known as "being Rogalised" by the managers. It was almost a badge of honour!

In October 1975, I was working late in the office one night, when I received a phone call from Dr Rogal.

"Hi David, I've just been looking at some of the test results from my examination yesterday. I'm not too happy with a couple. I really need to check them again. Can you come up and see me?"

"Of course," I replied. "Nothing wrong, is there?" I felt really fit, and bursting with energy.

"No! No! it's probably a faulty machine. I'd like to see you soon, though. Can you come tomorrow?"

This last sentence hit a nerve. "OK. I'll be there," I said, shocked at the urgency in his voice.

I spent half the day at Harley Street and an hour or two at the Middlesex Hospital where I had to run on a treadmill, undertake electrocardiogram tests, breathe into numerous machines, and have my blood pressure checked every ten minutes it seemed. I'd injured my ankle playing rugby the previous Saturday, so running on the treadmill was painful, but I put in a really good effort just to prove that I wasn't ready for the scrap-heap just yet!

When I got back to Harley Street late in the afternoon, I was asked to wait in the reception area for about half an hour before Dr Rogal could see me. My mind was in a whirl. I'd always prided myself on my fitness and never gave it a second thought that there could be anything wrong.

As I entered his office, he rose from behind his desk and offered his hand with a beaming smile.

"I'm delighted to say that you're fine. There is some abnormality in your heartbeat, though, but you won't have to worry about it until you're in your 50s."

"Why the extra tests, then? What made you make me take them again?" I asked.

"I think your body's producing too much adrenaline. We didn't understand the symptoms until recently. We were grounding pilots on the basis that this could be dangerous, but recent research has proved that it's not as serious as we first thought. See you next year." I floated out of his office in a euphoric state and found the nearest phone box to call Ann.

"Thank God you're all right!" she said. She knew how much I'd been worried. Dr Rogal's words, however, would prove to be uncannily prophetic.

In 1978, after four years at Lex Southampton, I was delighted to be asked to consider the role of General Manager at Lex Maidenhead again. Since I'd worked there last in 1974, the Rolls-Royce/Bentley, Jaguar, Austin/Morris and Rover/Triumph and Land Rover dealerships, together with a huge forecourt operation, had merged into one business and relocated to a "state of the art" dealership on the Slough Road. It was now the flagship within the Lex group, so I was deeply honoured. Although the salary package was outstanding, the job brought two problems.

The first was that the Lex HQ was just up the road in High Wycombe, so my performance would be highly visible. This didn't worry me as much as the second problem. Part of the contract was that I'd *have* to relocate within 12 months. Although I agreed, I was deeply unhappy about moving away from Winchester. I gambled that I'd do such a brilliant job that I could prove being close to the local community wasn't necessary. Apart from my love of Winchester and the rugby club, I'd have the added problems of relocating Ann's parents. Stephanie, too, had settled very well and was enjoying her time at the Romsey convent school. She moved there from Queen's Mead, a small private secondary school, when it closed down.

Although we were not Catholics, the convent accepted all fee-paying denominations and proved to be a good influence on Stephanie. We'd only just moved house too! We'd found a delightful detached house about half a mile from our existing home in Harestock – 21 Winslade Road was considerably larger than the semi we bought when we first came to Winchester, so we felt we were at last making progress on the property ladder.

I wasn't too daunted at first by the increased responsibility of the new job and was pleased to join up once again with Tony Gosnell and Robert Lloyd with whom I'd worked at the Rolls-Royce dealership four years previously.

Although I made quite a few changes to the physical structure of the business, I hardly changed the management team – I relied on my usual style to motivate and involve them in the major decisions. I found this much more of a challenge than in previous jobs. I had ten managers reporting to me, and maybe this was too much. I was spreading myself too thinly. However, after the initial honeymoon period, the worsening economic situation really conspired against me.

I didn't panic, but it was difficult to generate sales of cars in an environment that eventually led to another full-blown recession. This wasn't the biggest problem I faced though.

I was becoming increasingly alarmed at the number of customer complaints that landed on my desk each morning. During the first two years they were high, but manageable. By 1981, though, if I didn't have at least 10 letters complaining about the quality of the cars we sold, then I knew the postman hadn't called! This took a great deal of management time and effort to resolve and left little scope to plan the growth of the business.

My entire ten-year career at Lex was framed against the backdrop of probably the worst economic environment since the Great Wars. This, combined with the struggle for control of industrial relations between the government of the day and the communist-led trade unions, using British Leyland Motor Corporation as the "political football", really made life impossible for a dealer.

What really angered me when I received these customer complaints, was that in almost every case, they were not the result of the dealer's incompetence, although the customers seemed to think so. The quality of the cars being delivered, especially from Austin, Morris, Rover and Jaguar was appalling. Labour relations at the factories, especially during this period, were at an all-time low. "Wildcat" strikes (strikes without notice and not authorised by the Trades Union Congress, the TUC) were being called on the simplest of pretexts. This played havoc with production schedules.

The sloppy quality of cars from the British Leyland Motor Corporation I had first witnessed whilst at Lex Southampton was now at epidemic proportions. Matters escalated to such an extent, that in late 1978, the government and the TUC couldn't agree on the level of wage increases. This dispute spilled over from the car manufacturing plants into the public and private sectors. Workers from many different industries and utilities, such as the health service and refuse collectors, up and down the country went on strike. Rubbish piled up in the streets, and hospitals and government offices were blockaded. This period became known as the "Winter of Discontent". What a background to promote selling British Leyland cars!

There was also an anarchic force at work too, which I witnessed first hand. Graham Odey, our Service Manager, called me one morning and asked me to meet him in the workshop. As I arrived, there was a silver Jaguar XJ6 saloon parked outside his office with both front seats covered in seat covers to protect them. Graham opened the front door, and removed the driver's seat cloth to reveal a tan leather seat.

"Are you ready for this?" Graham said, as he moved round to the passenger side. With a flourish, he removed the seat cover to reveal a *black* leather seat! I was speechless! It was perfectly obvious that this had been done deliberately, but proving it would be impossible. Graham also pointed out paint runs on the front and rear wings! Whoever inspected this car and passed it good enough for delivery was surely determined to bring down the company.

We returned the car and made a forceful condemnation, but we got nowhere. It just led to another customer complaint for yet another late delivery. This was not untypical. It go so bad, that I resolved never to sell these cars to any of my friends – I valued them too much. I even got a hard time from the MD, John Tinker, when we found it impossible to resolve a recurring problem on his car affecting the steering. It was insoluble, despite sending the car back to Jaguar on several occasions. In the end they replaced it!

We subsequently heard of other cases, such as a Mini being delivered to another dealer who, concerned the gears wouldn't engage, discovered on stripping down the gearbox that it was full of oily rags! Another event that caused uproar in the media when discovered by the British Leyland management, was that many night-shift workers took their sleeping bags to work, never producing anything!

Just to add fuel to the already raging fire, in 1980, there was another oil crisis following the Iraq-Iran war which pushed the UK into recession. High interest rates followed and now we had

Margaret Thatcher in power, a hard-line, right-wing prime minister, with an anti-trade union agenda doing all she could to smash their power.

This was the era of Derek Robinson, known as "Red Robbo", a militant shop steward based at the Longbridge British Leyland factory, and Arthur Scargill, head of the National Union of Mineworkers, who was largely influential in bringing down the Heath government in 1974. They were members of the Communist Party and their activities caused almost daily disruption to the production of motor cars and coal in the late 1970s and early 1980s. The ultimate result was many factories and mines closing and unemployment worsening to record levels. Desperate times.

Trevor Chin, the dynamic, driven, charismatic chairman of Lex, was determined to prove to his father, Rosser Chin, founder of the group, that he could be a success. He undoubtedly was. He often came to inspect the dealerships and most of my contemporaries dreaded it – it was akin to a royal visit! I absolutely welcomed it! I'd spend days ensuring that everything was painted, cleaned and scrubbed, memorising some of the statistics from our accounts and ensuring I knew what our competitors were up to. I regarded the visit as the most marvellous catalyst. From the time he arrived in a chauffeur-driven car, he'd fire question after question, so you really had to be on your mettle. Sometimes, he'd challenge you to a controversial discussion about how you ran the dealership. This was the best bit – you got a chance to air your views directly to the top man. It was exhilarating and greatly enhanced my knowledge of the business.

Another highlight was that as Rolls-Royce cars now had to be marketed and promoted to make sales, we came up with the idea of sponsoring a prestigious polo match at Smith's lawn in Windsor. We had designed, exclusively for us, a magnificent glass trophy for the winners and invited polo teams from all over the world to participate. Most of the arrangements were made with Major Ronnie Ferguson, father of Sarah Ferguson, who became Her Royal Highness, Duchess of York, and he proved to be an excellent organiser.

So, on a quintessential beautiful summer's day, we hosted a magnificent champagne lunch and afternoon tea and watched the world's best polo players going through their paces. Our clients were most impressed to see Prince Charles' team win the "Lex Maidenhead Trophy" which was presented to him by Mrs Trevor Chinn.

Another champagne reception was held in the evening at the Dorchester hotel in Park Lane, London, where Prince Charles was introduced to our management team. I spent some time talking to him and found him to be utterly charming and very well-informed. Although none of us knew it at the time, he had just met his future wife, Diana Spencer, and it wasn't until a year later that his engagement was announced. A year after that, in 1981, he married her in Westminster Abbey. It was a great pleasure to have met him, and it remains one of the more notable events of my Lex career.

After three years, I'd successfully warded off the move to Maidenhead, but realised that if I had a future with the group, moving house was inevitable. However, I was decidedly unhappy with the products I was being asked to sell and maintain. I simply lost confidence in them, and as any salesman will tell you, if you don't truly believe in what you're selling, then you are conning your customers.

So I began looking around and registered with a head-hunter in London. Following a series of interviews with him, I heard nothing for a few months, then he contacted me and asked if I was interested in joining a property developer and house builder, quoted on the London stock exchange. They'd acquired a small building company two years earlier and a part of the business was a Volvo dealership in Southampton.

They'd tried to make something of it and lost a lot of money in the process but decided that rather than sell it, they'd recruit someone with my experience and use this dealership as a basis to create a car dealer network to offset any downside risks on property development.

After a couple of interviews, I was offered the job.

"Right, you've got six months to turn this Volvo dealership around. If you like us and we like you, I'll make a three million pounds investment available to you to expand the car business and we'll offer you a one-year rolling service contract. What do you think?" Stephen Hayklan, Chief Executive of Wiggins Group plc, said with relish.

It was a huge risk. I'd be giving up ten years' service with the market-leading dealer group. Also, no matter how much research I'd done and discussions I'd had, it was impossible to gauge the culture of the organisation until I'd worked in it. I could have been sacked after the first week with just a month's pay. They could have undermined any decisions I made. They could simply not keep their word.

On the other hand, what an extraordinary challenge! If it worked, I'd be able to put all my Lex training and experience to good use. And where else was I going to have the opportunity to build a dealer group with someone else's money and remain living in Winchester?

I trusted my instincts, as I spluttered the words, "I'd love to give it a try. I need to give three months notice, though." The other terms of the deal were quickly agreed and as I left his office, I already felt the excitement of this new venture welling up in my chest. I was aware that my heartbeat was more rapid than usual. In my most exaggerated fantasies, I couldn't have predicted what a roller-coaster ride was in store.

Those three months serving notice at Lex were purgatory. I lost interest in the job. The customer complaints were getting even worse. I couldn't wait to get stuck into the Wiggins job.

I was like a racehorse waiting to get into the stalls at the start of the race – nervy, tetchy and fractious. I had some regrets, though, especially about leaving a great bunch of dealership general managers with whom I was in touch regularly. Ed Oakley who'd taken my place when I left Southampton; Ken Easthope, General Manager at Weybridge was like a father figure to me; and Bob Clarke, General Manager at Epsom shared my love of rugby. Lex was a fantastic company to work for and they'd set me up for the next stage of my business career.

CHAPTER 13
A fresh business challenge!

The Volvo dealership I was tasked to turn round and expand was Rudds, located in Millbrook, Southampton. It was selling 250 new cars a year. I'd been used to running a company selling 2,000 new cars a year, so it was a very different experience.

One of my key concerns was whether the existing management were capable of running a much bigger operation. I spent a great deal of time with each of them and concluded that I only had to make one change – the management accountant. I found a great replacement, Peter Dashwood, who worked for a small group, and I persuaded him to join us on the basis of our planned growth. A big risk for him – he had to trust me!

The business was in poor shape. The staff were de-motivated, there was a lack of focus and very little had been invested in the physical structure. But the cars were great! Volvos were the exact opposite of the British Leyland cars – they were very well built, had a reputation for tank-like durability, reliability and safety. The styling in 1981, though, left a lot to be desired, but over the following six years, this was resolved and the franchise became much sought after.

One of the key things I learned at Lex was the potential income that could be derived from selling a finance package to fund the purchase of cars at the point of sale. Profit margins on cars is minimal, but there's always an opportunity to sell a finance plan, upon which the finance company paid good commissions. I'd successfully tapped into this area at Lex by setting up training sessions for all our sales staff and by me simply asking the salesman after each car sale, "Where's the finance plan?"

This meant every customer who bought a car was always offered an alternative way to pay We didn't want their cash or them taking a bank loan. This is one of the great myths of car dealing. Customers would often say, "How much off if I pay cash?" expecting a positive result. The fact is, we hated customers paying by cash. What we wanted was for them to take out a finance plan so that we could earn commissions. On many occasions, we sold a car at a loss, but made serious profit by selling a finance package.

So, one of the first things I looked for when I got to Rudds was to check how much finance they sold. I was delighted see the result – zero! I knew that for the modest investment of providing training for the four sales staff, I could add a considerable profit straight to the bottom line.

First, I had to set up a deal with a finance company. After interviewing several, I selected United Dominion Trust – UDT. Eric Cross was my contact and he shared my vision of making finance commission a major profit-earner for Rudds. This was another of those relationships, just like Ed Oakley at Lex Southampton, which has lasted to the present day.

Eric began training the sales staff who were sceptical at first, but when they realised how much commission they could earn, suddenly realised the benefits.

After the first six months, the dealership was humming! Not only was the income from finance surpassing all expectations, but despite a tough economic environment, sales, servicing and parts sales had all improved. The manufacturer was delighted.

Much more importantly, Steve Hayklan, my new boss, was equally thrilled. So much so that he kept his promise to make £3 million available to me and gave me free reign to expand the business. This was so typical of Steve. He backed people. I got to know him really well and he placed a lot of trust in me over the following seven years. He was also the quintessential entrepreneur.

As well as the chairmanship of a major plc, he had many other business interests. Although property development was his first love, he thoroughly enjoyed getting to grips and understanding any new business venture. He would start a conversation with complete strangers and pick their brains clean. He once met a chap on a flight to Cyprus where he thought there was a possibility of developing property and learned that he was a taxi driver who had the chance to buy out his boss's fleet. Steve spent some time with him and after a brief negotiation, lent him the money personally. The taxi firm became a great success and Steve enjoyed free holidays with his family in Cyprus for many years!

Fairly soon after he'd given me the go-ahead for expanding the Volvo business, he asked me to look at a sports club in Southampton he'd just bought and needed management. I explained that I knew nothing about sports clubs, but I'd have a look anyway. It was one of the first such clubs in the country and certainly the first in Southampton.

My interest in sports gave me a head start and so I agreed to manage it for him as well as expand the Wiggins business. There was no extra payment but we agreed on a 33% share of the business, which was very generous. I applied my business nous and usual enthusiastic, persistent approach and although I only worked on the club part-time, it did very well. We sold it a few years later for a good profit.

As I proved myself, he gave me more and more responsibility. He was so far ahead of anyone else I knew in spotting trends and acting upon them.

He once rang me in the office late one December evening.

"Hi David, I want you and Paul Llewellen, (the Finance Director) to fly over to Los Angeles. I've seen a great opportunity in a company managing mutual funds. I've booked a first-class flight for you both on the 19th. I'm already here."

"But Steve," I said, "haven't you heard of Christmas?"

"Don't worry, you'll back in the UK by the 24th, I promise."

This was typical. Although he was married with children himself, nothing ever got in the way of a possible business venture.

Paul and I got on exceptionally well. He was in his late 20s and had a very keen brain. Steve had organised transfers from LA airport to the hotel where we arrived at about 8.30 pm local time. I knew exactly what would happen next. Sure enough, as we checked in, the receptionist handed us a message from Steve to the effect that he'd be picking us up at 9.00 pm to see the sights and discuss business! At least we wouldn't have time to worry about jet lag!

When Steve turned up, grinning, he said, "I've just been talking to my limousine driver, Jake. Such an interesting chap. He's going to make a fortune taking *unusual* photographs of LA. He'll take us around town to see the sights." I couldn't resist a nod and wink at Paul.

Jake took us everywhere, including Rodeo Drive and Grauman's Theatre on Hollywood Boulevard. The forecourt has the hand prints of many of the great movie stars cemented into the concrete. It was an exciting place to be at night, especially so with fantastic Christmas decorations everywhere.

Eventually, Steve asked Jake to take us to best restaurant in LA.

"The best is *Rex's*. Mighty expensive though!" Jake said, looking at us through his rear-view mirror.

"That's fine, Steve said. "Only the best will do for my able lieutenants!"

As we drew up to *Rex's*, allegedly one of the most famous eateries in the US, Steve said to Jake, "Please join us for dinner. It's the least we can do."

"What! Me, dine at *Rex's*? Are you sure?" Jake exclaimed.

"Of course. Just get them to valet-park the car," Steve said.

As we approached, I'll never forget the smug look on Jake's face as he got out of the car, took off his chauffeur's hat, and thrust his gloves and car keys into it before handing it to the car jockey, saying, "Just park the car for me, please." The look of astonishment on the car valet's face. too, was something I'll not forget!

We had a great night, devouring wonderful Italian food, washed down with plummy glasses of Chianti and swapping stories about LA and London before returning to the hotel.

Steve had arranged for Paul and I to spend the next two days at the target company to learn how the business worked and to provide a report. It was a mutual funds company which tipped shares and persuaded their clients to buy them, taking up-front fees and sometimes a share in any profits or losses.

We were entertained at the home of the principal the next night and met his family. The house was magnificent, with great views of downtown LA. At the end of the second day, Paul and I prepared our report, which concluded that it didn't really fit with our UK operations and would dilute our management resources, especially being so far away. Steve accepted our findings and, as promised, we flew back home in time for Christmas. It had been a wonderful experience.

Volvo were so pleased with the performance of Rudds, they tipped me off about the sale of another Volvo dealership, Tamplins of Twickenham. This was a much larger operation and was very well established. Once again, I checked the finance commission performance; a paltry £10 per car sold. We were already earning over a £100 per car at Rudds. This was especially ironic since the dealership was owned by UDT, the main provider of finance!

I concluded the purchase at £1.5 million. I was delighted.

They were selling around 500 cars a year, so I knew that with little investment, I could add another £50,000 pa in finance commission to the bottom line quite easily. I applied this principle to every acquisition I made, with resounding results.

The existing Tamplins general manager was relocating to another dealership, so my first priority was to replace him. There was only one candidate as far as I was concerned – Ed Oakley. In our time together working at Lex Southampton, he proved to be an outstanding leader and competent businessman. It took a little persuasion to get him to leave Lex, but when I explained the opportunity with Wiggins group, he accepted. We were on our way. Ed travelled up daily from Southampton for a year and really got the dealership buzzing. This acquisition proved to be an outstanding success.

During the following three years, I went on a spending spree. In 1982, I purchased a Peugeot-Citroen dealership in Winchester. It wasn't my first-choice franchise, but geographically it made sense and it was available at a good price. I really wanted BMW and after a considerable amount of lobbying, I persuaded them to let me open up a dealership in Winchester, but first I had to find a facility they approved of. I came up with the idea that if I could buy out the local Fiat dealership, I could set up the BMW business in its place. Fiat was having a bad time in the market, and everyone thought I was mad to buy this franchise. I had to keep my plans top secret because the BMW franchise was really sought after. My persistence paid off, though, and we opened the BMW operation in Winchester in 1985.

I purchased another Volvo dealership in Croydon, South London at around the same time. This was a tiny operation but with great potential. I had to relocate the business and so purchased a large

Vauxhall dealership and after revamping it almost completely, installed the Volvo franchise. Alan Maiden was the kindly proprietor, who was in his 60s, and had inherited the business from his father, having worked for him all his adult life since leaving school. He was ready to retire and he'd punted the business around to a number of potential buyers. I spent a lot of time with him listening to his tales of how things used to be in "the good old days".

I learnt that for the whole of his life, he'd never purchased a car, any fuel, insurance or servicing.

This was all provided to him with costs charged to the business. I don't think he even knew how to fill a car with petrol! He seemed quite daunted by the fact he'd have to sort all this out. I was bidding against some big hitters but I came up with a plan that connected with his emotions. If he sold the business to me, then I'd agree that Wiggins would supply him with a fully-serviced car, changed every year, including fuel for the rest of his life. I can't say definitely, but I feel this swung the deal my way. I'd worked out the cost on the basis of a 15-year life span, and in relation to the purchase price of a million pounds it was insignificant, about £6,000 a year. Within three months, we launched the opening of Tamplins Croydon, with the gorgeous Miss Sweden 1985 cutting the tape!

So with five dealerships in the group, covering excellent franchises, we became very profitable. We quickly became the third largest Volvo distributor in the UK. We also won Volvo's prestigious Customer Service award, presented to me at a lavish award ceremony in Cannes, South of France. I promoted Ed to Managing Director and I moved up to Chairman of the Wiggins Motor Group. This gave me more time to develop some unique marketing ideas and to concentrate on a business opportunity I'd been thinking about a great deal.

Two of the ideas revolved around making the customer feel really good about our group. Based on the absolute reliability of Volvo, I suggested to the sales staff that we offer a 30-day exchange plan on any new car. We'd guarantee to exchange a new Volvo for *any* reason. This was common practice on used cars but no one had ever offered this benefit on new models. As soon as a new vehicle leaves the showroom, it depreciates heavily, so dealers didn't want to take the risk of losing a fortune.

My suggestion was met with incredulity by the sales staff, including the manager.

"But boss, we'll have every Tom, Dick and Harry changing their cars and we'll be stuck with a showroom full of metal worth a fraction of the new value!"

"I think it's worth the risk. The upside is taking away the fear of customers buying the wrong car, so we'll end up selling *more* cars and just look at the goodwill we'd generate," I reasoned. I didn't admit that I hadn't done a great deal of research – it was more of an instinctive feeling.

I insisted we try it out for three months, and as time went on, and very few cars were exchanged, the salesmen became more confident and used this policy to close more and more deals. Then we had a lucky break.

A husband had bought a new Volvo hatchback for his wife as a surprise birthday present. We were instructed to deliver the car, park it outside the house and tie a huge ribbon to it by 8.30 am one Saturday morning. This we did and thought no more of it. Until the husband returned to the showroom later that day, quite distressed. He explained that as he asked his wife to open the bedroom curtains that morning, he'd said, "Happy birthday, dear. I hope you like your birthday present." Apparently, his wife burst into tears, not because of the generosity of her husband, but because she hated the colour!

"I don't supposed you'd consider changing the car for this reason, would you?" he implored. We were delighted to do so and gained a customer for life! He told the local newspapers and all his friends. What positive publicity! It really set us apart from all the other car dealers.

This really convinced me we were onto something. Everybody felt good about the policy and sales continued to increase. By 1986, our group sold over 2500 cars and exchanged just 43. Each time we did so, we gained another loyal customer. As far as the exchanged cars were concerned, we always found a use for them, either as demonstrators or used as a special promotion. Certainly, the benefits far outweighed the costs but more importantly, our customer loyalty rates were amongst the highest in the country.

The second idea was really an extension of the first. I suggested we call *all* customers who'd purchased a new or used car from us within 24 hours to ascertain that they were entirely happy. Some of the salesmen went ashen-faced.

"But they may give us a hard time. Suppose they've got a problem with the car?"

I went back hard. "I'm sure you'd rather know about any problems within 24 hours and rectify them than have the customer slag us off to all their friends for the next two years!"

Once again, I insisted we try it out. Most of the salesmen subsequently told me they enjoyed making the "hit me" calls as they became known. They almost *wanted* the customer to complain about something so that they could put it right. It gave them a chance to be the "good guys" and so gain their loyalty for life. Some customers simply didn't expect the call and were waiting for another selling proposition, which was absolutely forbidden. Both these principles were applied to all my acquisitions with terrific results.

But the business opportunity I'd been thinking about for some time involved extending the range and flexibility of finance plans to fund the purchase of our cars at the point of sale. I'd already proved that with minimal training, profits could be considerably enhanced.

The catalyst for this thought was the first ever computer laptop, an Epsom HX 20, launched in 1982. It was A4-sized, with a four-line display screen, had a till roll, a typewriter keyboard, was battery-operated and had just 16k of memory, a tiny fraction of today's laptops. They cost £300.

One of our salesmen, Laurie Rutter, had a sister who was a programmer, and she wrote some simple algorithms (a series of logical steps for processing information in a pre-ordained sequence) that greatly enhanced the speed with which we could put finance deals together. I had absolutely no idea about computer programming, but I was totally sure about what I wanted to present to our customers. I wanted to start with what the customer wanted to pay each month and then be able to offer alternative quotes in a matter of minutes. This process of working out a finance plan from the monthly payment became known in the industry as a "roll-back" and we were the first to offer it in the UK.

Until now, the salesman had to use price lists for the cost of the car and accessories, then refer to printed schedules of interest rates, linked to the size of the deposit and the length of the agreement to arrive at a monthly payment. These tables were for 12, 24 or 36-month agreements only. If this was unacceptable, they'd have to call the finance company to get a special quote. It took forever.

Now, we could work back from what the customer wanted to pay each month by inputting this figure and the program would calculate the deposit required and the length of the agreement for a range of cars. With a few key-strokes, we could modify the proposal very speedily and give the customer several bespoke quotes within a matter of minutes, for example, changing the deposit or number of payments.

We first launched the idea at Rudds with just four salesmen and it immediately became successful. The finance provider, UDT, simply couldn't believe how many finance plans we were selling although we had to convince them to accept these unusual quotes. We pointed out that as long as the customer was credit-worthy (this was their responsibility) and that their interest rate yields were protected, it didn't matter how much deposit they received or how long the agreements were. The key factor was that we'd met the customer's monthly payment. No-one else was offering this service.

In 1983, I provided every salesman in the group with these computers and trained them in their use. They loved it! It added some kudos to their jobs. Now, they were finance experts and could operate a computer! Our figures continued to impress and so I thought, if we could increase our profits within our *own* dealerships, what about the other 7,000 operating in the UK?

I discussed this opportunity with Eric Cross from UDT who became very excited. I asked him to join our group and to set up a new business to offer all UK dealerships a package of training, hardware and financial expertise. He jumped at the chance and so Eric, with Laurie Rutter, headed up Leasemaster, a new wholly-owned subsidiary of Wiggins Motor Group.

Volvo, too, had seen what we'd achieved, and so they promoted the concept through their 250 dealers which got us off to a flying start. They set up regional meetings for a dozen or so dealers at a time where Eric and I presented the concept using our own achievements as a template. We travelled the UK and signed up a large number of dealers.

Other manufacturers and finance companies, having seen what was happening at Volvo, became so interested we decided to franchise the business to speed up our growth. By 1986/7, we had 16 franchisees in key locations in the UK with plans to grow to around 64. The franchisees, after a few days' training, promoted the concept to dealers of all makes of vehicle and we took a share of their profits based on the volumes of business they provided. Despite some early failures due to poor selection, Leasemaster began to be profitable.

My status within Wiggins and with Steve Hayklan was such that I was elected to the main plc board in 1985. This was a great experience and now I was exposed to the workings of the City. It was embarrassing too. At the monthly board meeting, Steve would ask me to report the motor group's figures, knowing they were often better than the property division!

He never let anyone forget that it was *he* who'd appointed me and given me my head! He became my mentor although we never ever discussed it formally – it just happened. I learnt so much from him – mainly to keep an open mind with everyone you meet – your antennae will usually pick up something that adds value to the business.

Me... the future Prime Minister...?

L – R: Grandad Jim, Mum, Uncle Les, Aunt Pearl and Nan in 1913.

L – R: Standing: Dad, Mum, Nan, Uncle Les, Aunt Pearl.
        Sitting: Cousin Pearl, Uncle Jack in 1943,
                   at 23 Brighton Road, Walthamstow, London.

Me... the king in the school play in 1953 at 11, Third Avenue, Galon, Uchaf, Merthyr Tydfil, S. Wales.

L – R: Me, Alun Jones and George McKinney with Rusty in 1954.

Cyfartha Castle – my very grand grammar school in Merthyr Tydfil.

Stylish sister Ivy with her husband Bob in London in 1945.

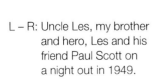

L – R: Uncle Les, my brother and hero, Les and his friend Paul Scott on a night out in 1949.

Mum and Dad, dressed to kill, outside a guest house in Hastings in 1955.

Party for elderly

EIGHTY old-age pensioners were the guests of Park Street Women's Institute at a luncheon party held in the village hall recently. They were welcomed by the president, Mrs Aileen Mullet, who said she hoped they would enjoy the lunch instead of the traditional tea party.

Mrs Ruby Henley from Caroline Sharpe House entertained them with songs (see picture above). The guests, from Vesta Lodge, Jane Campbell House and Fosse House, each received a gift from the institute members.

Mum doing what she loved best in 1979.

20 year-old me relaxing on holiday in St. Ives.

Fatherly duties sharing ice-creams!

19 month-old Stephanie – so cute!

Me, Ann and Stephanie on holiday in Genoa in 1970.

Old Verulamians XV 1965–66

D. Holland, D. Henley, B. Ullyatt, D. Hobbs, K. Tomlin,
M. Schroeder, D. Saunders, J. Trounce, T. Fellows, N. Woods,
C. Cole, G. Davies, P. Wood, A. Dawson, A. Crabtree.

Old Verulamians celebrating a win against Old Fullarians in 1971.
'Prime' having some fun at my expense – top left!

At work and play in the 1970's.

Above: a business jolly to the Isle of Wight.

Left: a photo for the press.

Murder on the Nile 1975 – acting my heart out with the Ropley Players!

Winning the Cup at the 1974 Embley Park Sevens.
I'm 4th from the left. Leroy Angel is receiving the cup.

Winchester Veterans in 1985. I'm 4th from left, standing, with slightly less hair than in 1974!

Lorraine and I on our Wedding Day – June 20th 1990.

Arnie, the cat, defending his territory from a safe location!

A little patch of paradise!
The Old Post Office in Knapp Lane, Ampfield in 1995.

Kai and Kasia from this...

to this...

...to this, with Stephanie, Dave and Lorraine in Melbourne, 2006.

Celebrating my 60th with Davies, my school chum.

L – R: Me, Cousin Pearl and Lorraine 2008.

Me, sharing the stage with 'Elvis' at my 65th birthday party.

Aaron's Wedding Day
– 15th July 2006.

L – R: Aaron, Lorraine and Max.

Stephanie and I in Los Angeles 2009.

The latest family addition
– Lewis aged 20 months.

CHAPTER 14
Guilt, family upheaval and a change of relationship

I visited my mother in her warden-controlled flat as often as I could, but not as often as I should. I still feel pangs of guilt 30 years later. I was always in a rush to get back to business, despite her imploring me to stay a little longer. She'd make me home-baked rolls filled to overflowing with my favourite fillings – cheese, tomato and Branston pickle. As if that wasn't enough to fill me up, she'd force me to have at least two chocolate éclairs, which she knew I couldn't resist! I'd waddle out to the car when I was finally allowed to leave.

"Oh, I've just learned a new tune, David. Please stay while I play it for you, won't you?" she pleaded on every visit, just to buy some more time with her precious one. She was so incredibly proud of me, despite not really understanding what I did for a living.

She just saw a confident, well-dressed man, with impeccable manners (thanks to her) driving the latest model cars, so I probably exuded a fair degree of success. I just wish I'd spent more time with her. She became renowned for playing the piano in her warden-controlled flat and even had a press article written about her.

All the residents loved a sing-song, mainly those melodies so popular during the war, and so Ruby was very much in demand.

In February 1981, at the age of 78, she died of a heart attack whilst playing for the residents one afternoon. This is exactly how I think she'd have wanted her life to end. She still grieved for Dad, who'd died 17 years earlier, and he was mentioned every time we met. Playing the piano and feeling needed was her lifeline. Her ashes were spread at Garston crematorium, near Watford, the same place as Dad's, so they were together at last.

Securing the Wiggins job based in Southampton meant that, at last, the issue of moving house to facilitate my Lex career was at an end. This was such a relief and so, buoyed by this fact, Ann and I moved to a larger house with space to build a granny annexe in 1981. We thought, or at least Ann convinced me, we should sell the apartment I'd bought for her elderly parents and they could move into the extension.

Ann and her parents had discussed the probability that in the event of the death of one of them, the other wouldn't want to live alone. I didn't really think it through thoroughly enough, so I just went along with it. Financially, it made sense.

We found a nearly-new detached house on a good-sized plot in a close of just three houses in Harestock, not far from our current house in Winslade Road. After the inevitably delayed planning consents, "The Firs", Rewlands Drive underwent a transformation with a granny annexe built by Gerry Rowe, my rugby mate. I split the garden up so that Harry could still potter in his own little "kingdom" and the annexe was designed so that each family had some privacy. Ann, Stephanie, myself and Zara, the golden retriever replacement for Ella who'd died a couple of years earlier, as one unit and Harry and Elsie, the other.

It started out quite well. I became totally involved – obsessed is probably a more accurate description – with the new job and carried on with my sporting pastimes of rugby, soccer and running, so didn't have a great deal to do with Ann's parents. But, over the following years, Ann and Stephanie became even closer to them than before. Partly my fault, I now realise, but I felt I was becoming ostracised with some important decisions being taken without my knowledge. For example, Stephanie, now 19, had a serious boyfriend, Danny. Without discussing it with me, they'd agreed that he could come and live with us. It wasn't a big deal, he only stayed a short time, but I felt it was presented as a fait accompli.

In 1983, less than a year after moving in, Harry, by now in his late 70s, fell ill. He was diagnosed with pleurisy, an inflammation of the membrane covering the chest and lungs. He'd been a heavy smoker in his youth, so it wasn't particularly surprising. He was unwell for several weeks, and admitted to hospital a few times, but seemed to be recovering at home.

I returned from rugby training one evening to find Ann, Stephanie and Elsie very tearful. They told me they thought Harry was dying and had called the doctor and would I go and see him in the annexe.

It didn't take me long to conclude that Harry was already dead. It must have only just happened. He was slumped in his favourite armchair. So for the third time in my life, I witnessed a corpse first hand; my grandmother in Wales, my father and now Harry.

I broke the news as gently as I could. They each became almost hysterical, sobbing into each other's arms. The doctor arrived and confirmed the sad news. Even as I was making arrangements for the undertaker to call, I recognised that life at "The Firs" would never be the same again.

Elsie didn't grieve too much for Harry — in my opinion their relationship was not based on love or respect so I wasn't surprised. Although she agreed that building the granny annexe was to account for just this possibility, she said she'd find it impossible to live in it alone. She wanted to live-in with us. I should have been stronger and resisted, but at a time like this, I found it impossible to put up a robust argument to prevent it. So, that's what happened.

Elsie was a kind woman who doted on Stephanie and Ann, but Ann and I had no privacy. Every evening, she'd sit with us, knitting and watching the TV programmes *she* and Ann wanted. I felt even more excluded than before and felt outside this triumvirate. The seeds had been sown right back when Stephanie was born and lived with Ann and her parents for four years before we became a family unit. And here we were, 21 years later, in exactly the same situation. I could have fought it, but I instinctively knew that it was an impossible task. I reacted by working exceptionally long hours and carrying on with my rugby passion.

My obsessive nature, with that clock inside my chest whirring away, driving me to become successful and to be regarded as such by my peers in business and sports, together with my feeling that I was now an outsider in my own home, led my relationship with Ann to seriously deteriorate. She really couldn't wait for me to slow down or even retire early so that we could spend more time together. Conversely, I felt I hadn't yet reached my prime. I was nine years younger, in my early 40s, fit, strong, and had an abundance of energy.

I simply fell out of love with her. It wasn't a conscious thing, more like a slow death. She just seemed happy for us to jog along as one happy family – I needed something more – something to stimulate me – something exciting.

I'd had vague thoughts about leaving Ann, which I'd not shared with anyone. It was too complicated and I didn't feel confident I could handle the upsetting consequences, so I just jogged along in the relationship too. However, this tepid situation was to change dramatically.

During 1981 and in my first year at Rudds, the Volvo dealer in Southampton, I met and became friendly with one of our customers, Frank Sweet. He worked close by and often popped in for a chat at lunch time. He was a leading light with the Worthy Players, an amateur dramatic society in Winchester. Given my earlier involvement in "amdram", I couldn't resist his invitation to read for a part in J B Priestley's *When We Are Married*. I got the role as Herbert Soppitt, the hen-pecked husband.

We rehearsed and performed at the Jubilee Hall in Kings Worthy and I found the cast and production team a great bunch of people. One, in particular, I found exceptionally attractive but far too extrovert for my taste. Lorraine Brown played the part of the flighty maid, Ruby, with gusto. She was so lively and full of fun almost to the point of exhaustion. She was married to Don, who was a member of the Worthy Players too, and they had two great kids, Max, aged ten, and Aaron, aged just six. Although I'd registered how beautiful she was with a great personality, I thought no more of it.

I didn't realise that at the time they were having some problems in their marriage, which may have accounted for her behaviour. We appeared together in a number of plays and music-hall events over the next couple of years and when I took over the management of the health club in 1982, I asked her to help out on reception.

She was perfect. By then, she and Don had agreed to separate but lived in the same house until it was sold. I still didn't realise that slowly, she was making a huge impression on me. She also worked part-time for the local Boys' Club and her boss, Mike Shearman, whom I knew vaguely, always asked Lorraine to call me to elicit donations. He seemed to know I'd be a soft touch!

When I sold my shares in the health club in 1984, Lorraine got a job working in Pitkins Wine Bar in Jewry Street, a trendy place which many local businessmen used as their watering hole. I'd moved my office from Rudds in Southampton to the Peugeot dealership, Wiggins Short in St Cross Road not far away. I'd purchased this dealership two years earlier, so Eric Cross, who by then was heading up our leasing operation, and I, used to lunch there occasionally. Lorraine and I flirted a great deal and I surprised myself by plucking up the courage to ask her out for a drink. I wasn't the only one – I had to wait in turn – she was very popular. I got firmly rebuffed.

"No way! I wouldn't want to upset Ann for a start." She knew I was married and knew Ann and Stephanie vaguely since they'd attended some of our productions at the dramatic society and visited the health club.

She's told me since, that although attracted to me, she, quite rightly, didn't want to get involved with a married man. This was despite my protests that I was unhappy in my marriage, which was practically over as far as I was concerned. I asked her out several times afterwards with the same negative result. By now, she'd split up from Don and lived in Parchment Street with the two boys and so was a free agent, although with a few boyfriends keen to get involved!

Later in 1984, a life-changing event presented itself when, as a donor to the Boys' Club, I was invited to a presentation evening at the Winchester Guildhall. As Lorraine was also attending, I asked her for the umpteenth time to join me for dinner afterwards. She declined, but after I pleaded with her, she agreed to have a "quick drink" at the Otter pub in Otterbourne. I think my typically persistent nature had worn down her resistance. We drove there separately as she was going on to make up a foursome for dinner in Southampton with some friends intent on matchmaking – I was inordinately jealous.

I loved being with her. We blended into each other's psyche, completing each other's sentences, occasionally uttering the same word simultaneously, and conversed effortlessly, so we arranged to meet again at the Montague Arms in Beaulieu in a few weeks' time.

We had a wonderfully romantic dinner and she was impressed when I described exactly what she was wearing the first time I saw her at the Jubilee Hall. As we walked to the car we held hands which sent an electrifying tingle up my arm. I was hooked.

I'd known Lorraine for three years but never felt this way about her before. I became obsessed with her. She told me, too, that she was concerned that her feelings for me were growing stronger – concerned, because she knew the situation wasn't exactly ideal and that there'd be some problems to overcome if these feelings grew any stronger.

At first, I was euphoric. I found myself singing or whistling to myself in the office. There isn't a better feeling in the world that that of being loved. I discovered even more deeply, her true nature – putting other people first, a capacity to make all those around her happy, open and trusting and, like me, only really got annoyed at something that wasn't "fair". She was always laughing and had many friends. She remains a terrific communicator.

She was 39, very pretty, with a great figure. I was 43. She'd emigrated to Vancouver in Canada with Brenda, her oldest friend from school, when they were both 18. Brenda stayed, having met and married Dave, a builder, but Lorraine, despite some romances, was homesick and so returned when she was 21. I'm so glad she did!

She'd been adopted by an older family when she was three years old, having spent her early life in many foster homes. Her mother, who lived in Bitterne, Southampton, had an affair, coincidentally, with a Canadian Air Force photographer during the latter days of the war and Lorraine was the result. When he'd returned to Canada her mother met another man who said he'd marry her, but, cruelly, Lorraine was not included in the package so she would have to be fostered out or adopted. Despite many attempts, Lorraine has never found her father.

When she was 28, she traced her mother who by now was living in Sidmouth, Devon with her husband. She also discovered a half-sister, four years younger, living in the same town and although she was in touch with her new-found family for a number of years, she never got over the fact that she was given away to strangers. They haven't been in touch for over ten years.

Her adoptive parents, Mr and Mrs Cornelius, both in their 60s at the time of the adoption, brought her up unnecessarily strictly, particularly Mrs Cornelius, who never really wanted to rear another child having had six of her own, the youngest being 16 years old. It was *Mr* Cornelius who insisted that she should not be sent to yet another foster home. He'd heard of Lorraine's plight from one of his daughters who worked with Lorraine's mother. There was little love in the house and sometimes Lorraine was treated cruelly. She's often told me about some of the beatings Mrs Cornelius handed out for the slightest misdemeanour, using a cane or a wet hand slapped across her legs leaving the imprint of her ring.

Mrs C delighted in pointing out the red wheals to the rest of the family as if to say "She was naughty and she deserved it!" I thought Lorraine was remarkably well-balanced given this difficult start in life and possessed a remarkable *joie de vie*. Once I got to know her better, I realised she had little self-worth as a direct result of her "Victorian" upbringing. She often remarked that I was born to redress the balance which is why fate had thrown us together!

I realised I wanted to spend the rest of my life with her. I left her a note to that effect following an evening at her Parchment Street home. She was both surprised and deeply worried about the consequences but she reciprocated my feelings. My euphoria quickly turned to anguish when I realised I now had to make a decision. I hated deceiving Ann and knew that I couldn't carry on this "double life" for long. I would have to confront the issue. Should I stay with her or move in with Lorraine? Staying with Ann was, overwhelmingly, the easier option. But that would do nothing to overcome my lack of love for her and hence the relationship. On the other hand, if I moved in with Lorraine, there were huge risks. Suppose the relationship, once we lived together, didn't work? What about the feelings of her two boys, aged by now 10 and 14 respectively, whom I'd inherit? How would the finances work?

The most difficult issue of all was how to break the news to Ann that I didn't love her any more. She had no real idea how I felt – we'd never really discussed it. I'd also have to explain my decision to Stephanie and Elsie, Ann's mother. I agonised over the decision during the first few months of 1985, tormenting myself with guilt until I could stand it no more. Wherever I was, whatever

I was doing, it was always at the forefront of my mind. I tried to blank it out. I immersed myself even more in the expanding business, sometimes working on the business plans until midnight at home. Even during rugby training or in the gym, still this agony wouldn't go away. Out running for miles, I'd weigh everything up, churning every aspect, trying to see a clear way forward.

"That's it. I'm going to stay." A mile later, "No, no, I'm going to leave." Another mile, "No, I'm staying." It was purgatory.

At the end of March, I finally plucked up the courage one evening to break the news that I wanted to leave, ending our 25 years together. Understandably, she took it *very, very* badly indeed.

She immediately accused me of having an affair and demanded to know who she was.

"There's no-one else. I just don't want to live with you anymore and think we'd both be better off if we split!" I blurted out.

"This is ridiculous! Look what we've got? A lovely house, cars, and your job's great. What more do you want?" she screamed back. "And what do you think Stephanie will say?"

"Stephanie's 23 years old. She's a grown woman!" I yelled back. She'd left school with 11 GCSEs and obtained a good job with the Independent Television Authority, ITA. She'd joined the Territorial Army and inherited my drive and generally optimistic outlook on life. She'd also had a number of boyfriends, so I figured she'd already had to cope with relationship issues of her own and was now a mature young lady.

Ann and I spent the next four to five hours into the early part of the next day emotionally discussing what to do. I found it difficult to precisely enunciate *why* I wanted to leave if it wasn't for another woman. I held onto the premise that Lorraine was just a catalyst. I reasoned that if I'd been deliriously happy in my marriage, we wouldn't be having this discussion. We were both in tears most of the time, my head ached and felt like exploding and my nerve-ends became jangled and frayed as we discussed over and over again why I should or shouldn't leave. I knew it would be difficult, but this was worse than I could possibly have imagined – without doubt, the worst evening of my life and probably Ann's too.

She finally persuaded me to give the marriage another three months before making a final decision. I agreed. I assumed now that I'd leapt the highest hurdle by making my intentions clear, actually leaving would be easy – how naïve!

When I told Lorraine what we'd agreed, she made it very clear that it was solely *my* decision. She said she wouldn't see me any more until the trial had run its course and I'd finally made up my mind.

The next few weeks were hell. I missed Lorraine and Ann tried everything she knew to please me. If anything, this only served to stiffen my resolve. She tried *too* hard in every aspect of our relationship. My favourite meals were always ready whenever I wanted them, we spent more time together on our own, as opposed to always having her mother present in the room, and we talked and talked and talked, continuously analysing where things had gone wrong. *I* knew for sure it was over and began to dread facing the final confrontation when I left.

This time when I told Lorraine of my decision about leaving, she insisted that in order to protect her boys, I should spend six months living on my own. This would help us finally determine whether we were right for each other and whether the impact on her boys was going to be positive. I agreed and made arrangements to rent a flat in Winchester from the day I left.

Until then, I hated being in this twilight zone – I was spending time with someone I didn't want to be with yet denying myself time to be with someone I did – so, on the evening of 25th April 1985, five weeks into the trial, I told Ann I was leaving. She immediately told Stephanie and her mother.

I still don't know how I built up the courage to begin packing in front of these three hysterical women. Ann followed me everywhere, hectoring me all the time. It was a huge shock to them so I understood why they were so upset, but instinctively I knew I was doing the right thing, despite being tortured with guilt. I kept telling them that financially, there would be no problem – I was happy to walk away with nothing. I was leaving a substantial house and good standard of living to move into a flat on my own, so I wasn't exactly running off with all the assets. This was obviously only part of the issue, but it was all I could think of saying to deflect some of the misery surrounding me.

I threw as many clothes as I could into a couple of suitcases and said I'd be back for the rest in a few days. I took no photographs or mementos, something I later regretted. I drove out of the drive with three tearful women and Zara, my lovely golden retriever, standing in the doorway. My emotions were a complete mess. It would have been so easy to turn back but I just gritted my teeth, telling myself over and over again it was the right thing to do, although I found it difficult to appreciate that I was on the cusp of a new, exciting relationship with someone whom I truly loved.

It wasn't Ann's fault or my fault, it was just that circumstances, right from the beginning of our relationship, didn't allow us to have sufficient emotional "cement" to bind us forever.

That night, I met up with Lorraine at Jill and Peter Welsh's house. They were her long-term friends and as there was a delay on signing the completion documents on the flat, we wanted a "safe house" to spend the first night of our life together. It proved to be an inspired choice. Jill and Peter had been through a similar experience and so knew exactly what we were going through. I was in a dreadful state. I kept bursting into tears, both through relief that I'd finally broken free and the overwhelming feeling of guilt.

Next morning, I went to work and explained to my business partner, Ed Oakley, what I'd done. He knew Ann quite well, but he made no judgement. I was still in a state of shock but he handled it well. For the next few weeks I found it difficult to concentrate on the business and Ed really ran the show for a while. Just as well, because Ann, who is uncannily perceptive, found out about Lorraine within days, and became understandably vitriolic. She visited the showrooms to confront me in front of the staff. She even called my boss, Steve Hayklan, to tell him what I'd done. Fortunately, I'd already explained the situation and although he was sympathetic towards me, he was more concerned about my business performance. She also discovered where Lorraine was working and visited her office for a confrontation in front of her employers, accusing her in unflattering terms of causing the break-up – although understandable, it was distinctly unpleasant.

There was no point in staying in the flat. I hated living there alone. I hardly knew where the kitchen was at home so had no idea how to cater for myself – I just filled the cupboards with cans of baked beans and lived on them for a couple of weeks! Lorraine took pity on me and agreed that I should move in with her and the boys, Max and Aaron, losing the remaining five months' rent paid in advance – that was the least of my problems!

I went back home on a couple of occasions to collect some more things and tried to get Ann to understand that it was finally over between us. I once again emphasised that I'd see that she had no financial problems but over the next few years, we had many vitriolic battles during the divorce proceedings. She considered that as I was the "guilty party", I should pay for my sins. She felt she should be compensated for what I'd done. I made many generous offers, all rejected, which meant the final settlement went all the way to court. I tried to reason with her that it would be best if we could agree the settlement ourselves since the mounting legal fees were eating into the sum available for us to share. She dismissed the idea. It seemed she wanted to make life as difficult as possible for me regardless of the financial split.

Lorraine and I dreaded the letters sent by her solicitor which were usually aggressive, threatening and demanding. Fortunately, my solicitor was able to place them into context once I was able to confer with him, but in the meantime, they were very unsettling.

Eventually, with a little help from our barristers and solicitors, we settled outside the Winchester Law Courts minutes before the case was due to be heard before a judge after four years of haggling. She was very badly advised in my opinion and although she received a considerable settlement, it was less than I'd offered in the early stages when my guilt was at its peak. The legal fees alone were close to £25,000! I was left with very little capital, but I was earning a six-figure income and had some valuable share options. At least, Lorraine and I could now plan our future.

I don't blame Ann for acting the way she did. I can see now that a combination of her changing hormones and the abrupt ending of a 25-year-long relationship drove her to do things perhaps she wouldn't normally have done. I think she was encouraged by her solicitor and by her mother, Elsie, who said, when I met her once after I'd left, "I hope you rot in hell!"

Stephanie, too, was very upset and made it clear that she didn't want anything to do with me, although I desperately wished to remain in touch. She was still living at home and had to handle all the emotional outpouring so it must have been very stressful.

This emphasised my feelings of guilt which continued to gnaw away to such a point that Lorraine persuaded me to undertake some counselling. At first I dismissed the idea but it got to the stage that my guilt was enveloping every aspect of my personality and threatening my relationship with Lorraine. She felt guilty too, so it became almost the only subject we spoke about. Finally I relented. I'm so glad I did.

By the second or third session of pouring out my heart to a wonderfully understanding counsellor, Jane Williams, I begun to realise, with her help, that it wasn't all my fault. I was taking *all* the blame for the failure of the relationship because I was the one who ended it. The relationship had broken down many years earlier and that was the fault of *both* of us. My infidelity, I learnt, was the *symptom* and not the *cause* of the break-up. This realisation helped Lorraine and I to deal with the situation.

I endured a tortuous, emotional process including breaking down in tears a few times before this simple truth finally seeped into my consciousness. Once it did, I began to feel a good deal better. I still experience some remorse today, but it is now manageable and in perspective. It still surprises me that I was capable of such emotions – I'd always thought I could handle anything!

I also had to break the news to my brother Les, and sister, Ivy. They were both very supportive. Ivy and Bob, her husband, had been to see one of our plays at the Jubilee Hall and when I told her, she said that she *thought* she saw a spark between us and wasn't too surprised. It shocked me. It must have been a subconscious reaction between us because it wasn't until about two years later that I began to have strong feelings for Lorraine. She was very happy for us.

Les's attitude was great, but his wife Peggy was very negative and quite rude to Lorraine when they eventually met. As she was a similar age to Ann, I think she perhaps felt threatened by these events and maybe feared that Les would travel down the same path.

I was especially sorry that my mother didn't live long enough to meet Lorraine. I'm convinced Mum would have approved and they'd have enjoyed each other's company immensely.

Life with Lorraine in Parchment Street was very different from Rewlands Drive. I was so pleased to be with her that I'd plan my day to get home from the office as early as I could. Previously, I'd put aside some jobs to work on later in the evening, I had no real incentive to do otherwise.

I also discovered that Lorraine was a great cook. My mother was, too, and Ann was excellent, so food had always been very important to me. Lorraine always had a sumptuous three-course dinner on the table for me and the boys every night. We sat at the dining-room table, which had been laid as if it were a Michelin restaurant, complete with tablecloth, napkins, cutlery and two bulbous wine glasses for the adults! The TV was turned off and we simply sat, ate and discussed our various days' activities. It was a great way to maintain contact with the boys, although I suspect at the time, they found it all rather boring. Now they've fled the nest, Lorraine and I continue with the custom.

Lorraine's an expert interior designer, too, and her flair shone through in this cosy 1930s terraced house she'd furnished with a fusion of warm colours on the walls and floors which seemed to reflect our happiness at being together.

My biggest challenge was how to develop a relationship with Max and Aaron. They were naturally suspicious of me at first, and I really tried to get on well with them. If anything, I tried *too* hard. I was always taking them running, suggesting a kick-about over North Walls park or taking them to the cinema. Although the relationship wasn't bad, I sensed I wasn't making much progress – I was desperate to make it work. I'd heard of many relationships being completely undermined by the "inherited" children who'd put every obstacle in the way of becoming a happy family unit.

I was chatting to Mike Shearman, Lorraine's ex-boss from the Boys' Club one evening, and I asked him, with his vast experience of dealing with teenagers, how he'd proceed.

"You just need to back off a bit, Dai," he said. "You'll put them off if you're always initiating stuff. Let them approach you with suggestions. They'll come to recognise that you are a permanent fixture as time progresses and they'll see how much their mother loves you. You'll see a big difference but you must give it time." These proved to be wise words and within the next few months, there was a considerable improvement in our relationships and we became very close. I'm so glad I took his advice.

Cosy though it was, I didn't really like living in *Lorraine's* house. I wanted us to make a fresh start, build a nest *together*. Lorraine agreed, so in July 1986 we moved into a brand new, south-facing, end-of-terrace house in Port Lane, Hursley, about seven miles west of Winchester. The development of just six houses wasn't complete when we purchased it, so we had a choice of colours for the walls and floors so Lorraine was able to apply her considerable skill in replicating the warmth of Parchment Street in a modern environment. The only downside was that the garden was a little larger than a handkerchief – not something I was used to! However, I researched a great deal and designed a courtyard garden, of which I became very proud.

We had some wonderful neighbours, especially Dot and Steve Waterman who'd moved in just before us. They've remained friends ever since and we are both godparents to their children.

Roz and Tony Baker had lived in Zimbabwe all their lives but decided to settle in the UK. Tony was another entrepreneur, always coming into my house to discuss his latest ideas. After we'd known them a few years, they decided to go back to Zimbabwe and invited us to visit them.

They lived just outside Harare in a beautiful house complete with maids and "the boy". He was aged 60 and called "Wattie", short for Watson. He ensured our every whim was met. We weren't ever allowed to help wash up, make our beds or brew our own cup of tea!

"No, you mustn't do anything, not even plump up the cushions after you've sat on them," Tony said. "He'll take it as a sign he's not doing his job and he'll think he's failed."

I'm sure Tony looked after him well, but we couldn't ignore the feeling of us being the "master" and he being the "servant". This was reinforced by the fact whenever Lorraine rang Tony and Roz, "Wattie" always answered the phone and before handing over the receiver, he'd enquire, "How is the master?" much to Lorraine's chagrin!

We were only a 100 yards or so away from one of Lorraine's friends she'd known for over 20 years, Linda House. Her two children, Chris and Catherine, had grown up with Max and Aaron when the families lived in Kings Worthy, just outside Winchester and so we had a ready-made "family" on our doorstep!

All our houses were close to the King's Head pub, just across the road, and it became our "local".

We spent every New Year's Eve at the pub when Arthur and Myra, the landlords, threw fantastic fancy-dress parties with most of the neighbours attending and generally made fools of ourselves. We could just about stagger the 30 yards home unaided!

The local recreation field was just across the road, and so many summers' evenings were spent playing football with the two boys and sometimes with other kids joining in. I remember Aaron and Max being very impressed when I crossed the ball firstly with my left foot and then, later on, my right. They were both as mad on football as I used to be, so this triumph was more than superficial. It represented the starting point of gaining their respect. I knew all that practising when I was young would pay off some day!

There were some great scenic runs around the village too – often I'd jog to Otterbourne or through the woods to Oliver's Battery when I got home from work, both about a five-mile round trip.

"Let's get married!" I said one evening. I'd been thinking about it for some time and was absolutely sure that I wanted to make the ultimate commitment but Lorraine was cautious – she was happy with the way things were and nervous, thinking that getting married might spoil things, but she finally agreed and we married on Lorraine's 44th birthday on June 20th 1990. With her typical sense of style, we invited only close family and friends to the ceremony at the Winchester register office and to a small reception at Keats restaurant in Ampfield, but on the day, sent a mock telegram to about a 100 of our other friends telling them we'd just got married and that they were invited to a celebration exactly a week later, also at Keats.

Lorraine looked fabulous in a stunning white suit trimmed in black and a hat to match. Obligingly, the sun shone brightly during the photographs and Max, then 18, and my best man, gave a wonderful speech, saying such kind words that cemented our relationship. We flew from Southampton to Paris on a day when the weather deteriorated badly throwing all four seasons at us – brilliantly sunny and warm one minute, thunder and lightning the next. It was just as well that Lorraine insisted on only drinking champagne at the reception because the flight was very bumpy as we encountered a high degree of turbulence for most of the flight.

I still don't know how she slept through it all except that Mike House, Linda's husband, had organised some more champagne on the flight, so an extra glass or two probably accounted for it! When we got to the Hotel Westminster in Rue St Honore, I'd forgotten that I'd arranged for some flowers and yet more champagne to be placed in the room! Lorraine's minimal capacity for alcohol was proving true to form and so she promptly fell asleep, once again, on the bed.

England were playing Sweden in the 1990 soccer World Cup on the same night, so, as I had nothing better to do, I tuned in to watch. The score was 0-0 and as Lorraine didn't wake until the next morning, I was able to announce at the second reception that on my wedding night, England failed to score and so did I!

The weather in Paris was dreadful, but after two days, I surprised Lorraine by arranging to travel south to Geneva on the TGV, the express train. The hotel was right on the lake with a view of the famous fountain. Here, the weather was superb with clear blue skies, clean fresh air and at last, some warmth on our backs. We hired a Renault Cabriolet and drove with the top down through lush meadows full of cows – I'm always reminded of this time whenever I hear cowbells – up through the Alps and round the vast Lake Leman that dominates Geneva – we were blissfully happy!

The reception, a week later at Keats, turned into a great party with just about everyone who was invited turning up. The bar bill was monstrous – my fault for inviting so many rugby mates! It was worth every penny!

Stephanie came to the reception, too. I was delighted! I'd kept in touch, phoning her and meeting up for lunch occasionally and although cool at first, I think she saw how happy I was with Lorraine and began to accept the situation. I think her main feeling was that I'd swapped her for two boys. I worked hard on explaining this simply wasn't true. Although, because of the circumstances of her birth, I wasn't perhaps as close to her as I could have been, the boys would never replace her. After all they were 10 and 14 years old at the time of the split – hardly a fair swap, I joked. Stephanie knew Lorraine from the health club days and I think they liked each other but understandably, she was concerned about her mother – she didn't want to appear disloyal. Attending the reception was a strong vote in our favour, and a major turning point in our relationship.

CHAPTER 15
Vet's rugby and touring – again!

Thank God for veteran's rugby! I don't mean a team of veterinary surgeons, who, when not attending very sick animals, play rugby. I mean the formation of a rugby team whose only qualification is to be over the age of 35! Terry Munford, with whom I'd played in the Second and Third XV at the club, realising that the physical part of the game was starting to take its toll on our aging bodies, decided that unless we could play against other old lags like ourselves, our rugby careers were finished.

So in 1986, Terry got together a team to play our first match against Portsmouth Veterans. The quality of rugby played was superb. We were slower and perhaps not quite so physical, but many of my team-mates were very skilful, having played to an excellent standard in their youth, and now swapped brawn and muscle for guile and cunning! Playing veteran's rugby extended my career by seven years.

Although we didn't take the matches quite so seriously, it was competitive enough to make it interesting. Terry lightened the mood by including some impressive gardening tips in his pre-match team talk! If it was very cold or wet, we'd share a tot of port straight from the bottle just before taking the field!

We won many more games than we lost mainly through a superb half-back combination of Keith Edwards at scrum-half and Dave Whatley at fly-half. They were both outstanding players. Keith could easily have played for a better side, but I think he enjoyed being superior to the rest of us! He kicked wonderfully well, whether from place-kicks or out of his hands. But most of all, he possessed a fantastic pass. If Dave Whatley, the receiver at fly-half, wasn't available to play, we'd argue about who would play in this position. We knew Keith only ever passed to you if you were in a better position and the ball was spun with pinpoint accuracy straight into your hands. He made the receiver look international-class!

Dave Whatley was a rugby genius. His reading of the game was always spot-on. He sensed when an opposing player was out of position and instinctively, was able to assess the other side's strengths and weaknesses and to exploit them. He was short, overweight and had no pace – except over the first five yards when he was electric! So playing outside these two experts in the centre three-quarter position was a joy! Dave Renwick was the other centre and we gelled together beautifully – he was brutally direct and confrontational, whereas I was more of an elusive runner, trying to evade tacklers!

Pete Langley also played for a few years either as wing or centre despite suffering a great deal from a weak back caused through a previous injury. He insisted the only remedy that worked was wearing his mother's corset under his kit! I was charged with the dubious pleasure of lacing it up as tightly as I could, almost to the point of stopping him breathing! At least he had the good grace to cut off the suspenders!

The changing room before battle commenced often resembled a scene from a world war medical station – bandages and supports were being meticulously wound round flaccid limbs, pungent liniments were furiously rubbed into ample flesh and, for some, a calming cigarette puffed to soothe the nerves.

On the pitch, all the talent we possessed outside the scrum was no use unless the "donkeys" in the ball-winning department did their job. Here, too, we were blessed with some fine players. Doctor Roddy Burlinson was a powerhouse and played until he was 61! Derek (ten-pint) Weaver, Pete (salmon-leap) Poutney and Pete (varicose-vein) Tuckey all combined to make sure we always had enough ball to win the game. This was a great period in my rugby career. I enjoyed using my experience to counter declining pace and anticipating where the ball was going, thus saving precious energy. Surrounded by such talented players, too, constituted a joyful Saturday afternoon.

Winchester Rugby Club wasn't my first taste of vet's rugby. One evening in September 1985, I was making my way home from a meeting in London. I'd just missed my train from Waterloo, so I popped into a pub nearby to wait for the next train – as one does! As I entered, I was amazed to find it packed with middle-aged men of just about every nationality, dressed in rugby shirts, singing songs, playing guitars and generally having a great time.

Then it dawned on me! The Golden Oldies rugby festival was being played in England. This annual international event is organised especially for guys aged from 35 upwards – some are in their 70s! The only concession to the older players is they get to wear purple shorts which means they can't be tackled! This competition was being held in London for the first time and attracted over 150 teams from all over the world. I remembered reading about it some weeks before.

I was immediately seized upon by a group of New Zealanders, who, when they discovered I played rugby, insisted on buying me a beer. We all had a very invigorating evening, each nationality trying to outdo the singing exploits of the other. I missed all my trains, except the last one that left at 11.30 pm. Just before I left, Des, the captain of Eden Wanderers from Auckland, asked if I would like to play for him the next day. He explained they'd suffered a few injuries in the warm-up matches and were especially weak at centre three-quarter, or second five-eighth as they call it – my position. I was delighted.

"Right Dai, be at the London Irish ground at Sunbury by 1.00 pm tomorrow with your boots. We'll provide the rest of the kit. Good on ya, mate!" I got to bed at around 1.00 am and couldn't sleep in anticipation of the game later in the day. When I got up, I thought perhaps I'd dreamt the whole episode. And then, realising it had actually happened, I had some doubts. Did he mean it? Was he joking? If he was having a joke at my expense, he didn't realise how determined and persistent I can be.

I called my secretary and explained that I had some urgent business to attend to so wouldn't be turning up at the office. I'd worked very long hours in the previous week so I felt I could take a day off without feeling too guilty. When I told Ann what had happened, although supportive, she was doubtful Des had meant what he said. "Well, I'm going. If I don't play, it'll be a good day out anyway. See you later tonight."

As I arrived at the stadium I felt nervous and I thought I might be about to be making a fool of myself. The ground was packed with players and supporters from all over the world, wearing a kaleidoscope of team colours. Des had told me to look out for a group wearing black and amber tracksuits, coincidentally the same colours as Winchester! I was relieved to hear Des's voice with his unmistakable Kiwi vowels shouting out over the din, "Dai mate, over here! We've been waiting for you!"

As I got changed with the other guys, there was a great deal of banter between them, all good-natured, and mainly directed towards me.

"Hope you're as good as you said you were in the pub last night. We're all hung-over,mate. We're relying on you to win the match."

My level of nervousness shot up a few degrees. What had I said? What was this team's playing standard? Would I be out of my depth? Were they just winding me up?

We were playing an Australian side, which increased my level of tension – they don't usually pull their punches against the Brits. No matter what level you play rugby, the physical nature of the game means no player wants to be second best in a confrontation and let the side down. Although I was 43, I was very fit but even so, my confidence was ebbing away.

I needn't have worried. I've explained earlier about extra special episodes that happen probably only a few times in any sportsman's career. That feeling of invincibility, of having time with the ball to perfect your skill and possessing almost ethereal powers. I'm glad to say this was one of those episodes.

The standard of play was very high. This helped. The ball was only passed to me if I was in space, and if I got tackled, the support play was quick to the breakdown to retrieve the ball. Within the first ten minutes, I made a break from close to the halfway line and the opposition seemed to melt as I weaved towards the line for a try. From then on, I played with confidence and thoroughly enjoyed my debut with Eden Wanderers in a match we went on to win convincingly.

Afterwards, I had another wonderful night of camaraderie in the London Irish clubhouse, not leaving until very late into the night. My new-found colleagues were full of praise for the way I played and I felt like I'd been a member of their club for years rather than just 24 hours.

"What are you doing Sunday, Dai?" Des enquired as I left.

"Well, nothing really."

"Right, we'd love you to play for us again. We're playing a combined Oxbridge University team at Richmond. Do you fancy it, mate?"

"Well, yeah, thanks Des. Are you sure? I'd love to play. See you there," I responded.

By the time I met the team on Sunday at the superb Richmond ground, I felt really confident. They all welcomed me like a long-lost Kiwi and were so friendly and chummy, I was entirely comfortable in my adopted team. As we were changing, I asked who was in the university veterans side.

"Oh, I heard they've got some guest players. Some old England international has-beens. You'll be ok."

"Well, who?"

"Some blokes called David Duckham and Jacko Page."

Was he serious?

These were, despite my Welsh background, my schoolboy heroes! They were not only former England internationals but legends of the game in the 1970s. This was a serious step up in class and they'd attracted a large crowd.

Although Duckham didn't play, Jacko did, and as I suspected they were far too good for us and I couldn't repeat my performance in the first game – in truth, I had a nightmare of a match and was really disappointed.

As the game ended, I was shaking hands with Jacko Page, when an announcement came over the PA system. "Carlton, from Australia, are short of two players. If anyone would like to play, please report to the official's marquee. Thank you."

Jacko turned to me and said, "Do you fancy it?"

I was desperate to make amends and as the games were only 20 minutes each way, I certainly felt fit enough to play two matches.

"Yeah, why not? I'd love to."

After we'd both registered, there was about a ten-minute wait before the second game commenced, and as I was stiffening up, I began doing some elaborate stretching exercises on the touchline. A BBC camera crew approached and asked me to carry on whilst they filmed. They told me they were recording the Golden Oldies event for the Rugby Special programme which went out every Sunday afternoon on BBC 2. I thought no more of it.

I had a much better game this time, with the Eden Wanderers team watching, so I felt I'd partially recovered their respect as a rugby player. When the match finished, I re-joined them and had another memorable night's celebration with all the other teams as this was the last day of the tournament. They were returning to New Zealand the next day and as I left them for the last time, I had a tear in my eye as I hugged all of them goodbye after they'd presented me with a club blazer badge and a club shirt. I made a note of some of their addresses and telephone numbers, but deeply regret that the list was mislaid during my break-up from Ann in April 1986.

A couple of weeks later, I turned up for a game at Winchester to be greeted by the team humming the Rugby Special theme tune.

"What's going on?" I said.

"Oh, don't you know. You're a TV star. You were on Rugby Special last week!" Jonesy said.

He went on to explain that when they showed the credits at the end of the programme, I was doing my stretching exercises at the side of the pitch whilst Nigel Starmer-Smith, the presenter, made some caustic, ageist remarks about us old men having to spend hours warming up before a match! And to think, this entire adventure only occurred because I missed my train at Waterloo station!

In May 1988, my Old Boys' club, the Old Vs, invited me to tour with them as a veteran to Berlin. They were short of players so they accepted Nosher Eames, my club-mate from Winchester, as an honorary Old V so he could also tour. Wives and girlfriends were encouraged, so Lorraine came too. Nosher was, and still is, a confirmed bachelor.

Berlin was chosen as a place to tour simply because one of our Old Boys, Mark Upsdale, worked for a German computer firm and so was well-placed to arrange everything. As I met him in the airport, I asked him what he thought of Berlin.

"Dai, it's great! I go to the beach some days, then other days I go sailing. I love it!"

"No," I said, "I don't mean where do you go for your holidays, I mean how is life in Berlin?"

"That's what I'm talking about. We have a fantastic river running through the centre and as Berlin was built on sand, we have great beaches. You'll see some tomorrow night. We're going on a riverboat cruise."

Berlin was fascinating. The western quarter, where we stayed in a contemporary boutique hotel, was vibrant, colourful and architecturally beautiful. One evening we were taken to a huge radio tower, the Funkturm, based on the Eiffel Tower in Paris, from which we could view from the 125-metre-high platform, the whole of Berlin. The contrast was extraordinary. The wall dividing east and west was still in existence. There was almost complete darkness looking east, but a scene more reminiscent of Las Vegas when we looked west.

We also visited Checkpoint Charlie and the graffiti-covered walls complete with heavily-uniformed, humourless, armed soldiers, both US and German, who looked intimidating and menacing. This was the only checkpoint where registered military personnel and tourists were allowed to enter East Berlin. The wall was erected by the communist-controlled eastern sector in response to the 2.6 million East Germans who'd escaped to the west since 1949. After the wall was built, which extended to 27 miles across Berlin with 302 watch towers, visiting the west was illegal and 392 would-be escapees were either killed or wounded in attempting to escape. The wall became the ultimate symbol of the Cold War.

Incredibly, and to the world's surprise, within 18 months of our visit, the wall was demolished amid scenes of delirious Germans at last being re-united with their friends and families. In a strange way, I was glad to experience the wall's existence. I could never accept the extraordinary idea of segregating the German people, including families, simply on the basis of the political beliefs of the ruling governments.

We played against a German club side as the warm-up match for the German national team taking on the Public School Wanderers from the UK. We won quite handsomely, and after we changed we watched the main event. All four teams, with wives and girlfriends, were invited to a trip down the River Spree on a huge vessel, where we dined on traditional German food – sauerkraut, frankfurters and pickled cabbage, all washed down with copious amounts of lager from a brewery with a German name impossible to pronounce! I saw for myself what Mark meant about his nautical pastimes. Although it was early evening, we passed numerous sailing boats and the beaches were wonderfully sandy and full of deckchairs!

Winchester Rugby Club veterans went on a weekend tour to Paris in 1991 where we were due to play a French veteran's team based on the outskirts – or at least that was the plan! Thirty players and supporters left on a Friday night in the middle of May, meeting at the clubhouse for the coach to take us to the Portsmouth ferry to Le Havre.

Clive Mansell, one of our players, turned up dressed as a woman complete with stockings, bright red lipstick and high heels, together with a pal who'd never played rugby before, who'd also temporarily swapped sexes! Clive ran a successful pub on the outskirts of Winchester and when he told one of his regulars, Pete Sands, earlier in the day where he was going, Pete insisted on coming. They'd decided that it might be fun to go through the entire tour as their other halves and so only brought their wives' passports.

"Clive, you'll never get away with it," I said. "You'll probably both be turned back at Portsmouth. Nice dress though!"

"Shut up, Dai. Just give us a kiss," Clive said, puckering up. I declined the invitation.

Surprisingly, they easily passed through the control point at the ferry terminal. I couldn't help thinking it would be different on the French side. Once aboard, there was the usual drinking, singing and playing silly games until the early hours.

Few of us will ever understand how Clive and Pete glided through the immigration authorities at Le Havre. I can only assume they either went along with the joke or truly believed these rather manly mademoiselles were the real thing. Either way, they were sitting in the coach swigging beer from a bottle before most of us had been processed!

We breakfasted at a motorway café on the way to Paris and finally reached the rugby ground at about 1.00 pm for a 3.00 pm kick-off, but to our dismay, the clubhouse was locked up. Terry, our captain, who spoke passable French, made some frantic phone calls and was told that the French captain had the key. He found his address and then we hunted him down – not easy in a Parisian suburb.

Once we found his house, Terry went to the door to be met by the captain's wife. I could tell it was bad news as, from the confines of the coach, I saw her shake her head furiously.

"I'm sorry, boys, but they've gone off to play a tournament in Belgium – the game's off." Terry was mortified and deeply embarrassed. So began the longest pub crawl I've ever endured. We returned back to Paris, checked into our two-star hotel opposite the Moulin Rouge in the Pigalle district and all met up in the bar, Clive and Pete still in drag. It was 2.30 pm.

After the first few bars, we split up into groups but miraculously, we met up with some of them later in the evening. I've absolutely no idea where we went, except we walked everywhere but rarely for more than a few minutes before we entered another bar. As I had a smattering of French from schooldays and had spent time at my flat in St Malo, I was elected to find somewhere to eat. The boys were most impressed when I managed to find a brasserie that would entertain a table of 12 at such short notice!

In one particularly seedy bar, we had to leave in a hurry. I opened my wallet, which was full of francs to buy my round and Keith Edwards, allegedly, spotted a couple of French "lowlife", as he subsequently described them, take a menacing step towards me. He grossly over-reacted as he blocked them and shouted out, "Everybody, quick, run, run, we must leave!" I thought there was a fire, and we all dashed outside immediately and ran to the next bar.

"Bloody hell, Dai, I thought you were going to get mugged in there and as it was your round, I felt I'd better do something to make sure we could all still get a drink!"

The last bar we visited was, by now, some way from the hotel. We named it the Bobby Charlton bar – the patron was a dead ringer for the former Manchester United icon, complete with the trademark comb-over! He was quite pleased to be associated with such a famous footballer and said he'd keep serving as long as we stayed there. Oh dear! The result was that Nosher Eames, Nick Rogerson and I, who were sharing a room, crashed into bed at around 4.30 am next morning, after an hilarious, fun-filled, beer-soaked night.

We spent the next morning nursing giant hangovers and slept on the coach as we travelled up to Le Havre for the ferry trip home, which I remember vividly. It was such an unbelievable event, I've stopped telling the story. People simply don't swallow it. I *know* it's true. I was there.

Returning on the same ferry was a golfing society with a couple of superb singers who performed a cabaret for us and the other passengers. They challenged us to respond, and this is when the fun really started. Clive and Pete had, once again, negotiated their way through passport control in Le Havre, still with their lady-clothes and make-up and now they were our cabaret!

They got up onto the tables and amidst great encouragement, sang, amongst other bawdy numbers, *Eskimo Nell,* a very rude rugby song, whilst prancing about like two genteel members of the Women's Institute – it was a hoot!

When they finished, they were accosted by an attractive, slim English woman in her mid-40s.

"How dare you take the p**s out of us! I'll show you what a *real* woman looks like!" With that, she jumped up onto a table and began the sexiest striptease act I'd ever seen.

Many passengers made their way from wherever they were sitting to see what was going on. She took off the last remaining piece of clothing to a deafening roar which attracted the attention of the ship's purser who told everyone to quieten down. He then turned to Clive and Pete and asked them to accompany him to his office.

We didn't see them again for several hours, and Clive later told us they were placed in the ship's *secure environment* – effectively a jailhouse – whilst they checked passports. When the purser realised what had happened, he gave them a very stern warning and told them they weren't best pleased to have been misled. Any further attempts to undermine Passport Control would lead to a custodial sentence! They'd had a good run though and given us a lot of pleasure.

The striptease artiste (I'm sure she must have been a professional) spent the rest of the night drinking and flirting with us – what a character!

On the coach journey from Portsmouth to Winchester early on Monday morning, we realised our other halves wouldn't believe the game never took place and would assume the tour was just a ploy to get away for a few days. So we all contributed to making up a press report of the match. It was all perfectly true! Some examples were: "The score was 0.0 – no one scored", "Our winger ghosted past the opposing player as if he wasn't there", "The French defence was non-existent!"

Unfortunately for us, Kit Neilson, a long-time member of the club who wasn't on this tour, was the deputy editor of the Hampshire Chronicle and he was bright enough to see through our charade – either that or he was tipped off. He still edited and published the report but removed some of the more obvious references to the phantom match. But at least a report appeared in the paper the next week, "legitimising" the tour.

CHAPTER 16
Thrilling business opportunities

As the blissfully emotional roller-coaster ride of my new relationship, punctured by the joys of rugby touring, was continuing, there were exciting developments in my business career.

My opposite number on the property development side was Jeff Fanstone, a fellow main board director. We were roughly the same age and shared the same values and as he lived in Southampton, we saw each other socially. He was also involved in the health club Steve had asked me to sort out. We got on exceptionally well and enjoyed our friendly rivalry for Steve's approval. I'm sure Steve picked up on this and he gave us a number of projects to work on together. He persuaded the board to offer us both some exceptional share option schemes and bonus packages based on performance, so Jeff and I were highly motivated. I thrived in this stimulating environment.

The Wiggins Group's property division became heavily involved in the new Canary Wharf development. This was, in 1986, the largest commercial development project in Europe, and Steve, our charismatic leader and never one to miss a commercial opportunity, almost shook with excitement whenever he discussed our company's involvement.

At one board meeting, he gave Jeff and I a project affecting this development, and asked us to report back at the next meeting. We'd also agreed at that same meeting that the group would take out Key Man life insurance policies with exceptionally large sums payable to the company in the event of a director's demise. So, caught up with Steve's enthusiasm, as soon as we got on the train from Waterloo to Winchester straight after the meeting, we opened our brief cases and spread our papers on the table and discussed the project earnestly.

Before I'd left home that morning, Lorraine reminded me that we were attending a Boys' Club presentation that evening, and she'd collect me from the station to drive us directly to the venue as we had a very tight deadline. Jeff and I became deeply engrossed in our project, but I'd mentally counted the number of stops as the train sped southwest, so after an hour, I began packing up my papers just as the train stopped. I rushed up the corridor, judging this to be the Winchester station.

It was a foul, dank, drizzly November night, and as I opened the door expecting to step onto the platform there was nothing but darkness. I looked back up the line, and *thought* I saw the station buildings and assumed the train had overshot. It started moving again and so, thinking of Lorraine waiting for me, and remembering that the next station was Southampton Central, I decided to jump down onto the ground and walk back to the platform.

The target was much further than I'd judged and as I hit the ground, I lost balance and felt myself rolling down a steep embankment clutching my briefcase! As I clambered back onto the track, shaken and badly winded, I noticed the train had stopped again about 100 yards ahead of me, this time, at what looked remarkably like Winchester railway station!

I heard a commotion and Jeff leaning out of the window shouting, "Are you all right? Are you all right?" He'd raised the alarm, fearing for my safety. I then saw the approaching outline of a man wearing a British Rail cap swinging a lamp from side to side saying, "Where are you? Where are you?"

When we finally met he really went for me.

"What the bloody hell do you think you're doing, jumping off the train before we got into the station? We're going to be ten minutes behind schedule now!" He never said I could have killed myself or asked how I was.

"Well, what do think *you're* doing, stopping the train a hundred yards *before* the station? I could have broken my leg," I yelled back.

"Electrocuted yourself more like," the stationmaster snarled, before leading me back to the station.

When I arrived at the platform, Jeff looked me up and down and said, "God, you're in a bit of a state. I think you ought to have a brandy to settle your nerves." I was wearing a long, white, mackintosh, which was now splattered with mud and patterned with grass stains. My hands were cut and bleeding. As I sipped my "medication", I suddenly remembered Lorraine and the Boys' Club presentation! I slammed the glass on the table and ran outside to the car park and saw her sitting in the car, drumming her fingers on the steering wheel with the engine running.

"Where have you been? You're in a disgusting state, you're late … and you've been drinking!" Of course, when I told her what happened, she was very sympathetic. I went back to the station washroom to clean myself up as best I could and we arrived at the presentation just a little later than planned.

At the next board meeting, under "any other business", Jeff recounted the incident and extolled my selflessness in my unsuccessful attempt to sacrifice my life in order that the Key Man life insurance policy would be paid out in full to the Wiggins Group!

My Motor division was performing well in 1988, some months making more profits than the Property Division. All the dealerships were ahead of their business plans and the finance subsidiary, Leasemaster, was writing millions of pounds worth of finance and contract hire agreements via other car dealers using our unique computer programs. We saw this as a major area of growth. The motor group's total turnover was around £40 million with profits just short of a £1 million and we had ambitious plans to gear-up the operation substantially now that the business model was proven − but it was not to be.

For probably the first time in his entrepreneurial life, Steve was too early, and too zealous in his pursuit of the likely profits from the property investment in Canary Wharf. This resulted in some serious cash flow problems, so when our merchant bankers, Barclays De Zoete Wedd Ltd, suggested selling off the motor division, he reluctantly agreed. He called me up to his palatial offices in Rutland Gate, not far from Harrods in Kensington, to break the news. He was very bashful, almost embarrassed, so when I asked whether he'd consider me heading a management buyout of the motor division, he was quite relieved.

I began the task earnestly, asking Ed Oakley, now Managing Director of Wiggins Motor Group and long-term colleague from my Lex days what he thought. He was very positive and said he'd be delighted to join me. Our Finance Director, Mel Hobson, whom I'd recruited two years earlier and played a major role in our performance, was also up for the challenge.

We prepared a five-year plan incorporating all the key elements of the Wiggins' model and presented it to our bank, Lloyds in Southampton, who were very keen to back us. They'd been involved since I appointed them our bankers in 1982 when I first joined Wiggins, so knew what we were capable of achieving. The buyout proved much easier to put together than I thought.

So, a month later, I went to the Wiggins main board meeting, and presented our bid. We offered £5.5 million, leaving £0.5 million up our sleeve for negotiating. When the meeting ended, we were told we had a good chance of being successful.

A week later, I was again summoned to Steve's office, to be told that our merchant bankers had been "putting out some feelers" and had a bid of £7 million on the table! Steve was even more embarrassed. He was in a difficult position. I knew that if the buyout was successful, he'd have invested in us personally, but as the Chairman of a public company, he had to be seen to do the best deal on behalf of the shareholders. This new bid had very few conditions. There was to be no significant due diligence exercise carried out, and they would provide the funds and complete the offer within four weeks. The only certainty was that, understandably, they didn't want me! They wanted a fresh start with their own management leading the business.

The purchaser was Pendragon, an emerging dealer group with the backing of Sir Nigel Rudd, a very well-known and successful businessman. We were amongst the first of their acquisitions that led to them becoming the largest dealer group in the UK with a turnover in the £billions! The deal was completed so quickly, I don't think they realised what they purchased! The Leasemaster concept was a new, exciting business model, and growing fast. Incredibly, they closed it down within six months! Also, in their haste to complete the deal, there were no covenants restricting me on setting up another business in the same locality, or employing any of the staff or management. This proved to be a serious oversight.

All that remained to be negotiated was the important matter of my compensation for loss of office. I had by now a three-year rolling contract and some worthwhile shares and share options granted to me as a reward for the success of the motor division. Steve and my erstwhile colleague and Finance Director, Paul Llewellen, did the best deal they could, ever-mindful of their responsibilities to the shareholders. We finally agreed a package in early January 1989. Although coming out of the business with a substantial payoff, it was with a heavy heart that I left my "baby". So much of my life had been invested in the growth of business and the plans I had to turn this company into a major player, but I was particularly disappointed to part company with the people I'd brought in and developed.

I also felt, in a strange way, that I'd let everyone down. Although I couldn't have matched the Pendragon deal – it would only have been trumped again, I'm sure – it felt like I was handing over an adolescent child to a new parent whom I didn't know.

During the following month, I had many offers to manage other dealer groups, and also thought seriously about doing something entirely different. Finally, I decided to go away for a few weeks with Lorraine and the boys and not give the future a thought – at least that was the idea. After the first few days my brain was working overtime charting my next move.

We went to Orlando, Florida, and spent time at Disneyland, Universal Studios, the Epcot Centre and lying on the beaches on the Gulf Coast. By the time I arrived home, I'd made up my mind. I was going to buy myself a dealership and put into practice all the lessons I'd learned over the past 20 years making money for someone else, but this time I'd be doing it for myself! Trouble was, what and where?

Fate took a hand. I was only back a week when my previous bank manager at Lloyds, John Veck, called me to say that he'd heard a whisper that Testwood Motors, a VW, Audi and MAN truck dealer in Totton, Southampton was possibly up for sale. I immediately wrote to the owner, Ray Dawes, and asked if I could visit him to discuss the possibility of taking over his company.

I met him during March 1989 and tried hard to put a deal together that would convince him to sell. It was incredibly difficult. He was a few years older than me and had bought the business around ten years earlier. He saw the sale as his single opportunity to make some serious money. He was a real worrier and anxious about selling the business too cheaply. We met many times in his scruffy office above the body repair shop and agreed certain details, which we both duly noted but then the next time we'd meet, he changed his mind and I'd have to re-negotiate all over again! This happened at almost every meeting and was exceptionally frustrating, but I was my usual persistent and dogged self. Finally, after a great deal of haggling, we purchased the dealership on 2nd May 1989.

I negotiated the whole deal on my own, because, although Mel and Ed had agreed to join me, they'd been kept on by Pendragon. I had to secretly communicate with them regularly to keep them in the picture. I wrote another five-year plan, incorporating some acquisitions, again following the Wiggins model. The bank were suitably impressed and couldn't wait to lend us the money to proceed. We paid £3 million for the company, Ed and I putting in £100,000 each and Mel £50,000, the balance being funded by Lloyds Bank. I'd previously negotiated for Ed and Mel some excellent bonuses and share options whilst with Wiggins, so they were able to invest in the new venture.

We had to offer personal guarantees to the bank, so that in the event of the business failing, the bank could look to us to recoup some of their losses. This included the possibility of selling our houses and quite probably the clothes on our backs, so it was a high-risk strategy!

I wanted Ed and Mel there at the start, so they had to time their exit from Pendragon very carefully. I knew once they'd resigned, they'd be paid off immediately. We gambled they wouldn't want the two main directors of the business they'd just acquired working out their three months' notice – their hearts and minds simply wouldn't be in it.

Pendragon had no idea they were going to work for a competitor less than two miles away. We also had the pick of the best sales staff, mechanics and office administrators, and many followed us into our new venture.

On the day of the takeover, we were euphoric! I was 47, had received excellent training in all the major business disciplines and been around the block a few times. I'd experienced recessions, appalling product quality, and handled many inter-personal problems in the car retailing business. So I strongly believed if I could handle that lot, I was ready for anything! Now, with Ed and Mel's help, we were going to make our fortunes.

On the day of the acquisition interest rates were around 13% but the bank's economic experts assured us they'd quickly drop back to around 8% and this assumption formed part of the business plan which showed a very healthy growth in future profits. There was no talk of recession.

Within three months of the acquisition, interest rates had leapt to 15% and we were paying the bank 3% over base rate! So before we opened the doors for trading, we were paying 18% on the purchase price loan plus some other loans to finance working capital. Our first year's interest rate bill was over £700,000! The business had made £200,000 in the year just before the takeover. Rates didn't return to single figures until three years later in 1992. The interest charges crucified our business plans and our dreams were in tatters.

We'd planned for Ed and Mel to run the dealership, whilst I sought to acquire others and build a significant dealer group but from day one, we were in survival mode, not grandiose expansion. This was a deeply worrying time for the three of us and our families – as well as the prospect of being sued by the bank for the guarantees we'd given, the job market wasn't exactly booming – a full-blown recession gripped the UK for the next three years.

We weren't the only company in trouble. The banks panicked. They foreclosed on many businesses, some of them run by very astute businessmen I knew well and I often wondered why we weren't amongst the casualties given the parlous state of our company's finances.

It reminded me of the time when I was a kid and went to the fairground. There was usually a shooting range with revolving, sitting metal ducks which made a loud "ping" when you knocked one over. They'd keep on coming round and round and if you hit three or more you'd win a fluffy toy. I now felt like one of those ducks – the one in front would be hit, then the one behind – but I'd keep going round and round surviving the rifle shots!

I believe it was because I'd learned from experience that the banks detest surprises. They need time to reorganise their finances and so I was constantly informing them about our cash flow predictions. I'd monitor our bank balance daily and forecast what it would be in the next few weeks and no matter how bad the figures were, I'd report this to the bank. It became an obsession. Sometimes I'd check the balance twice a day! They really appreciated this manic level of control, and I'm convinced they decided to make additional funds available to support us at the expense of other less well-managed businesses –or ducks!

John Veck, the bank manager, became our champion and supported us through these very difficult times. He was the old-fashioned variety, keen to know about the business and always on call personally to discuss any problems. He showed great faith in us. Sadly, he died of cancer at a relatively young age within a few years of the acquisition. Brian Thomas, his successor, however, was in a similar mould, and with his guidance, we survived.

We made substantial losses right from the beginning, but each succeeding year was less than the year before. We didn't make a profit until 1994, five years after the acquisition, but from then, right through until we sold the business in October 2004, we became a very profitable company.

The Audi franchise in particular was a huge success. We rode a massive wave of popularity. When we purchased the business in 1989, the national Audi market share was less than 1%. When we sold up, 15 years later, the national market share had more than doubled to around 2.5%, although locally it was closer to 4%, in a total market that was over a third higher. The reliability of both VW and Audi was superb, and this, together with some outstanding and motivated management in place, allowed us to command an excellent price for the business – around £5.5 million with all the loans paid off.

CHAPTER 17
Software developments – South African connections

When I came out of Wiggins, as well as wanting to find a business where Ed, Mel and I could operate successfully, I was keen to continue working with Eric Cross, Managing Director of Leasemaster, our finance and software company. Eric is an exceptional salesman with a great knowledge of financial products. He is always supremely confident too, and nothing ever seemed to phase him – a good man to have in my team. We both passionately believed that the concept of offering motor dealers multiple computerised quotation systems for finance and contract hire agreements at the point of sale was the way forward. So he and I, together with Ian Liesnham, who also worked with us at Wiggins as our computer systems trainer, formed a start-up company, Henley Systems Ltd. Ian was a solid, sound and precise manager and he complemented our collective skill levels brilliantly.

Eric and I spent the first few weeks plotting the future operation in my garage, which I'd converted to an office before moving to a room in a shabby, semi-detached house next to a Isuzu dealer in North Baddersley, near Chandlers Ford. The ceilings leaked and the pipes to the water taps rattled every time someone washed their hands. Its only merit was that the rent was very low! We visited second-hand furniture shops and bought desks, office chairs and filing cabinets, which Lorraine painted a fashionable milk-chocolate colour – she was always the artistic one!

We decided to offer a much more sophisticated system to Leasemaster, incorporating a detailed database covering every single vehicle supplied to the UK market from Mini to Rolls-Royce, together with all the factory-fitted options, extras, and respective on-the-road prices – literally hundreds of thousands of separate pieces of information that we'd need to compile directly from the vehicle manufacturers' price lists – a mammoth task.

We also decided to produce forecasts of the future value of vehicles in two, three or four years' time based on economic data and historical performance. These figures were a key ingredient in the production of a hire quotation and our system would be designed to easily incorporate them automatically.

Incredibly, up until 1989, all this information had to be sourced and *manually* calculated from complicated price lists before dealers could produce a quote, which in some cases took days. With our comprehensive computerised system, they'd be able to produce numerous quotes using different parameters to meet the needs of their clients almost instantaneously and directly in front of the customer. We regarded this significant development as a major business opportunity and were anxious to be the first to the market, so time was critical and we weren't exactly flush with funds.

Eric and Ian took out some bank loans covered by the dreaded personal guarantees to help fund the business whilst my contribution was to take no salary during this initial phase.

Once again, we raided Pendragon for the best staff and quickly recruited Kim Sandom, our former expert in setting future values of used cars and commissioned Steve Collins, who'd helped us to write the Leasemaster program for Wiggins, as a self-employed programmer, sharing the intellectual property rights with him.

We took on two girls to begin the gargantuan data collection task, joined after about a year by Sue Hanson, who had worked in the fleet department at Testwoods. The initial team was completed by Tony Carnell, a dynamic 55-year-old salesman and Simon Mills, our accountant, both of whom worked with us at Wiggins.

Pat Robins, my PA in Wiggins, also joined the team. She was a wonderful asset, really in tune with our culture and I'd never encountered a secretary who could type so fast so accurately! It was a big step for her to join our fledgling team but she proved a solid, loyal and important part of our success. She stayed with the company even after it was sold in 2000. After 14 years' service, she succumbed to the dreaded cancer in her early 60s despite a brave resistance.

So the team was hand-picked to deliver an innovative approach to selling finance and contract hire deals face-to-face with customers. Indicative of our approach was the selection of a swift as our company logo. A swift is almost exclusively aerial and rarely stationary – it does everything on the wing at high speed and with great agility – eating, sleeping, hunting and even mating! This would be us – except for the mating!

Comparing the differences in the two businesses for which I was responsible proved fascinating. One was a business almost overwhelmed with a huge debt mountain trying to generate enough cash to keep the bank happy, and the other, a fledgling, innovative company, trying to break new ground in the emerging market of contract hire where car *usage* as opposed to car *ownership* was becoming in vogue. No-one could say we weren't brave – and I know some thought we were out of our minds!

"Why on earth start a new company now? Haven't you heard? There's a full-blown recession ripping businesses to pieces. You'll never make it!" was a common lament from my peers.

We had some scary moments, especially in the systems company. We managed to just about keep within our overdraft limits most months, but on one occasion, I was forced into something that I'd vowed I'd never do.

"Sorry, David, I've just checked the banking figures and I don't have enough to pay the wages this month. We're right on the limit of our overdraft. What can we do? Is this the end?" Simon, our accountant, broke the news one morning after a particularly bad run of sales. I checked and double-checked the figures. I knew it was going to be close, but a couple of debtors had gone "belly-up", so it was true. I was already in debt, and lent the systems company £75,000, a major part of my severance pay from Wiggins. With the threat of Lloyds Bank calling in our personal guarantees if Testwood failed, I had no reserves to call on. I discussed the problem with Eric.

"Leave it to me," he said. "I'll talk to my brother." I don't know what he said, but Dave Cross, a successful businessman, on the basis of just a handshake, lent us the money, around £10,000, interest-free and with no time limit for repayment. This was a serious gamble but I instinctively remained optimistic we'd become successful.

Around the same time, Christmas 1991, we didn't have enough cash to hold a Christmas party and the outlook was particularly glum so we held one at our house, Bramble Cottage in Hursley. Instead of the traditional Christmas cake, Lorraine had baked a "survival" cake. This consisted of a sponge cake topped with icing sugar and showed a man swimming up onto a desert island complete with plastic palm trees with yellow and blue icing depicting the sandy beach and azure sea! The staff loved it, although they must have wondered what the future held for them.

From this moment, the business seemed to prosper and we were able to repay the loan from Eric's brother within six months. I will forever be grateful to him.

A year later, I was sufficiently confident about our prospects that I took out a lease on some beautiful converted farm buildings, Lake Court in Ampfield, between Hursley and Romsey. It was a huge leap of faith, but the setting was magnificent, overlooking meadows and woods. I felt this would help recruitment and be impressive for our visitors. Initially, we took a lease on one of the three buildings but as the business prospered, we eventually took over all three.

We achieved major growth when Network Contracts, a subsidiary of Barclays bank, having noted our efforts to franchise the Leasemaster business we'd set up within Wiggins, had decided that as Pendragon had since closed it down, they'd set up a similar operation. Backed by Barclays' resources, they wanted to develop a unique, bespoke computerised system based on the one we'd now developed for quoting for contract hire business and to franchise the concept nationally – much the same way we had done.

I held lengthy negotiations with a senior executive from Barclays who proved to be another difficult client. I certainly seemed to have had more than my fair share in my business life! He was irrational, expected the impossible and if things went wrong, he'd become aggressive and throw a tantrum, sometimes reducing my female staff to tears. He had a gruff, no-nonsense manner and had few social skills. When I remonstrated, he'd apologise profusely and he'd behave himself until the next outburst occurred. He also had a paranoia about us trying to sabotage his business by offering the same software to non-Barclays clients – nothing was further from our minds – but I had to deal with some angry, raging, accusative phone calls on several occasions.

However, he was totally committed to his company and drove his operation with the same intensity that I did. I think Barclays put up with his erratic behaviour because he achieved spectacular results. The underlying business strategy was sound and as they planned over the next five years to operate around 250 franchises (which meant 250 software and training sales for us), we put up with him.

Demand for contract hire was beginning to expand dramatically, mainly due to changes in government legislation to kick-start the economy. Leasing companies, usually subsidiaries of banks or vehicle manufacturers, were being set up to meet this demand and so, given our involvement in developing quotation systems, we were asked by many of them to expand the system to cover the complete management of a fleet of vehicles once the quotation had been accepted.

This meant designing a comprehensive, sophisticated and efficient program capable of accounting for each vehicle's running costs: servicing and repairs, replacement tyres and other spare parts together with reporting on mileages and fuel consumptions for fleets up to 100,000 vehicles. This was a huge project and we employed 12 new programmers over the following year to write the program.

So within five years of our start-up, we'd progressed from selling the original quotation software package for around £5,000 to a comprehensive fleet management system for anything up to £1 million.

We were once asked to quote for a worldwide system for Hertz, the major leasing organisation, which totalled around £10 million! Unfortunately, we didn't get it!

Writing the software wasn't the easiest of tasks – we had many sleepless nights trying to discover and eradicate the inevitable bugs in the system. We wrote hundreds of thousands of lines of programming code which had to be totally compatible with each other, so discovering these glitches would have tested the patience of Sherlock Holmes! One of our programmers once described the process as "wading up to your waist through treacle looking for a drowned fly!"

However superb our system, it would be completely useless without the data. It was vital that it was up to date so that the leasing companies could be confident that they were using only the very latest information. Any delays could prove costly because they had to honour the quotes they were providing to their clients. The information had to be accurate too. We'd be responsible for any errors so the data would have to be manually double-checked and then checked again before it could be released. In the early days, it was an essential, achingly mind-numbing process involving typing thousands of pieces of information into our system from a hard copy. As technology improved, we were able to input data electronically which saved a great deal of time.

I was very proud of our data girls. They made very few mistakes. Over a five-year period I can remember only two where we were responsible and had to compensate the client.

Initially, getting the manufacturers to supply the data in the first place proved very difficult.

"Why the hell should we provide you with all this information when you're not a dealer, you're not a customer and we don't know you from Adam!" one senior executive of a major manufacturer barked at me down the phone.

"Because if you don't, then the contract hire company won't promote your products. They'll tell the client that they don't have the information on their system. We make it so easy for them to quote for business on other makes of vehicles, so you'll lose out. We've already got three or four manufacturers aboard," I bluffed.

It took us a further year or so to convince all of them that our service was essential, helped by consistent lobbying from some of our early customers whose fleet sizes ranged from 5,000 to 100,000 vehicles. Once we made this breakthrough, the business grew significantly. By 1997, we provided quotation systems, with or without a fleet management package, to 15 of the largest 20 UK leasing companies. Between them, they had around three-quarters of a million vehicles under management. We'd achieved our goal of being the first to market this unique software and data – not a bad result for a fledgling company based deep in the Hampshire countryside – we were all immensely proud of this accomplishment.

As much as the early 1990s recession badly affected the Testwood dealership, it actually helped sales of our software. Many leasing companies were keen to update their systems to accommodate the growth of contract hire which was overtaking outright purchase as the preferred method of acquisition by cash-strapped businesses. Our system brought order, discipline and methodology to the management of vehicle fleets and our entrance into this market could not have been better timed.

From the first moments of acquiring Testwoods and setting up Henley Systems, I targeted myself to grow them to a point where I could sell them within ten years and retire before my 60th birthday. The 1990s recession made that impossible with Testwoods (which took five years longer) but with Henley Systems, I had a chance to partly achieve my goal.

In August 2000, after two aborted attempts, we finally sold it to a US organisation for a price in excess of £5 million – a good result, I thought, for a start-up from scratch 11 years earlier.

Part of the price was conditional on finalising a huge deal with BMW Finance with whom we'd just started negotiations. We were highly motivated to complete this transaction but it proved, once again, to be one of the most difficult negotiations I'd ever had to finalise. They were particularly demanding on the detail – every clause was minutely analysed, every word was thoroughly examined and every appendix was intensively scrutinised.

We had to agree the deal within a very tight deadline; the head of their IT department was getting married and he wanted the Agreement signed off before he left for his honeymoon. We worked all day and deep into each night of the week before the deadline and finally agreed all the details in the early hours of the Saturday morning of his wedding day.

He had to leave the meeting during Friday afternoon to attend the rehearsal for the ceremony so he left instructions on finalising the deal with his subordinates. We delivered the final Agreement to the church hall where the reception was being held for him to sign! I never discovered what his new wife thought of his commitment to the job but I'm convinced we'd never have reached a conclusion if this deadline hadn't existed.

The value of the Agreement was £1.2 million and we received an additional £200,000 for the business, so all this effort was worth it! It proved to be a good experience too, for when we sold the

Testwood Motor Group four years later – an equally challenging negotiation!

I could write a complete book about the negotiations for the sale of Testwoods, particularly the last four days – and nights! This deal was, without doubt, the most difficult to finalise of my business life. Part of the problem was that we split the sale between two purchasers which doubled up the number of issues, but the major problem was that one of the purchaser's legal team took his duty of due diligence to Olympic gold medal standard! I think he was completely out of his depth so checked and double-checked and fought over every last word of the Agreement.

After five months of tortuous negotiation, we'd finally agreed to complete the sale on Thursday September 30th 2004 and were assured by our advisors that all the outstanding issues had been agreed, so all we had to do was to turn up at our solicitor's offices in Bournemouth and sign the documents.

They weren't signed until lunchtime on the Monday 4th October after working on the Agreement most of the weekend and through the night on Sunday! Many times, we considered withdrawing but consoled ourselves that this was a great deal for us, especially given the pain we went through in the early recession-ridden days following the acquisition, 15 years earlier.

A few days after we'd completed the deal, I received a letter from one of the lawyers acting for the other purchaser, praising our team's coolness and professionalism under such procrastination – a collector's item, surely!

It took me some time to appreciate what we'd achieved by the sale of these two companies; for as long as I could remember since starting out in my business career, this was always my goal – financial independence at an age where I could enjoy it!

I'm often asked by friends and business acquaintances the "secret" to my business success. It's really straightforward. My dad's insistence that I become an accountant ensured that any risks I took, and there were a few, were fully evaluated. I'd inherited his obsession with figures and administration so I really focussed on the detailed cash flows and business plans in my company. I received some exceptional training and personal development in all the important business disciplines from one of my former companies, Lex, and I was unbelievably persistent once I'd chosen what I wanted to achieve. I became evangelically passionate about the products or services my company provided and had unequivocal belief in them.

But most importantly, I selected, developed and motivated my management team with extreme care. I continuously nurtured them to share my passion, beliefs and goals. I'd like to think I came up with a few innovative ideas for the businesses too, mainly to do with pleasing our customers – probably my mother's influence based on her appetite to please her friends and family with her piano playing!

Earlier in the development of the software business, we came very close to making our presence felt in South Africa. Ron Sewell, a motor industry expert and consultant who, with Joan his wife, became dear friends, asked if I would make a presentation about the UK vehicle contract hire market to a group of South African dealers he was entertaining in London. It was a great success and I struck up a close relationship with Errol Richardson, a senior executive with a large dealer group who also sat on the influential South Africa Automobile Dealer Council. He asked if I would go to South Africa and make some presentations to other dealer groups and major banks around the country. He thought our software could help them and we may make some sales.

So in 1991, Tony Carnell, my sales manager, and I spent two very demanding weeks, informing them how the UK market had developed and explaining our key role within it.

Errol's around the same age as me, but with at least three times my energy level – and *I* don't exactly sit around! He is never in the same spot for more than 30 seconds, and seems to get by on 3-4 hours' sleep a night. He's travelled the world investigating "Best Practice" ideas for the South African market. He must be close to earning the highest Air Miles collection ever since the promotion began! We're very much alike in wanting to make things happen.

One of the companies Errol introduced us to was First National Bank, a leading player offering vehicle financing and fleet management and Tony and I spent days working with their senior management, presenting our ideas and demonstrating the system in great detail. We put together an innovative proposal but we didn't get the deal. They decided to develop their own system.

I travelled to South Africa three more times to try to generate some business but without success. Most businessmen there have an unquenchable thirst for knowledge from the UK and USA. They're experts at picking up your ideas and developing them for their own use. Once we realised this, we held back a little on the details of our software but found it difficult, given our passion for the product. They are also very tough negotiators! But I found a great friend in Errol.

He often visits us whenever he comes to the UK. In December 1994, he was sitting in my lounge at home when he asked me what I was doing about the 1995 Rugby World Cup being held in South Africa the following May and June.

"I've only just been thinking about it. I've got all the details upstairs," I said.

"Well, bring them down and let's work out an itinerary for you. I'd love you to come and spend some time with me in Durban – it'll be great fun!" He scribbled out which were the best games to watch, where they were being played and how we could get there.

Lorraine was quite happy for me to spend two weeks following the tournament staying with Errol and his family and so, over the following few months, the plans were finalised. It was a rugby marathon!

On the first day, I watched four games! In the morning Errol and I went to see his sons, Brett and Shaun, play for their school, then on to Kings Park to see South Africa play England, and when we got back to Errol's beautiful house in Umhlanga Rocks, Glynis, his lovely wife, had taped two other matches! The entire Richardson family, including six-year-old Hayley, the youngest of the family, and I devoured them with as much enthusiasm as the accompanying pizzas! Not bad for day one of the tour!

Using Errol's home as a base, we travelled the country watching games – any games! Over the next two weeks, we watched matches in Pretoria, Johannesburg and in the delightful Rustenburg stadium we watched Ivory Coast against Tonga, where we had no allegiance whatsoever, other than savouring a good game of rugby! As a rugby "nut" myself, I enjoyed every moment and Errol and I became very close – almost like brothers.

I began to recognise that rugby in South Africa, especially amongst the whites, was followed with an incredible, almost religious, intense passion. Added to this was the pressure of the country's emergence from apartheid just three years earlier, which meant all sporting eyes would be on the nation led by Nelson Mandela, released from his 27 years' incarceration just five years before. For over ten years, South African sports were boycotted by almost every nation in the world, and this was South Africa's first participation in the Rugby World Cup. Many steps had already been taken to amalgamate the black and coloured populations into the mainstream of everyday life, including sports, so I, too, shared the excitement that many South Africans felt about the future of this magnificent country.

Errol was desperately keen to show me the progress that had been made in breaking down the apartheid barriers. It was hard to realise that simple pleasures, such as walking on certain beaches near Errol's home, were off-limits to black and coloured people just a few years before. Or that it was now possible for a non-white to play for the national team as Chester Williams did throughout the tournament.

I was so grateful to Lorraine, who recognised that this trip was really one for the boys, although after two weeks, I was delighted to return home and see her wonderful, smiling face once again.

As I watched South Africa beat New Zealand in the final on TV, I became quite emotional when Nelson Mandela, clad in the South Africa captain's No 6 jersey, presented the cup to him. South African rugby had been such a dominant symbol of white supremacy for generations and this moment captured the country's new era superbly. Errol rang me, almost in tears, to share the moment.

CHAPTER 18
Rugby coaching – dream cottage – health shock

During the 1989/90 season I picked up a rugby injury that, at first, didn't seem too serious. My right Achilles tendon began to ache after training and matches. By the next session or match it usually settled down. I thought it was just a strain but gradually, the more I played, the longer it took to recover, until eventually I was in constant pain.

I tried every remedy possible. The GP thought rest would be the cure, whilst a physiotherapist I visited suggested working it really hard to free up a possible bone spur! I applied every over-the-counter ointment available from Boots, and even had a couple of cortisone injections. Nothing would cure it. I didn't play for about three months and I was missing it badly. In desperation, a friend of a friend recommended a lady who said she was an expert in alternative remedies.

I arranged an appointment for 6.00 pm one evening at a small terraced house near Bedford Square in Southampton and experienced a bizarre treatment which was certainly an *alternative* to what I'd been used to! I was ushered into a tiny living room by an elderly woman dressed in a colourful flowing robe, a matching headscarf that covered her entire forehead and open-toed sandals. Lighted aromatic candles and night-lights lent a spooky aura to the room. The atmosphere reminded me of some of the séances I'd attended with my mother following my father's death in 1964.

After I explained my problem she told me to go into the next room and take off *all* my clothes and come back with a towel covering my private parts. I hastily explained that it was only my *heel* that needed treatment but she insisted it was absolutely necessary. She seemed to enjoy my nervousness.

When I returned, she asked me to lie face-down on the airbed that had been placed in front of the fireplace. She proceeded to give me an all-over body massage, unexpectedly vigorously, concluding at the offending heel. She warned me I might soon feel a burning sensation around the affected area and not to worry about the smell. I was intrigued to see her light what appeared to be a roman candle made of wax. When the wax liquefied, she rubbed the candle against my heel with elaborate strokes. I *did* feel an intense burning sensation, like tasting a hot chilli pepper on my tongue and the obnoxious smell *was* overpowering – something close to a scorched oily rag!

The whole process lasted about an hour and after I got dressed, she gave me the remains of the wax candle and told me to apply it twice a day for the next few weeks. I parted with my £15 and left with the feeling I'd just stepped back in time to the hippy era of Flower Power in the late 1960s.

When I explained to Lorraine what had happened, she wasn't too impressed on two counts:

"What were you doing in a strange woman's living room, practically naked? And what the hell is that smell?"

I religiously applied the wax until the candle was used up, which took three weeks. The net result? Nothing. I became really depressed.

Finally I went to see a specialist at Sarum Road hospital in Winchester who suggested "opening me up" to see if he could find the problem. I agreed. Within a week, he'd operated and said, "I found a few bits of grit but it's unlikely this is the cause." The net effect was six weeks in plaster. Whether it *was* the grit or the enforced rest due to the plaster-cast, the heel became less painful over time but it was the beginning of the end of my playing days.

I kept precise copies of my playing career whilst at Winchester (sadly, none at my only other club, the Old Vs). I played a total of 400 games from 1972 to 1990. I probably played a further 250 games for the Old Vs from 1961 to 1972. Although I'm very proud and grateful to have played so many times, I still miss it. For close to 30 years, playing rugby was not just a sporting pastime but an integral part of my life. I'd trained at least twice a week and played every weekend apart from when I was injured, which was very seldom. This is why it's no effort for me now to go to the gym or go for a run – if I miss a week, I feel cheated!

Now, what do I do? I'd considered refereeing but wanted more direct involvement with the players, so I decided to take up coaching. Initially, I helped the head coach at Winchester, John Prosser, purely on the fitness side whilst I took my coaching exams. After I passed my preliminaries, I got more involved and began coaching and managing the second XV, occasionally turning out as a player if we were short or a player got injured.

I took my intermediate exams at the end of a residential weekend in Wolverhampton. It was very thorough and intensive and I passed with a good grade. I felt unaccountably depressed driving back home and I couldn't explain why. I mentioned this to Lorraine and she was surprised. Coaching would keep me in touch with my friends and as rugby was my passion, what could be wrong?

It took me about a week to analyse the problem. The first issue was a realisation that when I started playing, coaching was almost unheard of at my level. The emphasis was on fitness and team tactics. I'd had the chance to be coached by the great Bryn Meredith of Wales and British Lions fame when he was my physical education teacher but then I was obsessed by playing football so it never happened As a result I had very few sessions on improving my individual skill level throughout my career. What made me feel sad was that I knew I could have become a far better player had I been exposed to coaching.

The second issue was that I thought coaching was as good as playing. It wasn't. As a player, you're a unique member of the *team* and however good the coach is, he is *never* a part of that *team*. He's an outsider. He has input and gets to know the players well but once the whistle blows at 3.00 pm on Saturday, it's the *team* that are together as one. I also realised that players perceive the coach as a leader and so will judge him far more harshly than a fellow player.

It's even more difficult if you're coaching a team for whom you've recently played. The players know your weaknesses too well and so it's harder to win their respect. I wasn't confident in my ability to win them over. Maybe I'd have felt differently if I'd moved to another club, but I loved Winchester – still do – so that wasn't an option.

Coaching is also incredibly time-consuming. Training in most clubs is on Tuesdays and Thursdays. You can't just turn up. You need to prepare the sessions to ensure 40-plus guys are fully occupied on meaningful drills lasting a couple of hours and designed to improve their skill levels.

And then there are Saturdays. You need to analyse the match to see what's necessary to improve results. So Sundays are taken up preparing the drills for Tuesday's session. Add in the fact that players get bored doing the same thing more than twice, so you have to develop different drills to ensure their active attention. Coaching is close to a full-time job, even at junior level.

John Prosser asked if I'd take over as head coach for the following season but for all the reasons outlined above, I declined. I carried on coaching the second XV until 1993. In my last-ever game, my 400th, I came on to replace an injured player and broke my collarbone in a match against Andover. Now aged 51, this really was the end of my playing and coaching career.

When I walked into the house with my arm in a sling and looking ashen-faced, Lorraine's shocked expression confirmed my decision. I'd also discovered golf, and was afraid any further injuries might affect my swing!

My connection with Winchester rugby club, however, was far from over. I sat on the committee as the fund-raising chairman in 1994 and was first elected as president of the club in 1998 and re-elected for the following ten years. I rarely miss watching the team play, home or away, every week — I just can't stay away!

I loved living in our first "love nest" in Bramble Cottage in Hursley. Although it was tiny, Lorraine had used her flair for style and design to wonderful effect. There's always something special about building a first home together. But she's a typical Gemini and one thing I've learned about this star sign is that they love change.

So I shouldn't have been too surprised when, in 1994, eight years after we'd moved to Hursley, she came home with some details of a thatched cottage for sale in Ampfield, a village four miles further west.

"I don't want to move," I pleaded like a spoilt child. "I'm happy here."

"Just come and see it. Pleeeese!"

When I walked up Knapp Lane to the cottage on a bright sunny day, I was immediately hooked by the sight of a chocolate-box lid picture. It was built in 1781, had whitewashed walls, bright red doors and window frames befitting a former Post Office (it was in operation until 1952) and had a magnificent cherry tree in full bloom in the garden. Inside, the owners had made a wonderful job of making it cosily contemporary, with a red wood burner and a timbered, mezzanine floor housing one of the bedrooms.

Lorraine uttered the immortal words in front of the owners, "I love it! I love it in every way!" Hardly the best negotiating strategy! I was left to pick holes where I could so that I could try to get the owners to lower the price. I was nervous about the fire risk of living in a thatched cottage but even this concern was overcome. There'd been a fire some two years earlier, so when the roof was re-thatched, the owners had to comply with the very latest building regulations which included housing all electrical cables in conduit and encasing the chimney breast in concrete. Damn! They'd thought of everything! We sold our house for £108,000 very quickly and within less than two months, we'd paid £179,500 for the cottage and moved in.

It was truly an idyllic place to live. Aaron was away at Farnham University studying journalism and renting a house in the town and Max was spending more time staying with his father in Winchester so we were alone apart from Arnie, the cat we'd had since 1989. He was huge and even as a kitten, he prowled menacingly. So he was named after Arnold Schwarzenegger, the giant body-building champion and movie star. Arnie thoroughly enjoyed bossing about humans and felines with equal ferocity. Everybody loved him except Lorraine. It wasn't her fault. For some unfathomable reason, he just didn't like her. Yet she was the one who fed and stroked him until he'd turn on her. She tried so hard to get him to stay on her lap, but five minutes was all he'd allow. He was really part-feral and some mornings the area just inside his cat-flap resembled an abattoir with parts of half-eaten rabbit and a couple of mouse heads usually left as a trophy. He died in 2006, aged 17 and was hunting right up to the end of his life, seemingly still determined to prove his prowess. He's sadly missed by all – except Lorraine!

Her flair for interior design couldn't be submerged despite her earlier exclamations. Over the following years we laid a new Portland stone floor in the dining room, put in a new bathroom, turned the garage into an office/bedroom and extended the kitchen!

I concentrated on the garden, and, between us, we turned the cottage into a beautiful home that was featured in a national magazine, *Homes and Gardens*. My office at Lake Court, Hursley was a delightful 20-minute walk away through the woods. My most abiding memory of living there is coming home from work on a summer's evening, walking through the white post and rail gate and seeing Lorraine sitting under the flowering cherry tree reading a book whilst sipping a glass of wine! This wonderfully enchanting life, was about to be disrupted in a most unexpected way.

One of the benefits of living in Ampfield was its proximity to several hundred acres of woodland with numerous paths weaving between the tall, mostly coniferous trees. I spent hours running through either dappled sunlight, light drizzle or heavy rain – nothing would interfere with my schedule!

During August 1995, I began to feel faint at the end of each run. At first I put it down to the heat. But then, the symptoms grew worse. Although I never blacked out, I often felt I was about to. When I had three such episodes, one after the other, I realised there was something wrong. I saw my doctor, Nigel Sylvester, a former rugby-playing colleague, and he carried out six tests, the last of which involved strapping a 24-hour heart monitor to my chest. The first five results all came back quickly and were positive. Lorraine and I sat at home anxiously one afternoon awaiting the results of the final heart-monitor test. She took the call upstairs and was on the phone for a long time.

"Well, what did Nigel say?" I asked anxiously.

Lorraine replied hesitatingly and, choosing her words carefully, delivered a very long, drawn-out explanation, implying that although the final test result was negative, it wasn't too serious, but I would have to have a small operation to implant something that would solve the problem.

"What you mean is, I have to have a bloody pacemaker fitted!" I blurted out.

"Well yes, but it's not the end of the world. Nigel said lots of people have them fitted!" Lorraine could see me getting agitated. I was. Me? Having to have a pacemaker fitted? One of the fittest chaps in the rugby club? Someone who exercises regularly? I was *more* than agitated. I was angry. I thought it was the end of my passion for keeping fit. Could I still go jogging? Would I have to "take things easy?" I felt I would no longer be "complete". I was 53 and considered I hadn't yet reached my prime.

I spent the evening going over all the questions I wanted answers to. Poor Lorraine. I must have been a complete misery. She consoled me as much as she could and suggested I spoke to Nigel the next day. He helped me put things into perspective, especially about my activities post-pacemaker. He said my heart was perfectly fine – the problem was having too slow a heartbeat. Usually this is a sign of fitness, but in my case it was causing me to almost black out. A pacemaker would resolve the problem. And yes, I could go jogging. And no, I wouldn't have to "take things easy". The operation to fit the pacemaker would be carried out under a local anaesthetic, generally took about 30-45 minutes and would involve an overnight stay in case of complications.

During our conversation, I remembered what Dr Rogal of Harley Street had said way back in 1976, when, following a routine health check, he'd identified a slow heartbeat, but said it wouldn't manifest itself for many years, so not to worry. How prophetic!

Within two weeks, I had an appointment at Chalybeate private hospital and the operation was carried out on 5th September 1995 by Dr Iain Simpson, a lively Scot, who also helped put my mind at rest by confirming that it was a very simple procedure he'd carried out many times – it all sounded so easy.

I was naturally apprehensive about the procedure because although I would be sedated, I was told I'd need to remain conscious as I may have to respond to some tests when the pacemaker was installed.

As I was wheeled into the operating theatre, I was surrounded by three nurses clad in pristine white gowns, white face masks, white caps and opaque, white gloves, giving them a ghostly appearance. Dr Simpson was dressed in a light-green gown, with matching headgear and mask. As a huge x-ray machine as big as a refrigerator was lowered over my prostrate body, I began to feel claustrophobic and then I started shivering, not through cold, but fear. I couldn't control it, although I really tried. I didn't want to look a wimp in front of the medical staff.

One of the nurses turned my head to one side whilst Dr Simpson injected me with something to make me drowsy. After some small talk through my chattering teeth, I was aware of him making the incision on my chest to take the matchbox-sized pacemaker he'd just shown me. He explained that the leads would be guided through my veins and attached to my heart muscle using the x-ray machine and he'd programme the pacemaker to "kick in" when my heartbeat dropped below 60 bpm (beats per minute).

I was facing a huge clock. I thought this was a good idea at first. I reasoned that I could put up with *anything* for 30-45 minutes and I could check the time as Dr Simpson and the team worked on me. Trouble was, as the 45-minute mark was passed, then the hour, then the hour and a half, and then two hours, my shivering got worse. Dr Simpson was obviously having some difficulty in threading the leads from the pacemaker to my heart muscle.

The nurses were very kind and kept talking to me, one of them stroking my head or my hand, which I found surprisingly comforting. Finally, with a flourish of the darning needle, Dr Simpson said, "All done!"

I was taken back to my room feeling very drowsy and fell into a fitful sleep. Later, Dr Simpson came to see me and explained that although there were some complications, the operation was successful and that Lorraine could collect me the next morning. She visited me in the evening but I wasn't particularly good company, apparently repeating myself and nodding off!

When I awoke next morning, I didn't feel well. I remember brushing my teeth and feeling very wobbly. I thought it was just a reaction to the drugs but as I was keen to get home as soon as possible, I played it down when the nurse came to check on me. Lorraine helped me down the stairs to the car and I sat nervously in the passenger seat.

We hadn't travelled more than a mile or so when I began to feel nauseous and faint. I shouted at Lorraine to stop the car. I got out and using the bonnet for support, I gulped huge breaths of air into my lungs. After a while, I felt slightly better, but we had to stop several times before arriving back at the Old Post Office, where I slumped in a chair.

Around 3.00 am I began to feel very ill. I was constantly feeling my pulse by placing my fingers against my wrist, counting the beats for ten seconds and multiplying by six to arrive at the number of beats per minute. My heart rate was incredibly erratic, shooting up to 300 bpm then dropping back to 60 bpm, before racing back to 300 bpm again. Lorraine implored me to let her call 999. I finally agreed but only on condition there were to be no sirens! I didn't want to cause any fuss.

Within an hour, I was in intensive care in Southampton General Hospital receiving some wonderful care and consideration. After a short while I began to feel better as my heartbeat settled back into a normal rhythm. They kept me in hospital that night and promised that they'd get Dr Simpson to see me as soon as possible the next morning to discover what was going on.

He explained that someone with a low heart rate sometimes developed a condition called atrial fibrillation or AF. The symptoms were exactly those I had experienced: a very erratic heartbeat that felt like a thunderstorm raging in my chest and blood draining from my head. Typically, the episode could last for any length of time, from two minutes to several hours, and stop just as suddenly for no reason when the heartbeat would return to normal. It is a condition affecting over a million people in the UK to varying degrees. It generally affects older patients and some have a higher tolerance than others. I hated the feeling and couldn't handle it.

The events of the previous few days, including the build-up to the operation, left me in an acute state of shock, so bad, I didn't venture outside the cottage for three weeks. Going into the office was out of the question. Every time I tried to walk up the lane or down the garden, I had to return within minutes. I felt so vulnerable and out of control. I became obsessed with constantly checking my pulse just to make sure it was still there! I was very emotional and often tearful – most unlike me. It was an experience I'd never even come close to in my life. Lorraine was fantastic. This was a very worrying time for her but she got the balance exactly right; cajoling me when I was feeling sorry for myself, and sympathising with me when I had an "episode".

Gradually, I began to venture further from the cottage. The turning point, after about eight weeks, was to attend the wedding in London of our dear friend, Janie. She's a sheer delight, and we became firm friends when Lorraine and I met her at a tea party in Hamble in the late 1980s. She's an expert on tea and travels the world giving lectures.

The ceremony was held at Chelsea Register Office with the reception later at the Waldorf hotel. I *had* to socialise and this helped to regain my confidence.

The groom was an 18 year-old Brazilian lad, incredibly good-looking but who could hardly speak any English. This, plus the fact that Janie was in her late 40s, didn't seem to daunt her! The marriage lasted about a year but broke up when Marcello left England to return to Brazil, ostensibly for three months, I think to set up a home for them both. Janie travelled to Brazil after about six months to see what was going on, but returned minus Marcello, so the marriage was over! We were all sorry it didn't work out.

I found the invidious and precocious nature of AF, starting and stopping for no apparent reason and without warning, very frustrating. I tried all sorts of diets, including cutting out red meat, alcohol and coffee, but nothing seemed to affect its course. My episodes sometimes lasted for a few minutes or, in my worst case, for 24 hours. It really affected my confidence. I felt so wretched when it cut in that I didn't want to be with anybody, or do anything. Medication helped to limit the number of episodes in the early years but as time wore on, they grew in frequency and intensity. Not pleasant.

Despite my health problems, I was determined not to let it affect my life and so gradually, over the next year or so, I re-commenced my running, although under very strict orders from Lorraine not to overdo it. I promised her I wouldn't and always gave her a time when I'd return. I tried as hard as I could to honour this arrangement realising that she must have worried every time I left the cottage. But for me, it was a great form of therapy and, although I am not in any way religious, I often raised my head to the sky when out in the woods and said out loud to someone, "Thank you!"

When I stopped playing and coaching rugby, along with some friends who'd also retired from the game in 1993, I decided to take up golf. After a few lessons, I was completely hooked, and within weeks, I'd bought some new clubs, golf shoes and all the relevant paraphernalia, joined a club, South Winchester, coughing up a £3,000 joining fee, and looked forward to a new sporting career whilst still keeping in touch with my mates, Nick, Nosher, Steve, Pete and Rod. We all became fanatical and played at least once or twice a week, sometimes more in summer. So when the pacemaker incident materialised, playing golf again was another big target.

My mates were very supportive and gradually, I got back into the swing — pardon the pun! — and for the next few years, golf became another outlet for my obsessive sporting odyssey. It became such a large part of my life that I've devoted a chapter to it later on.

We lived in the Old Post Office for six years, from 1994 to 2000. This period proved to be, AF excluded, as perfect a period of my life as one could wish for. Having survived the early years of recession, both the dealerships and the software companies were beginning to do well, and towards the end of this spell, I was able to spend less and less time at the office.

Max used to visit us often and sometimes stayed over. He had a variety of jobs including working as an undertaker for five years! He has a few grisly tales to tell! Aaron graduated with 2:1 degree in journalism in 1997. Lorraine had fashioned a new career as an image consultant, sometimes working from home. She was brilliant! I witnessed amazing transformations in the women she advised! On several occasions, we'd meet some of her clients in town who'd gushingly say, "Lorraine, you've changed my life! Thank you!"

Stephanie had set up home in Lyndhurst with Dave who was still in the Army. She'd left to have children and so on 22nd June 1997, Kai was born, followed shortly by Kasia on 3rd September 1998. Our relationship by now was excellent, and Lorraine and Stephanie got on really well too. When Kai was born one month prematurely (still weighing seven pounds!) we went to see him in an incubator in St Ann's hospital in Southampton. It was a worrying time but I think this really cemented the bond between Stephanie and I.

When Kasia was born, weighing a healthy eight pounds and four ounces, I was overjoyed to have a granddaughter, and even more so when Stephanie asked Lorraine to be "grandma" to them both.

They often visited us at the Old Post Office and we had some great fun in the garden with the little ones, Max and Aaron sometimes joining in too. Lorraine and I liked nothing better than when all the children and grandchildren visited the cottage together. Lorraine provided a sumptuous feast, enough to feed a whole regiment, not just one sergeant major, as Dave was at the time. We loved seeing all the siblings getting on so well.

CHAPTER 19
Golf – a four letter word ending in F!

If you find golf boring and want to skip this chapter, I won't blame you. But if you like tales of brilliance (sometimes), total incompetence (usually), laughter, tears, arguments, stupidity, infatuation and obsession, both on and off a golf course, then hopefully, you'll enjoy what follows.

Golf *looks* such an easy game played in glorious sunshine, blue skies and on grass manicured as if by a pair of scissors – even the bunkers filled with sand, resembling a tropical beach, look inviting!

This illusion betrays the truth. Golf is the most difficult and frustrating game that possesses evil intentions – it can make you feel supremely overjoyed or utterly disconsolate – it can give you ecstatic pleasure or make you feel deeply suicidal – it can make you feel like a supreme professional or a complete loser. It's the ultimate roller-coaster ride of emotions.

When I took up the game in 1991 I imagined I'd be quite good – after all, I'd played rugby, soccer, squash, and cricket, so I'd have an eye for the ball and I was competitive, right? How hard could it be to hit a golf ball with one of 14 clubs specifically designed for the purpose and make it go exactly where you want it to? On both counts, I was to become sadly disillusioned, although it took the best part of 14 years to finally realise that golf had become a "mistress" I needed to give up before she drove me insane.

Golf does have its good points. When the weather's fine and you're enjoying some excellent company, playing moderately well, not making a complete fool of yourself, then it can be very enjoyable. Trouble was, every time I went out to play, I always had an *expectation* that I'd play better than before. Surely, it's a perfectly reasonable *expectation*. It's entirely logical the more one plays and practises, the better one should get. This applies to every other sport I know, so why not golf?

I believe it's this *expectation* that screws up 95 percent of golfers. Golf has its own capricious nature – you may *believe* your swing is identical each time you perform it, but if it's the tiniest fraction out on timing, direction or posture, the result is disproportionately different. It makes no difference, either, whether you're full of confidence or in the depths of despair. You can go round the first nine holes in a personal best score, and then go round the next nine in your worst score. And vice versa. Having *expectations*, we put so much pressure on ourselves, the usual rules of self-improvement don't seem to apply. In other sports, you can be in form or out of form, but this generally takes place over a period. It's rare for a player to play a blinder one week and a stinker the next.

An example of golf's whimsical nature revealed itself early in my golfing career. I played in a mid- week competition at my club, South Winchester, one beautiful summer's evening and went round in my best-ever score. So good, I topped the leader board with 43 points and won the competition. I could do nothing wrong. I was, as golfers say, "in the zone". It was like those moments I've previously described in sport – I felt as if I was playing in a dream.

Full of confidence, I entered the following Saturday's competition. I played dreadfully! I was an embarrassment to my fellow players. I scored just 17 points, which any golfer will tell you is pretty poor, and I came last! The following week, the results of each competition were displayed on the club notice board. I regret not taking a photograph to prove all I've said.

Another example of golf's quirkiness is the time I scored a hole-in-one at Romsey Rugby Club's annual golf challenge at Dunwood Manor. I was having an unremarkable round until I hit a wonderful shot on the 116-yard par three 16th hole. With one bounce, the ball slid unerringly into the cup. I was ecstatic! Some players play for 50 years and not ace a hole.

As my foursome moved on to tee off on the 17th, I heard an almighty roar behind me. I turned and just glimpsed a ball drop into the 16th hole! The odds of two consecutive hole-in-ones are extremely long – I've since discovered it's around nine million to one! Back in the excited clubhouse, I discovered that my good mate, Nosher Eames, playing in the group behind us, had duffed his drive in between my shot and Romsey rugby club member Simon Kersey's ace, denying an incredible fluke.

Had the shots been consecutive, an entry in the *Guinness Book of Records* was surely possible, I thought, although I've subsequently discovered it's already been achieved. I had mixed feeling about this. Although happy to share the cost of a round of drinks in the clubhouse with Simon, as is the tradition, even in my finest moment of glory, *golf* couldn't let *me* have it to myself!

If you want to discover what someone's like, play golf with them. I've played with seemingly mild-mannered men who transform into bad-tempered tyrants on a golf course. It's like throwing a switch. Golf generally brings out the worst in people, not the best. It appears to be a blow to one's manhood if you play badly in front of other men. The ladies don't possess this genetic make-up and so probably enjoy the game much more whilst still remaining competitive.

As if the game isn't hard enough, strict etiquette must be followed.

For example, you mustn't stand in the line of a player's putt, no matter how far away you are and if you accidentally stand *on* the line between your opponent's ball and the hole, a single look from him will be enough to make you, literally, tread more carefully next time. And the same applies if you forget to rake a bunker after you've played out of it or fail to repair your pitch marks on the putting green. Golfers get disproportionately upset by these breaches of etiquette.

The rules of golf, too – 192 pages in the latest edition – need to be clearly understood and mastered. Playing your shot out of turn, accidentally playing your opponent's ball, having more than 14 clubs in your bag and forgetting to sign your card at the end of the round are all punishable offences, in the latter case, leading to disqualification! Even the pros slip up sometimes.

The dress codes in certain golf clubs and on certain golf courses are, frankly, laughable. I once played in a 36-hole competition, a round in the morning and one in the afternoon, where jackets *had* to be worn at both lunch and dinner despite a heatwave. This entailed changing clothes four times! Many other clubs insist on jackets and ties after 6.00 pm. On the course, one club insists you wear *long* white socks up to the knees if you want to wear shorts, which have to be knee-length. So all that's exposed is a pair of knobbly kneecaps! And don't even think about wearing your fancy designer golf shirt *outside* your shorts or trousers, even though some are designed for just that.

Having mastered the etiquette and the rules, you have also to cope with your playing partners, many of them having an extremely low threshold of concentration. I've known some (they'll get a mention later), who'll stop in mid-swing if a sparrow utters a peep, a player coughs or the drone of an aeroplane pierces the airwaves. The abrupt halt in the stroke is usually accompanied by a grounding of the club, an expletive, and a glare to the playing partners so fierce, Genghis Khan would be traumatised!

Club-throwing has almost become an art-form with some. Following a particularly poor shot, or to be fair, a series of poor shots, the offending club is either used like a hammer and driven into the ground, or it's literally hurled in the direction of their golf-bag, usually accompanied by the phrase, "You useless piece of s**t!"

I'm convinced it's down to the *expectation* issue – the utter frustration of knowing that you are perfectly *capable* of playing a particular shot having done so on many previous occasions; except this time, for no obvious reason, it's, let's say, less than perfect.

After 14 years I decided to drop out of the race. My obsessive nature had driven me to play and practise as often as I could, determined to get to a level I could be proud of. I discovered it was impossible. All I did was heap unnecessary stress into my life. Rarely, perhaps only a dozen times in this period, did I feel good after a round. I took it too seriously, perhaps. I reasoned that whatever standard I achieved, it would never be good enough.

My equally obsessive friends, with whom I'd played, toured and socialised were aghast when I told them I was giving up and only playing occasionally in future. They made me feel as if I was resigning from a religious sect! I felt such a weight off my shoulders and my mood considerably improved.

Now when I play, I have *no* expectations and simply enjoy the course, the exercise and the company. And guess what? I'm playing better than ever! I'm determined not to get back into the stressful, fraught relationship with this most difficult of mistresses!

Having made the decision to give up the game, I was committed to play with Rod Ellaway, my good friend and golf partner in one last pro-am charity match at Botley Golf and Country Club in Southampton. When we arrived I left my clubs outside the changing room whilst I went in to change into my golf shoes. This took less than seven or eight minutes. When I returned my golf clubs were missing! I'd left them close to six other sets thinking they'd be safe. I looked everywhere, asked around to see whether they'd been picked up by mistake and checked with the shop to enquire if anyone had reported anything suspicious. Nothing. They must have been stolen. By now, my tee-time was fast approaching so in desperation, I explained my predicament to the golf pro.

"I'm due on the tee in five minutes, can I hire a set? Mine have been stolen."

"What a bugger!" I'll set you up with some demos and second-hand stuff I've got in the back of the shop. Don't worry about the hire fee." I was very grateful.

He stuffed a brand new golf bag with a ragged assortment of clubs, some tees and balls and I rushed down to the first tee with a minute to spare. It was just as well I had no time to get nervous – there was a gallery of around 50 spectators and other players waiting their turn to tee-off watching me play my first shot of the day with an unfamiliar club and playing a course for the first time without so much as a practice putt!

I needn't have worried. My shot flew down the fairway to gentle applause and I went on to have one of the best rounds of my life, our team finishing just short of the prizes. After the round, I called the police to report the theft and then Lorraine to tell her what time I'd be home.

"Did you have a good time?" she said.

"Great! I had my best round for years with a set of borrowed clubs!"

"Why borrowed?"

When I told her the story she burst out laughing.

"You do realise this is divine intervention, don't you? It's obvious that someone up there doesn't want you to play anymore!"

Rod thought as I'd played so well, I might go back on my decision to retire. If anything, it confirmed everything I've just said. I'd played with my own set of clubs for years and "grooved" them in to my swing. How was it possible I could play so well with such an assortment of different clubs I'd never practised with? It's truly a crazy game.

My golfing odyssey was full of fun despite my love-hate relationship with the game itself. My group of friends were an extraordinary mix, thrown together by a love of rugby and then golf. We never stopped laughing – usually at someone's expense – and seemed to find hilarity in almost every situation we encountered. This became even more prevalent when we went on tour.

Twice a year for 14 years, six or seven of us travelled to the West Country, Dublin, Edinburgh, St Malo and Honfleur in France or to the Algarve in Portugal for a long weekend of golf, drinking and eating, all to excess! We felt like schoolboys again, free from responsibility, playing childish pranks and taking the p**s out of each other!

I usually borrowed a VW people-carrier from the dealership to cart us around the courses. A typical day would start with a cooked breakfast at the hotel or clubhouse, teeing off around lunchtime. Four to five hours' golf later, we'd shower, have a few drinks whilst discussing the game, and then drop off our bags at the hotel. Then we'd hit the town. We always seemed to discover which pubs/clubs stayed open the longest and rarely got to bed before 3.00 am, especially if the hotel bar was still open and there was a snooker table. I think we can claim the record for the latest receipted bar bill timed at 6.05 am in the Imperial hotel in Torquay! Unrealistically, we *still* expected to play great golf the next day and became predictably cross if we didn't!

On all the 30 or so tours, we played for the tour championship. Our scores were aggregated over the four days, and the handicap system we used meant they were uncannily close. This simply added to the pressure, especially on the last day, when cumulative hangovers and lack of sleep took its toll on the course!

The "hard core" tourists were Rod Ellaway, Pete Langley, Nick Rogerson, Steve Waterman, Nosher Eames and myself. Others "guested" from time to time – Phil Austin, Dave Crowther and Ged James.

Rod's the ultimate organiser. He arranged around 90 percent of the tours, usually superbly, but made one mistake in Torquay of which he is reminded about from time to time – more later! Rod has a great appetite for life, especially food and red wine. We call him "Red Ollaway". He'll have a go at anything and has an incredibly strong constitution. Late one evening, we were talking to a couple of Aussies outside a bar in St Malo, when Rod asked me to hold his pint whilst he excused himself from the conversation. He returned within four minutes saying he'd thrown up in the toilets and, taking back his pint, said, "Please carry on with what you were saying."

"Streuth, mate, that's impressive!" said one of the Aussies in obvious awe.

Pete is the exact opposite of Rod. He's our "social worker", always trying to ensure everyone's happy. He's a day-dreamer too – usually referred to as "Dolly Daydream". We were once being ushered out at closing time from the Rainbow club, a noisy bar and discotheque, coincidentally also in Torquay, in the early hours of a Sunday morning. Pete stood out in the middle of the road in his shirtsleeves trying to hail a taxi for us all in monsoon-like torrential rain for a good half-hour whilst we all cowered under the eaves of the club! Typical Pete!

Nick is a highly intelligent Geordie who works for the Audit Commission. Everything must be absolutely just right for Nick, so he's with the right organisation. He's a stickler for upholding the rules of golf and he's probably committed the whole 192 pages to memory! Unsurprisingly, he's known as "Rulebook". His general knowledge is extraordinary. I only ever enter quizzes if Nick's in the team.

Steve was my neighbour when Lorraine and I lived in Hursley. He's been playing golf for many years so had to put up with us novices in the early days. Iain, his son, joined the rugby club aged six, and made his debut in the first XV in 2008, aged just 17. It was a great personal thrill to see him progress through the age groups and grow up into a fine young man.

Steve's renowned for his "Stevisms" – comments or actions usually made without thinking through the consequences! Once, he was at a business function and spotted a dish of gourmet crisps on the next table. He leaned back in his chair, and reaching across, grabbed a handful, uttering, "You don't mind, do you?"

"Well yes, I do actually," said the fellow guest. "I've just paid £3 for them!"

Steve is one of the kindest men I know and sometimes feels highly embarrassed if his "Stevisms" have offended anyone. He just can't help it, much to our amusement.

Nosher was one of the first players I got to know when I joined Winchester Rugby Club back in 1972. As his moniker implies he's an enthusiastic consumer of food. He shares my view about golf and for the last few years has caddied for one of us rather than play. He never married, although came close a few times and never ceases to surprise us with his knowledge – especially sports. Another good man to have in your quiz team!

There are so many stories I *could* tell about out touring exploits. I'm ever-mindful of the expression we adopted, "What goes on tour, stays on tour." However, some experiences which aren't too incriminating are worthwhile relating!

We visited Torquay many times and it proved to be a fertile ground for memorable incidents. On one visit Steve volunteered to give Rod a break from organising the trip to Devon. As we drove down Steve expressed some concern about the hotel he'd booked and seemed genuinely worried – after all, Rod's was a hard act to follow. We thought it was yet another of Steve's wind-ups. My attitude on all our tours was to "go with the flow" and not get involved in *any* decisions.

As we drew up outside the hotel in the gathering gloom, I noticed it was in complete darkness except for one single light bulb hanging in the reception area. Inside, the furnishings were tatty and threadbare. The landlord welcomed us with the words, "Glad to see you, boys. As you're the only guests, you'll have to go to a hotel down the road for supper. Chef's off. He'll do you breakfast tomorrow, though."

My heart sank. My usual policy of "going with the flow" was about to be severely tested.

"This is awful," I said. "There's no ambience here. I vote we move on." I had no idea I'd be reminded of the word *ambience* many times in future years.

Rod took control.

"OK, I'll try to get us somewhere more exciting. I'll go to my room and call from there."

We all sat down in the lounge whilst the landlord ran around supplying us with drinks. At one point he disappeared to answer the phone. Steve, who was lingering around the reception area, overheard the conversation. Ten minutes later Rod re-appeared with a satisfied smile on his face.

"OK, I've managed to get us some better accommodation and the good news is that I've managed to get the same rate. We go there tomorrow."

As Rod finished the sentence, Steve said, "You daft bugger! I just heard the landlord take the booking. It was you! Did you dial 9 for an outside line?"

The landlord walked over to us and said, "Is there a golfing tournament going on, boys? I've just had confirmation for another six golfers. They'll be arriving tomorrow." He'd obviously intercepted Rod's call.

He couldn't understand why we all fell about laughing. He was even less amused to realise that his number of residents had started at six, been increased to 12 and was shortly to be reduced to zero!

We had no alternative but to stay in the hotel for one night and to sample the delights of the supper awaiting us in the other hotel down the road.

The waiter was a real "Jack-the-lad" type who was seriously unhappy in his job. We were just an interruption to his easy evening since the restaurant was empty. As he plonked down the main course he said, "If it were me, I wouldn't eat this." He had a similar derogatory comment whilst serving the apple pies and custard with his thumbs submerged a good inch into Bird's Eye's best product. "This is awful!" he said.

He also had a row with the wine waitress.

"No, not that wine!" he bawled, as he snatched the bottle from her hand. "They can make do with this," slamming down a cheap Rioja on the table. As wine was included in our menu price, we had to accept whatever they offered.

Despite my *laissez-faire* policy, I felt I *had* to take charge given that Steve had made a hash of the original plan and Rod had screwed up his attempted recovery. After dinner we went down to Torquay town centre and parked ourselves in an Irish bar.

"Right," I said, "I'm going to find us an hotel for the next three nights. Leave it to me."

On the way down to the pub, I'd noticed a small hotel, the Regina, which looked quite charming and overlooked the marina. I spoke to the receptionist who confirmed they had some vacancies at a very good rate.

"Do you have any parking?" I said.

"Oh, yes. We've got just one space so I'll reserve it for you from tomorrow night."

"OK. I'll take three double rooms, each with single beds please."

As I returned to the pub, I uttered the following words I've come to regret.

"Ok, boys. It's all *sorted*. Leave it to Henley if you want know how to organise a tour in future." I basked in the glory for the rest of the evening and the next day until …

My superciliousness was diluted when we returned to the original hotel in the early hours. The night porter made us some excellent ham sandwiches and poured us whiskies on the house. The bedrooms were large and had recently been renovated. Breakfast, too, was surprisingly good.

"Maybe we should consider staying," Rod said.

"You've had your chance, Rod. You blew it!" I was, unwittingly, setting myself up for some serious grief later on the tour.

The next day we played the picturesque Dartmouth course in stunningly beautiful weather. In the early evening we arrived back in Torquay to check in to our new hotel. As we approached and parked outside, I was dismayed to see the entire building covered in scaffolding! I'm sure it wasn't there the previous night. Every sea-view window was partially obscured by poles and timber. I joked that the scaffolding would provide excellent balconies – no-one laughed. The boys immediately doubted my judgement so Steve was volunteered by the others to come inside with me to check it out.

The same female receptionist greeted me warmly. "Can I look at the rooms, please," a stern Steve said.

"Of course," she said and they disappeared upstairs for a few minutes. I checked out the bar area, which was totally deserted. It was 7.30 pm.

When they returned downstairs, Steve looked glum.

"What time do you stop serving dinner?" I asked.

"Oh, you've missed it. It's usually about 6.30 pm. This is a SAGA hotel and the residents like to eat early, play some cards and then go to bed. Most of them are all tucked up by 9.00 pm." I could feel Steve's eyes glaring at me.

"Just one more thing. Where's the car parking space you promised?" I asked.

"Right next door, on the right-hand side. You can't miss it."

When we got back to the car, Steve recounted the sorry state of the rooms, which were the smallest he'd ever seen. He said a shower had been fitted in one of the cupboards, it was so tight for space.

"Dinner's off too. This place is the pits but we've got no choice. We'll have to stay tonight. Henley's cocked it up!"

"At least," I said, "they've got a car parking space right next to the hotel." I tried to sound positive. As I drove up to the space, it was taken up by a huge industrial skip, full of iron castings and concrete! This was serious. It meant we had to park in a public car park on the opposite side of the road and the meter required feeding with coins from 7.30 am *every* morning, including Sundays, or accept a £60 fine! I'll always be grateful to Nosher who volunteered for this duty.

The rooms *were* exceptionally small, the bar never opened, the breakfasts were awful – plastic eggs and rubbery bacon – no free car parking and the sea views were obscured by scaffolding! Most of all, as I was continuously reminded, there was no *ambience!*

Rather than change hotels again, we endured it for three nights. This tour became known as the "Ritz to the pits" and I have never been allowed to organise a round of drinks in future let alone a golf trip!

Steve has a habit of sleep-walking whenever he stays away from home probably due to the disorienting effects of consuming large quantities of alcohol. His nocturnal strolls became a feature of several tours. His room-mate, usually Dave Crowther or Rod, told us on many occasions they had to place a kit-bag across the hotel door to remind Steve not to go walkabouts. He did *escape* once in a Torquay hotel, wearing just a white T-shirt barely covering his assets! He walked down several floors before being discovered by the night porter, who kindly led him back to the room. We'd never have known about this but Steve, unbelievably, told us the next morning! The porter confirmed the story but denied us a copy of the CCTV!

We toured Brittany several years in a row. In 1989 Lorraine and I purchased a delightful 5th floor (no lift) apartment within the walled town of St Malo which has three great beaches and a lively nightlife. We enjoyed some wonderful holidays with Max and Aaron and sometimes, just the two of us, touring the Granite Coast in my 1967 Mercedes 230 SL convertible. We loved driving in Brittany with the top down, staying at gites and farmhouses, trying out our French and slavering over wonderful local cooking. We once stayed in a small hotel in Treburden, right on the north-west coast of Brittany, and after a sumptuous meal washed down with a Bordeaux Superieur, slept with the windows and shutters open to the sound of the waves gently washing the beach – quite magical!

St Malo is surrounded by some excellent golf courses that in the early 1990s were barely discovered, and usually deserted. It was a logical place for a golf tour. The first time we went, Rod, Pete, Nosher and I took the overnight ferry from Portsmouth, docking at around 7.00 am and were on the golf course at Le Tronchet in time for breakfast and a nine-hole competition before lunch followed by 18 holes in the afternoon. We usually got back to the apartment at around 7.30 pm, dumped our gear and toured the many bars after dining at a favourite restaurant. As the night wore on, if a bar closed, one of the locals would always know of another that stayed open later, so we got to know the bar owners especially well!

Mostly, we always returned to the apartment together, but we had a system where whoever went home the earliest would take the single set of keys, open up, but then leave the door slightly ajar, otherwise it would close and lock itself. I've always had a thing about keys and absolutely hated not being able to get access into my property. It happened a few times in the past! One night, Rod said he wasn't feeling well and asked for the key – he wanted an early night – it was 2.00 am! The rest of us wanted to stay in the Irish bar, one of our favourites, so in an unguarded moment, I relented.

About half an hour later, we all returned to the apartment, and tried the door – it was locked! We shouted and hammered at the barrier to our beds for ages – no response. Then I remembered, I'd left a spare key in the letterbox on the ground floor.

"Don't worry boys. I have a fall-back plan!" I stumbled back down the five floors to the ground floor. Nosher decided to come with me. I didn't have the letterbox key with me, so I tried to get my hand inside the tiny aperture to feel inside for the key to the apartment. It was impossible. My hand got stuck and I became angry, cursing my decision to let Rod have the key in the first place. When I finally managed to release my now-bloodied hand, Nosher, who was very impatient to get some sleep, smashed his fist into the plastic letterbox shattering it over the floor. The key was not amongst the debris! I must have used it previously in an emergency and not replaced it. I staggered back up the five flights of stairs in a foul temper. I hammered on the door once again without response. I don't think the boys had ever seen me in such a bad mood. They regarded me as "Mr Cool" – always in control of my emotions. Pete just laid outside the door, happy to "doss down" for the night.

"I'm buggered if I'm sleeping on a concrete floor outside *my* apartment. I'm off to find a hotel and Rod can bloody well pay for it! Anyone coming with me?" Reluctantly, they followed.

By now it was nearly 3.00 am and I didn't think I'd find anywhere to take in three glum men suffering the visible effects of alcohol. My anger had sobered me up sufficiently to put on a semi-coherent display of my schoolboy French. At the third attempt, a very kind, elderly, grey-haired lady, wearing a pink flannelette dressing gown took pity on us and gave us the keys to her last two double rooms in a run-down two-star Chamber d'Hote. This meant two of us sharing a double bed, which men absolutely hate, but we had no choice. Pete was in his usual daydreaming state after drinking copious slugs of calvados as well as beer so just picked up one of the keys to a room and vanished.

This left me with the dubious pleasure of bedding down with Nosher. At around 16 stone, and a reputation for snoring that's been known to take the plaster off the walls, I'd have resisted under any other circumstances!

Later, when I got up for a pee, I noticed Nosher's somnolent body clinging to the very edge of the bed. I probably did the same when I was asleep. We were so desperate not to touch each other, we must have left a corridor the size of a motorway between us!

After a fitful night's sleep with Nosher's reputation for snoring intact, we got up, dressed and went down to reception. Pete was nowhere to be seen and so we asked for his room number and went to find him. His room was a very grand apartment on the 6th floor with wonderful views over the old city walls. It was magnificent! He lay propped up in a four-poster bed surrounded by chintzy curtains in the honeymoon suite! He'd slept superbly, having completely forgotten the events of the previous evening. He greeted us with the words, "Hullo boys! What a great place. Can I have breakfast in bed?"

"No, you bloody can't. I'm going to settle the bill and then we'll go and have breakfast in our usual place in the town." I was still angry. The hangover didn't help.

As we were stuffing croissants and pain au chocolate into our mouths, Rod appeared, looking very bashful.

"Why the bloody hell didn't you open the door last night?" I shouted.

"I don't know. I didn't hear you. I wasn't feeling too well – I think I picked up a bug and I was absolutely shattered."

"Why didn't you leave the door ajar as I told you?"

By now, Rod was severely embarrassed.

"Sorry, I didn't think. The door just closed behind me and I suppose it locked itself."

"We had to shack up in a hotel at three o'clock this morning. I don't think we should pay for it, do you?"

"OK – I'll pay. I admit it's my fault."

He was so embarrassed. He's usually so "on the ball" and efficient. Nosher said, "Relax, Dai. One day, we'll have a good laugh about this." I didn't agree at the time but he was right!

We still tour once or twice a year, although the frenetic pace of the early years has been replaced with a greater appreciation of restaurants rather than pubs! That's not to say that we don't drink – we do – but the hours are now more sociable and the hangovers more manageable!

There are two facets of golf that I did appreciate.

If you're a footballer, it's unlikely you'll get to play at Wembley unless you're a professional. It's the same with cricket and rugby. The chances of playing at Lords or Twickenham are remote. However, providing you can afford it, the best golf courses in the world are available to players of any standard. As a member of the Motor Trades Golfing Society, for example, I've been fortunate to play many of the world's major courses: Gleneagles, Wentworth, The London Club, Woburn, Forest of Arden and Sunningdale. It's such a thrill to know you've played the same courses as Nicklaus, Palmer and Faldo.

The handicap system, developed over a long period, is an incredible leveller and uncannily accurate. This allows a lay-golfer to play a professional with an equal chance of winning the match – at least in theory. The major difference is in the capricious nature of the game I've already referred to. It only takes the novice to play well above his handicap for no apparent reason – earning the soubriquet, a "bandit" – and for the pro to have a nightmare round, to create a major upset! It does happen.

CHAPTER 20
The rugby club presidency

"You know, Dai, Pa's getting a bit old for the presidency of Winchester Rugby Club. I think you're the perfect guy to stand for election at the next AGM. After all, he's done it for many years." Jez Broadway, John's son, was calling me at home. I was very flattered to be asked. I'd played for the club 400 times, coached the players, worked on the fund-raising committee and after 26 years, knew practically everyone.

"What's involved?" I said, mindful that I was still having atrial fibrillation episodes and still involved in building my businesses.

"Nothing much. You're really a figure-head. You might need to bang some heads together or act as a peacemaker, but generally it's just handing out the trophies at the end of the year and being seen about the place. You'll need to make a few speeches as well, but that's it. Can I nominate you for election?"

"Who else is standing?" I enquired.

"Oh, no-one else. If you don't like it, you needn't stand for re-election next year, so it's not too onerous."

"Ok. Put my name forward," I said.

I was very proud to be elected president at the AGM in July 1997. I was only the seventh since the club was formed in 1929. John Broadway had done a wonderful job and would be difficult to follow but as events unfolded, the timing of this change for the club couldn't have been better orchestrated.

A year previously, the club had nearly folded. We'd been relegated several divisions, had huge debts and poor revenues. We were at the lowest point in the club's history. John recognised his limitations in the world of commerce so he set up a rescue plan with a local businessman, Ashley Levett. In return for paying off all the club's debts and providing investment to improve the facilities, he took over the club's assets, which included the clubhouse we'd built in 1973. Rugby Union was just entering the professional era and players at any level in the game could now be paid. Ashley took this opportunity to attract players on a semi-professional basis, appointed a full-time manager and an excellent coach, Phil Davies, with whom I played in the early 70s.

My initial role was exactly as described by Jeremy. I supported the "buyout" fully and watched with interest the way Ashley went about transforming the club's fortunes. He was a commodity broker and made a fortune – allegedly £50 million – in one deal involving large amounts of copper. His six-year-old son played at the club so Ashley was aware of the financial crisis.

On the pitch, the next four seasons were the most exciting I've known. The semi-pros who'd joined from more senior clubs steamrollered the team to four successive promotions to reach the fringes of the national leagues. In 1998 and 1999 we won the Hampshire County Cup, something we'd only done once before in 1976. We travelled much further for our matches, to Norwich, Cambridge and Thanet in Essex. The rugby was a joy to watch.

However off the field, things did not go all our own way. At first, the appointment of a full-time manager was a success. He and his team dealt with everything – our amateur input was no longer required. If we had a financial problem, we'd just call Ashley and he'd write a cheque for £20,000 as if it was petty cash. This happened numerous times. I wondered how long this could go on.

Shortly after investing in our club with the promise of making it successful in this new professional era, Ashley saw a similar opportunity to develop Richmond Rugby Club. Formed in 1861, they already played at the highest level but were struggling to survive in the professional environment. Over the next two seasons, Ashley reputedly invested £8 million in ground developments and signing several key players in the Premiership, including internationals like Ben Clarke.

I never discovered whether Ashley had a plan to make money out of these investments or whether it was an ego trip. I never got to know him well – he was cool and indifferent with me and although I tried to get close, I never succeeded.

Nobody's quite sure why, but by 1999, Ashley fell out of love with rugby and the governing body, the Rugby Football Union.

He walked away from both Winchester and Richmond losing his investment. He informed us he would no longer provide the cash required to run the club or pay the players and coach. To his credit, he paid off all our debts and leased the clubhouse at a peppercorn rent but we now had the responsibility of operating the club. It was a difficult transformation. We'd had four years of being spoon-fed.

This was just the sort of situation made for my business skills so my role became much more hands-on. I got involved in every aspect of the club, especially financing, accounting and setting up a management team to take us forward.

We had no funds to play players so they left for more lucrative contracts. The effect was almost the reverse of the previous halcyon days – two successive relegations! At least, we didn't fare as badly as Richmond. Despite the investment, they became bankrupt and were relegated to the lowest tier of the league structure – an ignominious fate for one of the oldest clubs in the country.

I immersed myself in the club with Lorraine's blessing and support. With over 700 members, and open every day for functions, it became a business requiring organisation, funding and management. I took full responsibility for driving the club forward and this became another obsession.

I endured many ups and downs in my ten-year presidency. I made many difficult decisions, not always to everyone's agreement.

One example was when I proposed a change of management which involved the termination of employment of our Chief Executive, who hadn't delivered the business plans, together with the Finance Officer, who happened to be his wife! I'd known them for many years and proposed them to their positions initially. It was a very difficult decision, but I had to act in the best interests of the club. They were understandably very unhappy and the issue was only resolved using expensive lawyers and calling an extraordinary meeting of the members where my decision was upheld by a large majority. It was an unhappy time for all concerned.

I found running the club more challenging than operating my businesses. Maybe I was too close to my colleagues. I worked hard to instil my passion for the club throughout the membership and didn't always succeed. To many of our members, the club was not as important to them as it was to me – as long as the bar was open and they could play or watch rugby, that's all they wanted. Many of them had no idea of what it took to provide these facilities.

But all the pain was forgotten when Saturday came – sharing a good lunch with the opposition management, watching my team play and, best of all, sinking a few beers after the game with some club- mates, who *did* share my passion for the club made it all worthwhile!

In June 2008, I stood down from the presidency. I'd given it my best shot and felt it was time to let someone else come up with fresh ideas to take the club forward. I left the club in an excellent condition with the finances in good shape and a capable management team. I was overwhelmed with the wonderful ovation I received at the AGM and honoured to be elected as a Life Vice President, one of just eight such members.

I hope John Broadway would have approved. Unfortunately he died in 2003, aged 73. His wife Audrey had died two years earlier and I know he missed her badly and was very lonely. On Sunday mornings after a match, he'd call me at 7.30 am to discuss the previous day's match! He wanted to chat about who played well, who should be dropped and the coach's tactics.

He died immediately after a match against Harlow played on a miserably cold, wet and dull March afternoon. We'd had lunch in the clubhouse as usual and I spent the entire match standing next to him, commenting on the game and exchanging the usual banter with the players. As the game ended I went off to help put away the corner flags and post pads.

"I'll see you in the clubhouse for a drink, John," I said.

"OK, it's your round," were probably the last words he ever said. As I headed back to the clubhouse, I noticed what I thought was a heap of playing kit lying under the rugby posts – everyone else had disappeared.

I cursed under my breath. I'd have to make a detour to take them into the clubhouse. I was deeply shocked to see that it was John struggling to breathe. At that time, I didn't know how to perform CPR, so I rushed into the changing rooms. "Quick! Quick!" I screamed. "Can someone help. Broadway's having a heart attack!"

Several players, including the Harlow scrum-half, who happened to be an Army physical training instructor, rushed out and began performing CPR and shouting to John, "Hang on in there!" John never regained consciousness, although he was not pronounced dead until he arrived at the hospital. I followed the ambulance to the hospital in shock.

I called Lorraine. I was tearful and must have sounded awful as I breathlessly said, "I'm in the hospital." Lorraine's reaction was close to hysterical.

"What's wrong with you! Is it your pacemaker?"

"No. It's John. He's dead." I explained what happened.

"Oh no! I'm so sorry." She'd empathised with his loneliness despite the early Sunday morning calls!

At the funeral held in St Peter's Roman Catholic church, Winchester, there were over 500 mourners inside and many more spilling out into the grounds. I was honoured to be asked to perform a eulogy and spent a great deal of time preparing it.

John was a great man, whose vision and drive was as huge as his massive build and I hope some of his kindness and spirit have rubbed off on me. His Barbour-coated, towering presence, bellowing instructions to the players in his public-school accent, is still missed at the club.

CHAPTER 21
Another house move, another health scare

"I'm a bit bored with the cottage. I fancy a change of scenery." Oh no! Here we go again, I thought. Why did I marry a Gemini who thrived on change?

"Lorraine, it's great here. We've done everything you've wanted to do to the place and it's perfect."

This conversation was remarkably similar to the last time we moved. I was determined to dig in this time so after a few weeks of these heavy hints, I said, "OK. If you can find somewhere better than this, I'll consider it." What a dumb remark! This was just the opportunity she wanted. Whenever we went out walking, she'd spot a house or location she thought might be possible, sometimes putting a card though the door.

It was on one such walk in the autumn of 1999 we discovered a beautiful location in Romsey. The garden was a large meadow with a lake – it was difficult to see the house, which was set close by the River Test in idyllic surroundings. We made some general enquiries but were told the owners had only just finished building the house so were unlikely to want to sell so soon.

Almost exactly a year later, we were sitting up in bed reading the papers when Lorraine said, "I don't believe it! That house in Romsey is on the market!" She was almost reaching for the phone before she ended the sentence! Two hours later we were the first to view it.

A month earlier, in August 2000, I'd sold my software business so it seemed almost like divine intervention – as if the vendors were waiting for the deal to go through before putting their property on the market!

Willow Grange, a name we didn't like, was very disappointing. The owners had built it on a speculative basis and although the basic structure was very sound, some of the fittings were poor quality. They'd also maximised the number of rooms – a separate kitchen, dining room and sitting room, all minute. The same applied upstairs with five tiny bedrooms. There was a mock-timber frame in the lounge and swirly, Artex plaster on every ceiling – absolutely not our taste.

However, the house was set in the most magnificent four-and-a-half-acre meadow and within it, a huge one-acre lake complete with mallards and coots. There were two giant willow trees, one at the front and one in the rear of the property, whose leaves shimmered in the autumn breeze. The views across the countryside to the hills in the distance were Constable-esque. And all within a five-minute walk into the charming country town of Romsey.

Although the guide price of £750,000 was far beyond what I thought we could afford, I turned to Lorraine halfway around the lake and said, "We've got to have this – I don't care what it costs!" Although she was very disappointed about the house, she'd already seen where she could improve it and my brain was working overtime on how we could cultivate a wonderful garden.

I immediately made an offer of the guide price. It was refused. The owner was a tenacious negotiator but after several weeks of haggling, in October 2000 we finally agreed a price of £785,000. Lorraine was furious. I pointed out that if he'd asked this price in the first place we'd still have gone ahead. It turned out to be a very good move.

Lorraine's training as a colour analyst and knowledge of style really transformed our new home. Every ceiling in the house was re-plastered to overcome the dreadful Artexing, walls were knocked down to provide greater use of space and even the kitchen, which was less than two years old, was ripped out and replaced with a more country-contemporary look, including a cream-coloured Aga, much loved by Lorraine.

The work was carried out by a good friend, Keith Ashley. Keith had done a lot of work for me in the car showrooms and at the cottage. He has the rare quality of being both an expert builder and full of innovative ideas. It was fun to see him and Lorraine animatingly discussing the best way to enhance the property.

The project took over three months but we were fortunate to be able to afford to stay in the cottage whilst it was being carried out.

Very few days went by during winter of 2000 and spring of 2001 that we didn't check on progress. Some days I jogged from the cottage in Ampfield to the house, about an eight-mile-round trip – I was becoming as obsessed as Lorraine!

Whilst she was up to her neck in plaster, timber and paint, I spoke to my good friend's wife, Gill Ellaway, a gardening and landscape expert, to see what we could do with this huge plot. She produced numerous schemes which we pored over during the dark, wet nights of winter and finally agreed on a plan. It was very bold! Decking around part of the lake, a new patio area fronting the south-facing house, 100 new trees dotted around the lake and some huge shrubberies with pergolas looked fabulous, even on the plans!

At the end of April and the beginning of May, huge trucks turned up with the all the plants and trees we'd ordered. Gill began planting them out with a little help from me. She was so precise, using a tape measure to ensure they were in the correct place according to the plan. It looked very sparse – we seemed to have under-ordered.

"Gill, this is hopeless," I said. "It's going to take forever for them to grow. Can't we infill a bit more?"

"Don't worry – just wait a few years. You must be more patient, Dai," she mocked. She was right. She knew exactly how big these plants would grow. Her skill and knowledge in terms of texture, colour and spacing has proven masterful.

Nine years later, and having developed a real passion for gardening – Dad would have been proud of me – we have a superb garden which we've opened to the public for the National Garden Scheme Yellow Book Cancer charity. We receive such wonderful comments from the hundreds of visitors each year. Sitting on the deck by the lake on a summer's afternoon, drinking tea, watching the kingfishers provide an acrobatic aerial display, seemingly just for us – it's a paradise.

Lorraine's vision, too, has resulted in a wonderful home, re-named The Lake House, where we've enjoyed entertaining our friends and family. In total we spent around £200,000 on the changes, which left a big dent in the proceeds of the sale of the business, but every time I walk round the gardens, I have an immense feeling of satisfaction. We worked hard and took a few risks in the business and this is the pay-off.

Whilst living at the Lake House, I had some more serious health scares. Following my pacemaker implant in 1995, the atrial fibrillation (AF) episodes began to increase significantly. I was warned this might happen as I got older despite the medication I was taking. The effect is debilitating. The thunderstorms going on in my chest continued to reverberate. Added to this was the stress of knowing that patients with AF are at a much greater risk of having a stroke than people without this condition and the stroke is twice as likely to prove fatal.

It destroyed my confidence. I was always making business presentations or speaking at rugby club lunches and dinners and became quite stressed at the thought that an AF episode would kick in just as I got up to speak – it never did, but I never felt comfortable. I was also concerned about continuing jogging.

I visited a cardiologist at the BUPA Chalybeate private hospital in Southampton who specialised in my condition – he's respectfully referred to as the "electrician" within his peer group. Dr John Morgan, now Professor Morgan, has transformed my life. It took three operations over a two-year period but eventually, he achieved something I really didn't believe was possible.

"I think the best route is to perform an ablation. This is an empiric pulmonary vein isolation procedure," he said after a thorough examination including an electrocardiogram.

"What the hell's that? What's involved?"

"Oh, it's fairly simple. I send two wires up through an artery in your groin and place them over the muscles of your heart where I think these electrical pulses are leaking, causing you the irregular heartbeats. Once they're in place, I zap them with a radio frequency catheter to seal up the orifice. It takes less than an hour. I can do it next week."

My face must have registered fear. I said, "Sounds painful. What odds do you give on it being successful?"

"Don't worry. I can give you something to make you woozy, but you'll need to be conscious because you'll have to react to certain commands. Two thirds of these operations are successful."

These seemed good odds and I was desperate, so early in the morning of 28th January 2003, I entered Southampton General Hospital and went down to the operating theatre after a morning of preparation. In the theatre, surrounded by heavily-masked nurses, wired up to highly sophisticated machines and bathed in the blinding whiteness of the lighting, I found it all incredibly unnerving.

I remember shaking just a little, reminiscent of having my first pacemaker implanted.

"Would you like a little gin and tonic to relax you?" the "electrician" asked. I liked his euphemism for a shot of diazepam – a form of Valium.

"Rather have a couple of pints," I spluttered nervously. "But, yes please." As I began to feel light-headed I felt a sharp stab in my right groin as the wires were inserted before making their journey up to my heart. I soon felt as if I was floating in mid-air, like an astronaut in space, hearing voices, but not the actual words, being aware of people all around me, yet feeling detached. Although I never lost consciousness, I was surprised to realise I was back in an intensive care ward with a dozen or so other patients, all the private rooms being occupied. I was wired up to a machine monitoring my heartbeat and blood pressure and a "thimble" on one of my fingers to measure the amount of oxygen in my bloodstream. I began to feel well and was soon tucking into a shepherd's pie with relish – I hadn't eaten for 24 hours before the operation.

Lorraine came to see me and remarked how well I looked but like me, was anxious to see Dr Morgan to see if he thought the operation had been successful. The degree of care I received was superb. It seemed every 20 minutes, a nurse came and checked on my "vitals" as they called them and kept assuring me everything was fine. One of them told me Dr Morgan would be round in the morning to discuss my case.

I found it difficult to sleep for two reasons. Firstly, the nocturnal noises from the other patients were very intrusive – coughing, snoring, some groaning, wind-passing and even some talking in their sleep. As it was an intensive care ward nurses and doctors ministered to some of the patients, clattering up and down the ward throughout the night.

Secondly, because the wires in my groin had travelled up a main artery, the orifice was "plugged" with a hard substance which made my groin feel very sore. I was advised to lay on my back and told it was very important not to move unnecessarily for fear of a leak from my artery – not the perfect formula for a good night's sleep!

Dr Morgan is an urbane, venerable man, with bright eyes and in his late 40s. As an expert cardiologist he lectures all over the world as well as performing minor miracles in Southampton. We'd established an excellent relationship once we discovered we were both Welsh and shared a love of rugby. For now, that's as far as it went – I got to know him a great deal better over the next few years.

"I feel pretty upbeat about the procedure. We won't know for a few months whether we've stopped the fibrillations. Don't forget, your heart's just been subjected to quite an ordeal. But I'm quite optimistic. You can go home this afternoon and start jogging again in a couple of weeks if you feel like it but take it easy at first."

Lorraine and I were very happy to hear the good news, but in the next four months I had several more episodes. One was especially bad on the evening of the 18th May. My heart rate shot up to 150 beats per minute and stayed there! I felt terrible. I was breathless just getting up from the chair. I felt as if I was having a heart attack. There was no pain though, so I assumed things would settle down. They didn't. Lorraine was very concerned when after four hours, nothing had changed. She wanted to call an ambulance, but I demurred, eventually settling for her taking me to the A and E department in Southampton.

I was treated as a priority as a heart patient and kept in for two nights for observation. They increased my medication before sending me home. I was still breathless walking up the stairs and sometimes in my sleep. I saw Dr Morgan once again within a few weeks and he said he still felt good about the ablation procedure.

During the next few months, I had many more episodes. So after yet another meeting with Dr Morgan, he decided to try another ablation. On 22nd January 2004, I went through an identical procedure. At least I knew what to expect.

Unfortunately, the number of episodes in the following months increased again! Since having the first episode back in 1995, typical of my analytical and persistent personality, I kept detailed notes on the date, duration and level of discomfort of every single episode I'd had, so I was able to note any patterns emerging. One was about to.

On the evening of 5th February, sitting quietly at home, I felt absolutely wretched, my heartbeat, this time, sticking at over 170 beats per minute for three hours. Lorraine insisted on calling an ambulance. I was in no position to argue.

When the paramedics arrived they looked shocked and asked me if I always looked "this colour" – an unwelcome comment. By the time I'd arrived at the hospital, my heat rate was back to normal, but they kept me in overnight as a precaution. Dr Morgan came to see me and suggested it was too early to assess the success of this second ablation and that I should monitor progress over the next few months. I reluctantly agreed. I never lost faith in Dr Morgan. We'd become quite close, especially when he told me his mother was born in Dowlais, South Wales, about two miles from where I was born in Merthyr. In all our subsequent meetings we discussed the rugby results first before we got onto the more serious subject of my health.

Matters didn't improve. During the next few months I maintained my detailed records and was able to prove that the running-rate of episodes after each ablation had increased from two a week to almost every other day. I was getting depressed. I didn't go jogging for weeks, fearful I might be making matters worse. I didn't go to the rugby club either unless I had to – I was concerned that anything the slightest bit stressful would set off another episode. I rarely went to work, relying on Ed and Melvin, my business partners, to run the dealerships. Lorraine, too, was also becoming very anxious although I sensed she was putting on a brave face. It must have been very worrying to watch my usually optimistic and positive personality deteriorate.

I saw Dr Morgan on 8th July and presented my detailed notes and asked what other options were available.

"Look, John, I'm desperate. Despite taking many different medications, having numerous modifications to my pacemaker and having two catheter ablations, the episodes of AF have actually worsened in the last five years as you can see from the record I've kept. What other options are there?"

"Well," he said, peering at his notes, "I think there is one more treatment we can apply which has a 100% success rate."

Suddenly he had my full attention. "We can carry out an *AV node* ablation. I guarantee that you'll have no more symptoms."

"Sounds too good to be true! Why's this different from the others?" I beamed.

"Well, the procedure is similar to the previous ablations except that this time we'll zap the AV node, cutting off your *natural* electricity supply to your heart, so it's a permanent and irrevocable procedure." I pulled a face.

"Then, we'll replace your pacemaker with one that will *always* be switched on. We'll use this to ensure your heart rate is always even. We can still program it to match your activity level so when you go jogging, it'll react accordingly."

I asked what I thought was an intelligent question. "So, what happens if the pacemaker stops? Do I stop?"

"In theory, yes. But the failure rate is extremely low and I can program it so that you're not 100% dependent on it. Your heart's in good condition, it's just that we can't control the fibrillations by medication, so this is the only option left. The downside is that you'll still be having the fibrillations. It's just that you won't feel the symptoms or know anything about it."

"When can you do it?" I asked.

"Let's get it done soon. I can do it on 5th August," he said, flicking through his diary.

When I left the hospital, I was in a very mixed state of mind. If he was right, the thought of not having that dreadful feeling of my chest wanting to explode almost every other day was something to look forward to. But having my natural electrics cut off and relying on an artificial computer no bigger than a matchbox took some time to accept.

His prophecy proved accurate. After this third operation I felt wonderful for the first time in many years. It was as if a brake had been released. Although nervous, only jogging round the garden at first, I gradually ventured further, getting back to the distances I used to run – about four to five miles. It was so important to me – I'd been exercising and running all my life since the age of 11 – I loved the feeling of fitness and can't imagine life without it. Mentally, it took a while to get over the fact that my heart was only pumping due to the pacemaker, but after six months, I didn't give it a second thought.

I only have to see the "electrician", Professor Morgan, once a year and every time we meet I always tell him how grateful I am that he's transformed my life. I'm back to the same positive, confident and happy guy I was before the fibrillations took over. It's a complete joy not to experience the stressful impact of the symptoms of AF. I no longer take my pulse a dozen times a day just to see that it's behaving itself!

My only concern is that the fibrillations *are* still occurring and the spectre of having a stroke still flashes into my mind occasionally. So I live my life as fully as possible, trying not to put off anything that gives me pleasure and trying to always remain positive. Lorraine's the perfect foil for this approach to life. She's *always* lived by this mantra!

CHAPTER 22
Happy families – business and pleasure!

"We're thinking of emigrating to Australia." Stephanie broke the news to us in the summer of 2003.

"What! You love Lyndhurst and the kids love their school. And what about your mother?" I reacted not angrily but with genuine surprise.

Stephanie and Dave went on to explain that Dave could transfer from the British Army to the Australian Army and extend his military career by five years. They'd investigated every facet of the move before they told us and as we learnt more, it seemed to be a good idea. He'd be posted initially to Melbourne and be supplied with a generous relocation package including free housing.

The only remaining issues were personal. Kai and Kasia were just six and five years old respectively and we'd seen a great deal of them since they were born. We loved them so much and hated the thought of them being so far away from us. They were the catalyst that led to improving relationships with us and Stephanie and her mother following the split back in 1985.

Ann and I only spoke to each other if we had to during the acrimonious divorce and financial settlement. Even after the grandchildren were born, we avoided each other as much as we could, to the point that we'd visit them separately on their birthdays! We'd see them from 2.00 pm to 4.00 pm and she'd visit from 4.30 pm onwards.

She'd married Rod, a very kind and gentle man, in the early 1990s. This softened the angst of the split, and so I called her one day, shortly before Kai's christening where we *had* to be there together at the same time and explained how stupid it was to keep avoiding each other.

"We'll both be going to school sports days, concerts, birthdays and Christmas carol services at the church for ages. Why can't we just be like normal grandparents and see them together?"

She agreed and after the christening, Lorraine and I and Ann and Rod spent some time chatting. Lorraine was great and we were glad we made the breakthrough. The relationship is so good now, Lorraine will call Ann for a chat on the phone! It's made life so much easier now we all get along.

Lorraine and I both felt especially sorry for Ann when Stephanie broke the news about emigrating. She'd lose close contact with her only daughter and the grandchildren whom she loved. She has a particularly close relationship with Kai and Kasia. When they were both at pre-school ages, Stephanie was posted to Aldershot and so she dropped them off at Ann's house in Harestock on the way up from Lyndhurst and collected them on her return. Understandably, Ann was very upset.

In December 2003, once they'd obtained all the necessary papers, they left the UK for their first posting in Puckapunyal, near Seymour, a garrison town about 60 miles north of Melbourne. They rented out their Lyndhurst home which at least gave the "grieving" grandparents some hope that they might return. We also reasoned that with emails and web cams, we could all stay in touch and be able to check on the grandchildren's progress through life. Ann's vacuum was filled by knitting clothes and sending them with other goodies to Australia every few weeks.

Although good to see them on camera, there's nothing to compare with seeing them in the flesh, and so I arranged for them to come to see us and Dave's family in 2004 and 2007. Ann and Rod spent three months with them in 2005 and we visited them at Christmas 2006.

They've since moved to Sydney and have all taken Australian citizenship. They have a wonderful life and Stephanie has proved to be an excellent mother nurturing her children in much the same way my mother nurtured me – giving them the confidence to tackle anything.

They've become the epitome of Australian children – fit, tanned, healthy, bright, sporty and always seem to have beaming smiles. They're both sports-mad and swim as if born in the sea. They're educated at a private Catholic school with a strong academic record as well as promoting sports. Kai, with his mop of blonde hair and manly physique, despite being just 12 years old, would be perfect as the "face" of Australia. Kasia's dogged "I'll try anything" attitude to life sums up the Aussie's psyche completely. They both have strong Australian accents too! I don't see them returning to the UK so we'll just have to keep up the visits for as long as we're able.

On 15th July 2006, Aaron married a stunningly beautiful girl, Jo, at Hillier's Arboretum at Ampfield with the reception held in a marquee at our home, The Lake House. It was a magnificently sunny day and having spent hours in the garden, there wasn't a leaf out of place, or a rose not dead-headed! The preparations didn't go entirely to plan though!

The marquee was erected on the Thursday, prior to Saturday's wedding, and all the tables were set up together with cutlery, glasses and crockery by the time night fell. Adjacent to our garden is a 12-acre meadow used mainly for cattle and was the only access for an electricity generator to be installed on the strict condition that the gate between the meadow and our garden should be securely locked each night.

At 12.30 am on Friday morning, we were jolted from our bed by the phone ringing. It was Grace, our wonderful neighbour.

"Do you know you've got some bullocks rampaging in your garden?"

"What? Oh my God, the marquee! The caterer must have left the gate open!" I exclaimed.

"I'll get dressed and help," Grace said. I was grateful. She'd been brought up on a farm and would surely know what to do.

Lorraine and I threw on some clothes, picked up a torch each and scurried down towards the marquee with trepidation. The bullocks were nowhere to be seen at first, but I heard them rustling amongst the trees on the other side of the lake. As I pointed my torch at them, they turned towards me and their eyes sparkled back. This seemed to be a signal for them to charge towards the house with the marquee in their path.

There were at least a dozen of them, and the sound of their hooves clopping on the ground was un-nerving – the last time I'd seen a stampede like this was in the Western movies! I really thought they'd run straight through the marquee – I could almost hear the crockery smashing – but at the last second, they split into two groups and ran either side of both the marquee and the house to the double gates at the front which were open.

Fortunately, Grace was able to guide them from there to another field where they could be secured, but not before they'd trampled over her vegetable patch and broken down a fence!

Next morning, I surveyed the damage to Grace's garden and offered to have the fence repaired. I was just grateful that, literally "a bull in a china shop" situation had been averted. The only real issue was that our manicured lawn was covered in cow dung. So I called Aaron's brother, Max, who was to be his best man.

"Hi Max, I need your help. Can you bring a spade to clear up some bull-s**t. You'll recognise it!" This incident provided great material for the wedding speeches.

The following June, Aaron and Jo came to lunch and produced a black and white photograph which was difficult at first to decipher. Lorraine finally realised it was a feotus and collapsed with excitement.

"Oh my God! Is it really what I think it is? Oh, my God! Oh, my God!" She was overcome with joy. She'd dreamt of this day ever since they'd married.

"What is it? Do you know?"

"It's not clear from the photo and really we don't want to know until it's born," Aaron said.

So Mother's medical and mental state became the centre of Lorraine's universe for the next few months until a healthy boy was born, Lewis Brown, weighing six pounds, nine-and-a-half ounces on November 5th 2007, just three days after my 65th birthday. Lorraine and his Uncle Max, still single and waiting for Mrs Right, are besotted with the little chap, as indeed am I.

Being adopted with no close family, having a grandchild as a direct descendent had a very special relevance for Lorraine. She's always loved babies and has been known to cross the road to say hello to one on many occasions. She's always been excitable, but I've never seen her so joyful and emotional whenever she sees Lewis.

In 1997, Lorraine received a letter containing some unbelievable information from New Zealand. She'd been chosen by the BBC earlier that year to visit Toronto in Canada to try to trace her father for a programme called *Private Investigations.* A small account found its way to the local paper, the Southern Evening Echo. A cousin, who lives in Southampton and whom Lorraine didn't know existed, had read the article and realised that Lorraine was the same person who was the subject of a tug-of war between two sisters, Lorraine's mother and aunt.

You'll remember Lorraine was the result of an affair between her mother and a Canadian GI during World War Two. When he returned to Canada her mother wanted to marry someone else who wouldn't accept another man's child. Lorraine's Aunt Mary, who'd helped look after her until the age of two, offered to adopt her and take her with them when the family emigrated to New Zealand. Her mother wouldn't agree and instead Lorraine was adopted by a family of complete strangers.

The letter was from Aunt Mary's daughter, also called Mary, Lorraine's first cousin. In it, she explained how her mother hadn't given up trying to adopt her and had tried to trace Lorraine when they visited the UK some years later. Apparently she often spoke of her love for "that little girl". The cousin still living in Southampton had contacted Mary who wrote to the Echo and asked them to pass on the letter. Sadly, her mother, Aunt Mary, had died just a few years earlier.

Lorraine was astounded. She had absolutely no idea she had any family other than her mother and half-sister in Sidmouth, Devon, let alone one in New Zealand! So began a sequence of events that led us to travel to Auckland later that year to meet up with a most amazing family.

Cousin Mary, who's just a few years older than Lorraine, and Pete, her husband, made us feel most welcome. There were the inevitable tears when they met us off the plane and there were more to come. They had two children who'd produced between them seven daughters whose ages ranged from 3 to 11 years old. They are a wonderfully tight-knit family who couldn't believe that the "mythical" Lorraine was finally in their presence.

I became very emotional too, when we were having tea at Mary's house. She'd inherited it from her mother and on the wall was a faded photograph of two beautiful blonde two-year-old girls.

"On the left is Pat, my sister, and the one on the right is you, Lorraine. My mother loved you so much and always wondered what had become of you. It broke her heart to leave you in Southampton knowing that you were being brought up by strangers. That photo's been on the wall for 50 years," Mary said, wiping a tear from her eye. I choked too, thinking of all the time Lorraine had spent looking for her father without success and that here was a ready-made family she never knew existed and who really wanted her.

Meeting all her cousins, first and second, once and twice removed, and some with a degree of likeness, couldn't have been more thrilling for Lorraine. We've visited them twice and each time it's been a great pleasure. Like most Kiwi's they love their rugby, so we shared a common bond there too! Grant Fox, the great All Blacks player in the 1970s and 1980s is a neighbour and so they arranged for me to meet the great man on our last visit – what a thrill!

The software company I'd set up in 1989 included a module for forecasting the prices of cars in one to four years' time. Our main clients were the car manufacturers. So, whenever a new model was launched, we were invited to appraise it along with the dealers. Locations chosen to launch these vehicles were usually exotic, exciting and expensive!

Other trips included attending dealer conferences or as a reward for achieving sales targets within our own dealer group. We stayed in opulent five-star hotels and were wined and dined at the best restaurants. This created an insatiable appetite for travelling, except, since selling the businesses, the trips now have to be paid for by me, so we appreciate them even more than ever!

One of the locations we visited was the Atlas Mountains in Morocco where we spent a day driving pre-launch Volvos through precarious passes. We stopped halfway at a market selling fruit, vegetables, carpets, and assorted trinkets. We'd become split from the rest of the group and parked a short walk away. As we returned to the car, two swarthy, dirty youths wearing turbans and those slippers that curl up at the front, menacingly demanded I pay them 30 dirham (about £2) before I could drive off.

"We've looked after your car, mister. We want money!" I remonstrated that I'd not asked them to look after the car and as I moved towards the door, one of then blocked my way, holding out his hand.

I reached into my pocket and thrust the only change I had, a 5-dirham coin, into his outstretched filthy palm. He looked at it disparagingly, spat at my feet, and uttered what I assumed to be a curse.

"If you don't want it, I'll take it back," I said. He begrudgingly curled his hand around the coin, spat at my feet once more and stormed off, followed by his lieutenant-in-crime.

Volvo put us up at a fabulous hotel in Marrakech, Les Jardins de la Koutoubia, a magnificent hostelry build on the site of a 13th century palace, rebuilt in the same style, just minutes from the city centre. In the evening, they hosted a sumptuous feast under a huge marquee. This was followed by a very authentic swordfight on horseback by turban-wearing, swashbuckling Berber warriors bringing the *Tales of the Arabian Nights* to life. We spent most of the next day fending off vendors purveying anything from carpets to cheap jewellery. Lorraine's fear of snakes prevented us entering the souks and bazaars – a wise decision – we later heard they were plentiful. Given our experiences, we weren't too impressed with the Arab culture!

Driving Nissans in Southern Spain, passing through gleaming white Moorish houses in the hilltop villages and across the arid desert, was fun. We started at Jerez, headed north to Granada and then west to Seville, and stayed at the superb Alphonso XIII hotel. It was built by King Alphonso of Spain in 1928 as Europe's most luxurious hotel. We love Seville which is the capital of Andalucia and the city of Carmen, Don Juan and Figaro. It's truly beautiful with the wide Rio Guadalquivir running through the centre, a magnificent cathedral and stunning architecture in ochre colours that contrast vividly with a usually blue sky and brilliantly reflect the sun's rays – so typically Spanish.

We've attended conferences in Barcelona and Madrid too, both vibrant and colourful cities, but Seville remains our Spanish favourite. In Barcelona, we stayed at the Arts, a contemporary hotel, with some fabulous modern paintings and works of art displayed everywhere. It's situated in the 1992 Olympic village and has great views of the ocean.

Hurling Citroens round the corniches of the Cote d'Azure was exciting – as long as you had a head for heights! We knew this area very well. We'd spent many holidays in Provence and on the coast when Stephanie was young. Our accommodation was very different now – staying in the five-star Hotel Martinez in Cannes compared to roughing it on a campsite in Cavalaire!

We've travelled in style to some of the most exotic locations in the world, courtesy of the vehicle manufacturers. We've sampled the pink, sandy beaches of Bermuda, enjoyed the strongest rum punches we've ever tasted in Barbados, spent the week before Christmas in a fairy-tale chateau in Banff in British Columbia surrounded by thousands of snow-laden fir trees, and thrown snowballs at each other when we stopped at Innsbruk station as we journeyed from Paris to Venice on the Orient Express. We also heard the Vienna Boys Choir singing in their cathedral and swam in the Aegean Sea surrounding the Greek Island of Skiathos. The car manufacturers certainly knew how to entertain us!

There was only one car launch that was a complete disaster. Whoever decided to launch the British Leyland Metro on the Isle of Man in *February* 1980, sailing from Liverpool across the Irish sea on the cruise liner *Vistafjord* must surely have been fired! The demonstration cars were all lined up in Douglas for the dealers to test drive, but the sea was so incredibly rough, we couldn't get into the harbour! At the gala dinner, the ship rocked so much, some of the plates and cutlery flew off the tables and it was almost impossible to walk anywhere without having something to cling on to. Many guests were sea-sick. Other trips carrying the dealers were successful, but our contingent of around 500 were distinctly unimpressed.

During the 1990s and early 2000s, Lorraine and I travelled to the USA, partly on business and partly for pleasure. The National Association of Automobile Dealers of America (NADA) holds an annual convention of workshops and an exhibition each February which attracts over 23,000 delegates from all over the world.

The convention centres large enough to hold such events are in Las Vegas, San Francisco, Atlanta, New Orleans and Detroit. We visited all of them at least once, apart from Detroit, which for some reason we missed.

I visited these conventions at my own expense because I believed I'd either learn something from the seminars or pick up some information or a contact that would lead to conducting enough business to at least cover the cost of the trip. It always did.

For example, I purchased some brush-less Hercules car washes from a USA supplier and arranged to have them imported and installed in all our dealerships. They were incredibly efficient and being brush-less, they didn't affect the car's paintwork. We were the first dealer to use them in the UK.

Louis, the Sales Manager, and I got on really well, and when he came to the UK to supervise the installations, he bought his wife, Ramona, with him. She was an attractive brunette, and wore an incredibly short leather mini-skirt to a dinner Lorraine and I hosted at a restaurant in the New Forest. They were great company too – a memorable night!

Once the four-day convention and exhibition closed, we'd hire a car and just head off in any direction for a couple of weeks to discover the real USA. We loved it. Lorraine's such a wonderful companion. My best memories are driving along listening to country music together on the radio, stopping for a coffee or a burger whenever we felt like it and choosing somewhere that looked exciting to stay. We had so many adventures – it would take another book to recall them all, but one or two stand out.

From Atlanta, Georgia, we headed north and found ourselves in a town called Helen, built entirely in the style of a Swiss chalet ski resort. We were just short of the Blue Ridge Mountains, and, being February, the whole town was covered with a fine smattering of snow as we drove down Main Street. We came across a delightful hotel, and were checked in by an overwhelmingly friendly young man full of Southern charm.

"Glad to meet you English folks. Whatcha doing tonight?"

"Well nothing. What do you suggest?"

"Well, we got a show on tonight in the local theatre. There'll be some singing and plenty of food. We're raising funds for a new library. Everyone's bringing a book to sell, but you don't have to worry – we'd just like to see you folks there."

After a quick change of clothes, we strolled the few hundred yards to the theatre and the young man introduced us to some of his mainly white friends. We scoffed cold meats and bread rolls, washed down with a couple of Budweiser beers and the music began.

First up were a group of elderly men whose a cappella harmony was mellow, mellifluous and memorable. Next on stage was a group of musicians with, reputedly, Elvis Presley's ex-pianist as their leader – they really rocked!

This was followed by the most unlikely star of the show whose stage presence was more like that of the theatre cleaner ... until she opened her mouth. I don't think we'd ever heard such a pure, wholesome, natural voice as she sang some deeply moving gospel songs. We met her afterwards.

BJ was a totally unassuming 19-year-old white girl, dressed in a most unflattering smock. We told her we thought she really could be a singing star but she didn't want to know. She was quite happy singing in the church choir and at occasional concerts. At the end of the evening, our, by now, close friend, the receptionist, went on stage.

"Would David and Lorraine Henley, all the way from England, please stand so that we can give them a good old-fashioned Helen, Georgia welcome." As everybody clapped and hollered, we felt distinctly embarrassed, but happy to feel such warmth.

This experience was common and highlights what the American people are all about. They love the Brits and it made us feel good to be welcomed in their country. To some, their openness is sometimes interpreted as being somewhat shallow. I don't agree. It's so refreshing to be greeted politely. At least they make the opening gambit and it's up to you how you respond and how far you want take the relationship. When you part, "Have a nice day" is, I'm sure, well meant.

Another example of this "special relationship" occurred on the same trip. After travelling east, through South and then North Carolina, with churches almost every mile, or so it seemed, we once again found ourselves stumbling into another unforgettable experience.

Driving along with the radio blaring, we heard an announcement on the local country music programme.

"Tonight at the Silver Fox club, in Greensboro, North Carolina, we're sponsoring a talent show. Country music lovers, this is a night not to be missed!"

I don't know why this announcement registered with us amongst all the other ads and promotions, but within the next hour or so, I said, "Hey, look Lorraine, there's that Silver Fox club! What do you think? Shall we go?" She was enthusiastic.

"Yeah, it'll be interesting. Let's drive round to find somewhere to stay." We were running short of time and there wasn't much choice so we checked into a place which reminded me of Bates Motel in my favourite movie, *Psycho*. The proprietor looked just like an older Anthony Perkins who played the psychopath, Norman Bates. He was sitting on a rocking chair on the veranda outside the office, chewing on an almost-expired cigar.

"Do you have a double room for tonight?" I asked in my poshest English accent.

"Might have, I'll just have to look and see in my book here," Norman Bates drawled in the most Southern of Southern accents. There were no other cars on the lot and I'm certain the place was deserted.

"Yep. There's a room right next to the office." I swear I saw Lorraine shudder. We handed over our credit card and he creepily pointed out the room in silence.

We quickly changed and made our way to the Silver Fox club about ten minutes' away. As we entered we nudged each other as we spotted the men wearing Stetsons, open-necked shirts displaying gold medallions, jeans and cowboy boots. The pony-tailed girls wore tight blouses, blue jeans and invariably white stilettos. The place was packed. I went to the bar to order a gin and tonic for Lorraine and a beer for me. I returned with an enamel jug holding four pints of the local microbrew, the only drinks being served.

"What have we let ourselves in for?" Lorraine said as the master of ceremonies invited the first entrant to the stage.

"Well, it'll be a good laugh," I responded, happily sipping my beer. What happened next was a brilliantly performed concert from ten superb artistes, backed by an outstanding country band. Our smirks turned to rapturous applause by the end of the evening. Suddenly, it all became clear why the standard was so high. This was the state's final audition for a recording contract at Mercury studios! After the winner was announced, there followed an evening of line dancing before we headed back to the motel.

It was in complete darkness, apart from the office light, which confirmed we were the only guests, which made Lorraine increasingly nervous. I'm sure she thought "Norman" would appear in our room armed with a knife at any moment as she took a shower!

Next morning we checked out.

"D'ya know, I wanted you folks to stay for months." Lorraine and I looked at each other with an expression which intimated "not a chance!".

"I just love to hear ya talk." That was it! He'd rarely, if ever, heard English accents before and he was obsessed by them. But this was another example of discovering the *real* America which never fails to surprise and delight us.

The convention in San Francisco was very special – not just for the exhibition or the workshops but because we took Aaron and Max with us. They were 13 and 17 respectively and were overawed by this iconic city they'd seen countless times on TV and in the movies. The Golden Gate Bridge, which we walked over amidst nauseating automobile fumes, Fisherman's Wharf, Pier 69, Chinatown, the largest colony outside China, and numerous trips on the famous trams up and down the vertiginous hills were essential attractions for us. The most memorable, though, was a visit to Alcatraz, the prison island less than a mile from the coast.

Lorraine sat outside as we three were fitted up with an audio system that explained the history as we walked through the prison cells and gantries. It was last used as a prison in 1963 and the atmosphere created by the audio tape was compelling. What drove the prisoners mad was they could often hear the hubbub of the city when the wind was in the right direction and some could even see the lights at night, emphasising their incarceration. Many escapees were shot in the attempt, but in June 1962, Frank Morris and the Anglin brothers, it's alleged, survived a hazardous trip to the mainland on a home-made raft made from raincoats used by the inmates whilst in the exercise yard. This was an incredibly audacious escape planned over a three-year period and involved making lifelike dummies to replicate their sleeping bodies at night whilst they worked on removing ventilator grilles! Nothing more was heard of these escapees, they'd just disappeared and the intriguing mystery of their escape is still being explored and discussed.

Whilst we were wining and dining in the fabulous Italian restaurants of North Beach, the boys ordered room-service at the hotel, usually king-size pizzas, played pool and watched American TV – they loved it!

Probably the most exciting conventions, though, were those held in Las Vegas – often described as a Disneyland for grown-ups! We stayed at the Flamingo Hilton which, like most of the hotels, has its reception deep inside the building, forcing you through a plethora of gaming machines. As you enter, the first thing you notice is the noise – bells clanging, levers clunking and metal cash tokens striking the scoop underneath the machines. They're not known as one-arm-bandits for nothing – we spent hours on these monsters without winning a thing! They seem to be programmed to pay out just enough times to keep you interested and so you keep playing. They're everywhere. I don't think we ever encountered a shop or a building that didn't have some.

Each hotel tries to out-do the other in the entertainment stakes. There are circus acts – trapeze artistes fly over your head as you gamble, a pirate show involving the sinking of a ship, a Venetian-themed palacio complete with canals and gondolas, a Parisian quarter, including a one-third-sized Eiffel Tower, and our favourite, outside the Bellagio hotel, hundreds of fountains that are choreographed to music. It's all designed to attract the tourist dollars and it works. Las Vegas was recently announced as the fastest growing city in the United States.

We've also seen some wonderful shows there too: Neil Sedaka, Robin Williams, Bette Midler and Barry Manilow. It's a magical place at night. It's hard to realise this whole city is built in a desert with nothing else for miles around. The Strip is a neon kaleidoscope of colours, almost blinding you into submission. The pace of life is electric too and after four days we were usually exhausted and ready to move on.

On our usual tour afterwards, we discovered, amongst many other locations, Palm Springs, a golfer's Mecca, with over 80 courses and Joshua Tree, an 800,000-acre national park which boasts a civilisation going back over 5,000 years, giant granite monoliths and 40-feet-high giant Yuccas. We loved the desert climate and drove for miles in this area full of sand dunes, parched valleys, extraordinarily rugged mountains and occasional oases. We promised ourselves we'd re-visit when we retired, which we did!

CHAPTER 23
The travel bug

Having visited wonderfully fabulous locations courtesy of the vehicle manufacturers, I developed a passion, shared by Lorraine, to travel as much as possible. This became easier to do once I'd fully retired but before then we fed the travel bug whenever we could with relish! I've tried hard not to make this part of my story too much like a travelogue, but more a kaleidoscope of adventures.

We toured many parts of France which, although three times the size of Britain, has the same number of cars on the road which makes it a pleasure to drive, except in the major cities. We love the contrast between the idyllic country backwaters and the madness that rules in Paris.

We spent our honeymoon there in 1990 and Lorraine's surprise 50th birthday at La Coupole, a famous brasserie in Montparnasse, so it has a special affection in our hearts, despite the traffic problems.

Lorraine had no idea on June 20th 1996 that I'd secretly arranged for her sons, her mother and 14 of her friends to travel on the Eurostar train to join us for lunch, carrying her birthday cake. As they entered the brasserie one by one, she was overwhelmed with joy. The restaurant, which serves hundreds of superb gastronomic meals a day, was packed with fellow diners and the atmosphere was lively.

Following a long, boozy lunch, I had a job to make anyone hear my welcome speech – it reminded me of rugby club dinners! The guests finally poured themselves back onto the Eurostar carriages for the return trip at around 6.00 pm. They'd left home at 6.00 am, so it was a day-trip and lunch to remember!

We often took my 1967 230SL Mercedes convertible and meandered through Brittany and Normandy stopping at chambre d'hotes or small hotels deep in the countryside.

We were once persuaded to enter a classic car rally driving through France from Le Havre and finishing at Carcassone in the south-west, a 600-mile journey. Although we considered ourselves Francophiles, we were complete novices as far as car rallies were concerned and should have realised that as the trip lasted only five days, it was more like a race. There was little time to savour the journey, leaving early in the morning and sometimes not arriving at the designated hotel until after 8.00 pm at night. After the first three days we decided not to compete but just to take our time and enjoy the glorious sunshine with the Mercedes convertible top down.

However, the rally took us to places we'd otherwise have missed. We discovered a small village in the Limosin area, Oradour-sur-Glane, which became infamous as the place where German brutality during World War Two reached unprecedented heights. On 10th June 1944, just four days after the Allied invasion of Normandy, 150 SS soldiers entered the tranquil village of 330 inhabitants and a roughly equal number of refugees. Hitler's elite troops massacred almost everyone and destroyed every building in this peaceful village and is regarded as one of the worst war crimes committed by the German army during the war.

The recently erected museum records that all the women and children were herded into the church at gunpoint whilst the SS systematically looted their homes before killing all but seven of the men and setting fire to the buildings. They then began firing at random into the church – the bullet holes are still evident – before releasing some gas containers and then setting fire to the wooden pews. Just one woman miraculously escaped and she was later to give evidence against the perpetrators. The village has been left in exactly the same condition it was on that day as a shrine to 642 innocent men, women and children who lost their lives.

At the Nuremberg war crimes trial, the Germans explained their actions suggesting the village was the centre of the local resistance organisation that had recently killed a high-ranking officer and 73 other soldiers after they'd surrendered and this was their revenge. There's no record of anyone being held responsible, which seems incredible. Whomever we believed, this was brutality on a scale we'd never encountered before close up and had a profound effect on the whole group.

In 1992, Lorraine booked a week's holiday in Elat, in Israel, just to get some winter sun. I had no idea this trip would lead to one of the most memorable days of my life. Elat sits at the head of the Red Sea and is bounded by Egypt, Saudi Arabia and Jordan. It's a lively, bustling seaside resort and the hotel was full of contemporary modern paintings and artefacts.

We were persuaded by a tour operator to take a one-day trip to Jerusalem, leaving by coach at 5.30 am and returning by a small aircraft at around 9.00 pm. Neither of us are religious and I'm hopeless at getting up in the morning but we decided to do it. We're both so glad we made the effort.

The tour guide was excellent. As we settled into our seats on the coach, he said, "I don't care what your beliefs are or, indeed, whether you have any. I'll make no pronouncements about what's true or what's false. I'll try wherever I can to explain the facts and I promise not to favour any one set of beliefs over another. You're all free to make up your own mind." This was great, I thought, and everyone on the coach seemed a little more relaxed.

As we headed north through the barren desert countryside, we made several stops. At one, the tour guide insisted we got out of the coach and pointed down to a sandy path skirting a mountain ridge.

"We can't be sure, but there's evidence to suggest this is the exact spot upon which the parable of the Good Samaritan was based. Even if it isn't, I'm sure you can visualise this is exactly the type of terrain referred to in the Bible." He made countless other references to the good book, bringing the scriptures alive – it was fascinating.

When we arrived at the Dead Sea we were encouraged to float in the sulphurous, steaming water but the gaseous atmosphere had most of us squinting our eyes and trying not to breathe in too much. The "bad egg" odour stayed with us for an hour or so afterwards. The experience wasn't at all as we imagined.

The highlight of the trip occurred once we reached the City of Jerusalem. Nothing could have prepared us for the experience of following in Christ's steps up the hilly Via Dolarosa to the place of His crucifixion. The guide spoke all the time, asking us to imagine what Christ went through on this journey, carrying and dragging the heavy wooden cross to His certain death. At the top of the hill, we entered the Church of the Holy Sepulchre, sometimes known as the Church of the Resurrection, originally built in the 4th century on the very spot where, allegedly, Jesus was carried after being taken down from the cross and buried in a tomb. At this point, many of our party knelt and cried – it was incredibly moving, and not as embarrassing as it sounds. I learnt that this is the holiest Christian site in the world, so pilgrimages were especially important.

Later, we visited the Wailing Wall, and once again, some of our new-found friends of a Jewish persuasion prayed and left notes wedged into the crevices.

We moved on to the Mount of Olives, Jericho and then to Bethlehem, where many more biblical stories were explained, especially those surrounding the birth of Jesus. Because we'd now visited places that were just names to us we'd learnt from the Bible, our parents and at school, Lorraine and I agreed we'd discovered so much more in this single day and gained a better understanding of some of the problems of this region. Even for complete agnostics and atheists, we believed this trip could make one consider alternative views of history and religion. Lorraine and I discussed our experiences at length, and decided we were still unsure what to believe.

In 1995, we visited Australia and New Zealand. We loved Sydney, little realising that this would be Stephanie's home within nine years! We also had no idea that within the next two years, Lorraine would discover an extension of her family in Auckland.

From Sydney, we travelled north and took a short cruise on a small boat with just 50 passengers departing from a very humid Cairns to the Great Barrier Reef, which was everything we expected it to be as one of the Seven Wonders of the World. We spent a couple of memorable days on a remote island where we learnt to snorkel. We'd never seen such incredible fish or coral before and it took us a long time to realise that no-one could hear our *oohs!* and *ahs!* under water!

When we disembarked in Cairns, we decided to visit the Daintree rain forest high in the mountains, travelling there by train but returning by cable-car, which is where the trouble started. It usually took about 45 minutes, scudding over the canopy of tall trees as you looked down on multi-coloured parrots flitting between them. After about 20 minutes, the open-sided cable car suddenly juddered to a stop, rocking precariously. Lorraine and I were the only people in our car which had stopped right at the highest point of the journey!

From this vantage point, we could clearly see the occupants of the other cable-cars. Some began shouting, some made a joke or two to ease the tension and some just sat there ashen-faced. For the first ten minutes, it all seemed a bit of fun, but at time progressed … 20 minutes … half an hour … 40 minutes, the mood began to change. It was beginning to get dark and now rain was being driven by the wind into the car. Suddenly, without warning, the whole chain suddenly lurched forward and very slowly made its way back to the ground. I was just beginning to panic, wondering how they'd have got us down if they hadn't got the apparatus working. I asked the attendant immediately we were safely on terra firma.

"If the machinery's buggered, we'd have to use a manual winch which is what we did. If that didn't work, then we'd send up a helicopter and bring you down in style, mate!" I didn't enquire if he was joking – I was just glad I didn't have to spend a night 1,000 feet in the air listening to the nightlife of the rain forest!

In New Zealand we visited all the usual tourist spots, but the highlight was the boat trip up Doubtful Sound in the South Island. Our most abiding memory was of the steamboat gently chugging on a mirrored mill pond, reflecting the sunny, cloudless sky and being followed by shiny, grey dolphins leaping out of the water as if synchronised. We passed acre after acre of almost vertical steep-sided emerald forests, which, the guide explained, had never had a human foot set upon them. Deep into the valley, the captain turned off the engines, and asked everyone to keep quiet for five minutes and to experience the uncanny, eerie silence of this vast inlet. It was a special moment.

I'd never considered the benefits of cruising before. I imagined old people in bath-chairs with blankets wrapped tightly around them to keep warm and being bored with nothing to do but look at the sea all day. Lorraine's view was different and so as part of this same trip she persuaded me to break our journey to Australia by spending some time in Singapore and to take a seven-day round-trip cruise with the Gemini Line which travelled up the Straits of Malacca, hugging the west coasts of Malaysia and Thailand calling at Port Klang (for Kuala Lumpur), Langkawi, Penang and Phuket before returning to Singapore.

The 19,000-ton Gemini Superstar carries 800 passengers, quite small by modern standards, so I thought it would be a good test. The ship was beautifully designed and enhanced by vibrant colours in the public areas and the well-appointed cabins. I grew used to sitting in the open-air restaurant at night, eating wonderfully prepared exotic meals, drinking fine wines in still-warm temperatures, with a 15-knot breeze cooling me down as the ship cruised to its next destination. The after-dinner entertainment was superb with first-class singers, dancers and cabarets.

The clientele were not at all as I'd feared – in fact, quite the opposite. Most were Aussies and Europeans, and a small number of Asians and it was all very relaxed. One night in the bar, Lorraine was being chatted up by a gnarled, slightly uncouth Aussie.

"Lorraine, do you like oysters?"

"Well yes, I do. Why do you ask?"

"I can eat a hundred of 'em in one go. Mind you, you know what they say about oysters?" He winked.

"Well, yes," said Lorraine, rather nervously.

"They make you go to the toilet too, mind you." Lorraine's opinion of Australians was impaired forever!

The ports of call were disappointing with the exception of Phuket. Langkawi's picture-postcard idyllic castaway island image had rubbish everywhere and the buildings were decidedly Third World.

We didn't even disembark at Port Klang. We were tipped off it was just a commercial port and that the coach trip to KL took nearly two hours, so we stayed aboard and luxuriated in having the ship almost entirely to ourselves.

Phuket was delightful and although commercialised, there was no mistaking we were in a different continent with ubiquitous elephants, bead-sellers and temples aplenty.

Back on the Gemini Superstar, I was never bored; there was a library, lectures, several pools, a putting green and always plentiful food with six meal-times a day, including a midnight buffet! If we wanted to escape, we sat on our stateroom balcony during the day and caught up on some reading.

Now fully converted to the delights of cruising, in 1996 we couldn't resist an outstanding offer from British Airways to fly to New York by Concorde, board the QE2 for a 10-day cruise up the Eastern seaboard calling at Bar Harbour, near Bangor, Maine, Boston, Massachusetts, and finally to Halifax, Nova Scotia before returning to New York for a flight home on a normal jet. The extra cost for Concorde was just £250 each, the usual fare was £2,500!

The surge of power I felt from the back of my sculptured grey leather seat as the missile accelerated through and beyond the sound barrier and reaching 2,000 miles per hour was unforgettable! We knew the speed precisely – there was an airspeed indicator in the passenger cabin. I couldn't believe we landed in Kennedy airport, New York just three and a half hours after we'd left Heathrow!

I was very disappointed when Concorde was grounded forever in 2003. Since their launch in 1973, just 20 were built and 14 served as airliners. They were never commercially viable, which surprised me, and not environmentally friendly. Many of them have been sent round the world to final resting places in museums and airfields.

The QE2 was a grand floating palace with dark-grained wood panelling, chandeliers and charming crew. The passengers were nearly all older than us which is why, when we were queuing to meet the captain on the first night, dressed in our finest, we began talking to George and Donna, an American couple around our age, late 50s, living in Doylestown, Pennsylvania. Thus began a very close relationship. They were an attractive couple. George was a well-known character actor who'd appeared in over 30 movies and TV shows. His movie and TV credits include: *Back To The Future*, *Close Encounters Of the Third Kind* and *Murder She Wrote*. He also ran an acting school in New York City. He'd been invited by Cunard to give a series of lectures about the movie business on this trip.

He was very handsome with dark skin and brown eyes, a deep, mellifluous, voice and exuded a brooding presence, yet possessed a great sense of humour. Donna was tall, elegant and beautiful and we weren't surprised to learn she was a former model. She was previously married to Harvey Korman, a huge TV star in the 1960s and 1970s, most famously appearing in the award-winning *Carol Burnett Show*, a comedy sketch programme and the movie, *Blazing

Saddles. So both she and George had experienced Hollywood. They were delightful company and we dined with them often, exchanging details of our very different lives.

Every time Lorraine has a lobster, she invariably compares it unfavourably to those we had at Bar Harbour. We sat on a high terrace with wonderful views of the sea, waiting for the Maine lobster we'd previously selected from the huge sea-water tank located in the main restaurant. It was served, grilled to perfection, with a knob of butter on paper plates and napkins – so simple yet utterly delicious! Afterwards, we strolled around the small town admiring the wonderful fall colours made especially vibrant by the addition of bright red maple leaves.

Shortly after arriving home, we received a phone call from Donna to say that she and George had split up. We were devastated. We thought they got on really well, but George had met someone else and that was it.

Donna and Lorraine got on so well, that Donna and her close friend from Los Angeles, Sharon, decided to visit the UK to celebrate Donna's 60th birthday – 25th January 1997. Although she was deeply upset about the split, we cheered her up with our British "quaintness" as she called it!

Later that year Donna invited Lorraine to join her and some of her friends to spend a week on a cookery course in Provence. Lorraine was delighted. However, just before she was about to depart Donna phoned to say she couldn't make the trip as she had a problem with her back. So Lorraine decided to meet Donna's friends at Heathrow for the onward trip to the South of France. She was nervous about spending a week with complete strangers, so I said I'd travel down in my classic Mercedes sports car to meet her at the end of the course and we'd spend some time touring one of our favourite parts of the world.

She needn't have worried. She had a week of great fun and friendship – I don't think much cooking was done. Apparently the hosts insisted that the local wine had to be thoroughly sampled first! Lorraine and Lelia, Donna's closest friend, also became very attached and together with Paul, Lelia's artist husband, they've visited us in the UK and we've seen them many times in New York, their playground, and New Jersey, their home.

Donna married Richard, a retired investment manager and the owner of the house she bought after her split with George and they, too, have spent time with us in London and Romsey. Donna and Lelia have introduced us to so many of their friends over the years and we feel we now have our very own American family.

In 1998, Max and Aaron, then aged 25 and 21 respectively, decided to travel the world as part of Aaron's gap year. He'd just graduated as a journalist from Farnham University and Max was still deciding on a career. We encouraged them and they returned as mature young men with many tales to tell! They spent three months travelling, sometimes staying with Lorraine's new family in New Zealand – it was a great success. We decided to fly to Thailand to spend a couple of weeks with them as they made their way back to the UK.

We met up in what I consider to be a version of hell – Bangkok. I hated it! It was shirt-drippingly humid, smelled of diesel and the roads were chaotic. I particularly disliked the tuk-tuks – fume-belching, three-wheeled motorised "lawnmowers" with two-stroke rattling engines that passed themselves off as taxis, speeding on rutted roads as if they were ambulances on emergency duty.

One rainy night, we hired a couple – they can only carry two passengers at once – to take us to a kick-boxing event on the edge of the city. The atmosphere was more reminiscent of a cock-fighting pit! The brightly-lit ring was surrounded by hundreds of short, brown, sweaty men, many of them wearing white singlets, cheering on their favourites. We watched in astonishment as the Thai bookies continuously shrieked out the betting odds trying to make themselves heard throughout the contest. It was the noisiest sporting event I'd ever encountered. It was exceedingly humid inside the building and the boxer's bodies glistened under the spotlights. The boys and I really enjoyed it but Lorraine, one of just a handful of women there, felt hugely intimidated.

Most of the Thais we met outside Bangkok were kind and gentle, gracious even, but those in Bangkok were always hassling and trying to rip off the tourists. This brazen, in-your-face street life of Bangkok contrasted startlingly with the beauty of the magnificent temples that we only fleetingly visited – I think we'd had enough!

We took the overnight train up to Chang Mai in the north of Thailand, a 12-hour journey, and stayed in the Regent Palace hotel, a luxurious resort just outside the main town. It was surrounded by rice fields worked by straw-hatted coolies and we went elephant-trekking through the nearby forests. Although it was still fiercely hot and humid, the people were delightful – so different from those we'd experienced in Bangkok. In the main town, ubiquitous young, orange-robed, shaven-headed monks carried out their early-morning daily ritual, walking around the streets with their begging bowls, collecting food from faithful citizens who believed that by giving sustenance to monks they will be blessed by their gods. Thailand was a great experience for us all, but especially for the boys.

As a reward to ourselves for selling my software business in August 2000, we visited South America and cruised around Cape Horn from Valpariso in Chile to Montevideo in Uruguay, via many interesting ports including Port Stanley in the Falkland Islands. Before joining the ship, we spent a week in Buenos Aires. I've always been fascinated by this part of the world and it was everything I expected it to be and more. Lorraine was more concerned about the journey around the Cape – she'd heard some horror stories about mountainous waves and heavy seas and of one cruise that had to turn back because it was so dangerous. It's where the Pacific and Atlantic oceans meet, but I was assured that in February it was usually very safe.

Buenos Aires is a mixture of Paris, Madrid and Milan, yet with its own distinctive flavour. The boulevards are wide and straight with great shopping arcades, the restaurants noisy and boisterous and the evocative tango is played everywhere! I felt invigorated every day. Almost every bar or café we visited had tango music playing – usually by a swarthy bandoleon player, passionately throwing his head back when emphasising the strident beat. Alternatively, they'd be playing a recorded version. Once you get the tango rhythm into your brain, it's impossible to get rid of it!

One evening, after devouring one of the best steaks we'd ever tasted, washed down by copious glasses of Argentine wine – total cost less than a fiver – we visited a tango show in one of the seedier parts of the city with some new-found friends, Nick and Rose from Kent and Herb and Roberta from New York City, who were to join us on the cruise. It was a lively, noisy and colourful show and we had front-row seats. Unbelievably, Lorraine fell asleep! I couldn't understand how this was possible, but her drinking capacity is close to zero, so I should have realised. At one point, she shook herself from her slumbers and began clapping earnestly. Trouble was, the dancers were in mid-flight and this completely threw them!

They stopped for a second before recovering their poise and continued.

"What did you do that for?" I hissed.

"Sorry, I must have dreamt they'd finished," she meekly replied. We never let Lorraine forget this night and it became a standing joke when we joined the cruise.

We loved the Argentines and they seemed genuinely pleased to see Brits. Many of them, once they knew we were from the UK, made a point of apologising for invading the Falkland Islands. They were deeply embarrassed by the policies of General Galtieri, leader of the military junta which ruled the country from 1976 to 1983. They pointed out that he was defeated in the elections held after he'd lost the battle and the country embraced democratic rule. Once they'd made their point all they wanted to talk about was football! They were obsessed by the European leagues and the British clubs.

Once on the cruise, we headed south from Valpariso, Chile and had great views of the Andes with their jagged peaks seemingly piercing the sky. We saw huge glaciers, some dripping into the sea and occasional ice floes, brilliant white above sea level, and a translucent turquoise hue below. We were joined every day by giant albatrosses gliding over the sea looking for an easy meal from the ship's flotsam and jetsam.

At the very tip of Cape Horn lies the world's most southerly city, Ushuaia, from where most of the Antarctic expeditions start. It was bitterly cold and bleak and is snow-covered for nine months of the year but had a surprisingly good selection of shops and even a soccer pitch! We found it hard to believe the South Pole was still 1,000 miles further south.

Having successfully negotiated the Cape in the most tranquil conditions the captain had experienced – much to Lorraine's relief – I felt a bit of a fraud as we were presented with our certificates proving we'd met the challenge.

The next stop was the Falkland Islands. Our first impression was, why on earth anybody would want control of this depressing, cold, bleak, windswept island stuck out in the Atlantic Ocean? We learnt that its strategic position was vital to protect the trade routes from South America to the rest of the world.

We were impressed by the immense patriotism of the islanders. There were Union Jacks draped at practically every window of every house. The pub served the best fish and chips we'd had in a while but the feel of the whole island was of being stuck in a time warp, circa 1950s. The clothes people wore, the houses and the few shops all looked colourless and faded. Once again, though, the natives were exceptionally friendly, probably realising that these cruise ships brought valuable trade to the island!

Next stop proved to be the highlight – for me anyway. We docked at Peutro Madryn in Patagonia and took a bus inland to visit Gaiman where the first Welsh settlers made their home in 1865 following religious persecution and a threat from the English of colonising the Welsh way of life. Patagonia was sufficiently far away, over 8,000 miles, to avoid any other European settlers at that time and it was not a British colony. We drove for a couple of hours through inhospitable desert and scrubland before reaching a beautiful lush valley, some 90 miles inland.

We learnt the story of the hardships endured by the first 153 settlers who walked there after disembarking from a sea journey on the *Mimosa* that took nearly three months, pushing wooden wheelbarrows containing their entire belongings, taking many days before stumbling across this oasis. They often ran out of water, reduced to near-starvation and attacked by the native Indians. Several died on the way but enough people survived to start what is today a thriving community of 20,000 inhabitants. Many are still Welsh-speaking, and in the small town there were chapels and flags showing the red dragon everywhere.

We were greeted by a choir who sang some hymns I remembered from my childhood. We sat down to a typical Welsh tea including Welsh cakes and drop-scones – both my favourites. We spoke to several members of the choir after the concert who were intensely proud of their heritage and possessed names like Trefor Pedro Rodrigues Jones and spoke English with a slight Welsh accent! I became quite emotional meeting these descendants of the settlers from almost 150 years ago and so far from their ancestors' birthplace and yet I could have been back in Merthyr Tydfil!

CHAPTER 24
Retirement and round-the-world trips

One of the fellow guests we shared a table with each evening on one of our cruises gave us some invaluable travel advice. He told us that many airlines sell a first-class round-the-world ticket for under £5,000, which we thought was great value. The only rules are that you have to always travel in the same direction – clockwise or anticlockwise – and the journey has to be completed within a 12-month period. There was no limit to the number of stopovers.

When I sold Testwood Motor Group in October 2004, and so effectively retired from day-to-day management, I thought this would be a great way of rewarding ourselves. Lorraine and I spent hours deciding where we wanted to go and for how long. We didn't need to be specific, the ticket was open so we could always detour or stay longer in a place we loved or move on if we wanted to. Lorraine had always wanted to go to Sri Lanka, so as part of a six-week trip, we set up a three-week tour of the whole island. We'd arranged to depart on December 27th 2004.

Our plans were, literally, washed away with the breaking news on Boxing Day that the worst tsunami ever had taken place just north of Indonesia and affected the coastlines for thousands of miles, including Sri Lanka! The devastation we saw on our TV screens was truly shocking as were the increasing number of deaths being reported on every news bulletin. We considered cancelling the trip, but there appeared so little we could do to affect matters that the very next day, we took off from Heathrow and travelled to New York, our first stop, without knowing how the rest of the journey would be affected. I couldn't speak to my travel agent until 2nd of January because of the Christmas break but it was obvious that it was impossible for us to travel anywhere near the affected areas. When we made contact, we hastily put together an alternative plan, spending more time in the US and South Africa.

In New York, we ate lunch at Rockefeller's ice rink in Manhattan with Roberta and Herb whom we'd met on the South American cruise. The muffled-up skaters gliding and swirling on the ice, as we enjoyed the warmth and conviviality of the restaurant, reminded me of the paintings of matchstick men by L S Lowry, renowned for his early 20th century industrial scenes. The next day we spent walking for miles in snow-covered Central Park which was a special memory as was the sight of a noisy, brightly-lit Times Square, looking and sounding even gaudier than usual, festooned with Christmas decorations.

After spending New Year's Eve with our good friends Donna and Richard and Paul and Lelia in Philadelphia, we decided to fly to San Francisco, and after a few days exploring parts of the city which we hadn't previously discovered, we planned to drive down the Pacific Highway to Santa Monica via Monterey, Carmel, Big Sur and Santa Barbara. This proved impossible! Southern California was suffering continuous torrential rain resulting in creeping mud slides running onto the highway, causing a great deal of damage and some fatalities. We asked a local travel agent where we could get some guaranteed sun on our backs. They suggested San Jose del Cabo, a small fishing town about 50 miles east of the more famous resort of Cabo St Lucas in Baja California, Mexico.

Baja is the finger-shaped peninsular running 1,000 miles south from the Mexican border and is renowned for its Pacific Grey Whale-watching expeditions as they migrate for the summer. Every year, around 27,000 of these huge mammals travel over 5,000 miles from the food-rich waters of the Arctic to the bays of Baja California to breed and to rear their young.

We spent a week in San Jose at a beautiful resort. The Presidente Intercontinental is set right on the beach and next to a wildlife haven. The town was full of typical Mexican bars, with dark-wood cladding, giant circulating ceiling fans and jet-black-haired men wearing huge sombreros, playing mariachi music. The beautiful, equally dark and mysterious women invariably wore black shawls, long skirts and broad grins.

We hired a car and drove up the peninsular visiting dusty, dirt-tracked towns set in arid desert populated only by huge cactus plants and where it only rains three or four times a year. Many of the white stucco-clad buildings were run-down, but we always found somewhere good to eat the staple diet of tortilla, fried chilli beans and hot peppers and rice – delicious! Many of the people we met were poor but very friendly and happy. This always seems to be the case in warm climates.

In a surfing and artist colony, Todos Santos, we stumbled across *the* Hotel California, allegedly, a house of ill-repute, made famous by the *Eagles* in their 1970's hit record of the same name. Don Henley (sadly, no relation) wrote the song whilst hanging out there in the late 1960s. We simply *had* to sample the atmosphere which was strangely subdued for a former brothel!

Back in the resort, I persuaded Lorraine to take a romantic sunset horse ride on the beach – she's nervous of these creatures but I'd been exposed to them when I went riding with Stephanie when she was a child. Despite her reservations, Lorraine enjoyed it, but the real bonus was in meeting some fellow riders who came from New Zealand – a mother, her grown-up daughter and friend. We got on so well, after sunset, we spent the rest of the evening in the hotel bar exchanging our life stories! We'd never been so intimate with anyone in such a short period of time. I can't explain why – it seemed so natural. They became such good friends, we subsequently visited them when we travelled to see Lorraine's family and they've visited us in London and Hampshire. We just "clicked".

A week later, we flew back to San Francisco and learnt that the weather had greatly improved so we rented a car and headed down to Los Angeles on the Pacific Coast Highway. This was a fabulous drive in beautifully sunny conditions, in sight of the Pacific Ocean's pounding surf practically the whole way. We made many stops to admire the scenery, but the Post Ranch Inn in Big Sur is possibly the best place we've ever stayed. It's set right on the ocean's edge, a thousand feet above sea level. It used to be a working cattle ranch but now operates as an upscale inn with many of the rooms built as tree houses but with every modern convenience and fabulous views.

Billy Post, the proprietor before he sold the business, is a genial 80-year-old who still takes guests on a walking tour of the ranch every day as he has done for 20 years since he retired. He delights in telling tales of how his father came to settle here after the gold rush following the Great Depression of 1929 when millions left the desperate times in the east to seek their fortunes, either panning for gold or breeding cattle.

In Santa Monica, we stayed at Shutters, a stunning white, wooden, clapperboard building right on the beach. This is another of our favourite hotels, and Sheila, Lorraine's friend from school days who's lived in the US for many years, joined us. We also met up with Donna and Richard again. They'd flown out from New York to spend some more time with us and with their friends, Sharon and Mike who lived in Fallbrook, between Los Angeles and San Diego. They're all such fun to be with, breakfasting, lunching and dining at their favourite haunts.

Our original itinerary had always included a visit to Tokyo. One of our friends, Marcus, had, a year earlier, accepted a three-year contract working for the Japanese branch of his company. He'd always been fascinated by the Japanese way of life.

I didn't give this visit much thought. I was looking forward to seeing Marcus again, but nothing could have prepared us for the experience that followed. I've never visited anywhere so completely different to the Western world. Our first impression was the complexity and size of the infrastructure.

Tokyo is the world's largest metropolis, with over 35 million inhabitants. We saw miles of raised motorways and overhead railway lines running, it appeared, just a few feet between skyscraper office blocks as if someone had threaded them between the buildings. They were perpetually busy. The underground system, together with the rail network and monorail, is the largest transportation system in the world with over 2,500 kilometres of track and extends far beyond the inner city. One station, Shinjuku, has over 200 exits! It all became clear why this immense transportation exists when I read that over 22 million people a *day* enter and leave the city!

In three days, we saw less than a dozen Caucasian people and English was spoken only in the best hotels or restaurants. Thank goodness Marcus had picked up a rudimentary smattering of Japanese otherwise I think we'd have starved! He proved to be a wonderful guide and took us to some amazing places off the tourist map.

We met him at about 7.00 am one morning to visit the fish market. I have never seen such a weird collection – it was as if you'd asked five-year-old kids to draw a fish using only their imagination. The result was on sale here! One, known colloquially as a helicopter fish, literally has its fins coming out of the top of its head. Others had the most incredible scowl on their faces as if they'd objected to being caught. There's a fish whose name, when translated into English, is Bastard Halibut, a bright red apparition – I actually had some for breakfast – it tasted like wallpaper paste!

He also took us to the public baths, known as Onsens, which literally means spring water. Although they're losing their popularity, we thoroughly enjoyed the experience. After selecting a kimono, men and women bathe separately, probably just as well as you're encouraged to be completely naked once you're inside the bathing area. There's a series of pools maintained at various temperatures and treated with different salts and lotions, aimed at either curing any ailments or invigorating aching muscles. I felt sorry for Lorraine. She had to endure the odd stares from a hundred other Japanese women as she was the only Caucasian in the baths! At least I could hide behind Marcus who seemed quite oblivious to the Japanese men's curiosity.

After bathing, we were advised not to shower, but to let the effect of the spring waters work on our joints. We then joined up with Lorraine in our kimonos in a public area where, in common with a hundred other spotless, inquisitive bodies, we were encouraged to lie quietly, relax and drink jasmine tea. Very civilised!

Next stop west was Kuala Lumpur, capital of Malaysia. We stayed a few days in the Oriental hotel in sight of the Petronas twin towers which were, until 2004, the highest building in the world before being taken over by Taipei 101, a single tower in Taiwan. Although as busy as Bangkok, KL exuded a great deal more charm. The city-based Malaysians seemed less frenetic and more relaxed than the equivalent Thais. KL possessed more of a Western influence although we were reminded how often the Muslims worshipped as we heard the evocative call to prayers five times a day from a nearby temple.

Our original trip always included a safari in South Africa, linking up with my good friend Errol. Because of the aborted trip to Sri Lanka, we extended our stay from one to three weeks. We flew into Cape Town and drove along the Garden Route taking in the south and then the east coast to Durban to stay with Errol and his family.

Cape Town is one of our favourite cities. The only blight is the drive from the airport to the Waterfront where you pass close by the corrugated roofs and walls of the shanty town where a million or more coloureds and blacks try to make a living. This scene is repeated in all the major conurbations in South Africa, but somehow, the comparison between the ramshackle homesteads and the magnificence of the seemingly eternally sunny Cape Town, with pristine yachts moored in glistening harbours and the majestic Table Mountain as a backdrop, brings the contrast sharply into focus.

We took a boat trip to Robben Island, a former leper colony just off the coast from Cape Town, where Nelson Mandela was sentenced to 20 years' hard labour for his struggle to free the country from apartheid. Seeing the conditions in which he was held really added to his legendary status. My remaining impression was the thought of him working every day, hacking at the face of the limestone quarry where the whiteness of the rock, greatly intensified by the direct rays of sunlight, led him to become partially blind. We stood at the very spot, and witnessed the effect first-hand. He was only allowed one letter and one visitor every six months. Following his release and subsequent cult status, Robben Island is seen all over the world as a symbol of freedom.

In Durban, we spent a week with Errol, who'd arranged a whirlwind list of things to do and to visit (as usual!), most of it business-oriented, visiting some car dealerships, which I didn't mind at all as the rugby season had finished!

Then, on up to the Phinda centre in Kwazulu-Natal which Errol had recommended as the best place for our safari. It's marketed as a high-class resort, with separate luxury villas dotted about the main camp, but with particular emphasis on the fact that you can usually always spot the "big five" animals – elephants, lions, leopards, buffalos and rhinos. They're known as the "big five", not because they're the biggest or most dangerous, but simply because this quintet are regarded by hunters as the most difficult to track and hunt. Although Lorraine and I aren't particularly intrepid travellers, we were looking forward to this part of the trip. The only wild animals we'd seen were in the zoo. It turned out to be a major disappointment.

Each day after breakfast at 5.00 am we met our assigned guide and the driver at 6.00 am and they'd take us out into the bush, returning at around 10.00 am. Then we'd leave again at 4.00 pm, returning at 8.00 pm. It usually got dark at about 6.00 pm so the Land Rovers were fitted with huge spotlights. So if you wished, you could spend eight hours a day looking for animals, which many of our fellow-safarians did. So far, so good.

On the first morning, we were given instructions about how to behave in the open six-seater Land Rover. If we spotted an animal, we had to keep very quiet and still and if we saw an elephant at close quarters pawing the ground and throwing dust up in the air with his trunk, we had to hold tight because the Land Rover may have to take some avoiding action very quickly!

We saw elephants, lions and leopards on the first morning but what began to irritate us was that if we spotted a pair of leopard cubs with their mother, we'd stop a while and then the guide would contact the other Land Rovers on their radio and give them the location. Before too long there would be four or five other vehicles full of people surrounding the animals. This process was repeated every single trip. On one occasion at about 5.00 pm we'd seen a lioness with her three cubs playing in a small wooded area. We stopped for a drink at around 6.00 pm just as the sun was going down and then the guide took us back to the same spot to watch them again under searchlight. Once again, as we backed out, another Land Rover came to take our place.

Inside, I was screaming, "For goodness' sake, let them have some peace!" I counted 16 Land Rovers at base camp so these animals were being gawped at and photographed for most of the day and night.

After the first day, Lorraine stayed in the camp all day reading. There was nothing else to do if you weren't tracking and gawking at animals. She hated safari. She found it boring after the first dozen or so sightings and shared my view about giving them some peace. It didn't help when later that evening two snakes entered the reception area whilst we were dining and caused some consternation. Lorraine's phobia is so deep she can hardly utter the word snake, so she locked herself in the toilets until I swore on my mother's life they'd been dealt with!

Although the accommodation was lightly fenced, we were warned that, occasionally, the wild animals would gain access, so if we wanted to go to the main reception area for meals, we had to call them up and they'd send an armed escort to make sure we'd arrive safely. We thought this was done to create a sense of truly being in the wild, but we heard from one of the rangers that a woman who'd ignored the instruction had her arm bitten by a lion in the same camp just a few months before!

I went on the night safari again and experienced a little too much wildlife. It's impossible to see much at night, even with the searchlight, but we'd located a lion and a lioness with some cubs and spent the usual 20 minutes ogling them. We set off back down the track, and within 100 yards we had a puncture! The guide is always armed, so he told us to get out of the Land Rover and to stand in front of the headlights, whilst he stood guard, rifle in hand. The driver had the unenviable task of replacing the wheel in almost pitch-darkness. Just then, we heard some elephants trumpeting and then the swishing sound of their trunks, unseen, but clearly not far away. I was so glad Lorraine was safely back at camp – she'd have been terrified. The guide put his finger to his lips to signify we should maintain silence.

The disturbing noise carried on past us amongst some trees – within a few feet I guessed – and we could see that even the guide was nervous. I was more concerned about the lions, but within about 20 minutes we were on our way back to camp, not exactly hanging about! The incident provided a good talking point over dinner!

After our three-day visit, we headed back to Durban, said our goodbyes to Errol and his family and then travelled onto Johannesburg for the flight back to London. This was a truly memorable trip around the world, experiencing so many different cultures and meeting such interesting people.

Each year since the world trip we've travelled extensively, mainly to the USA, except we spent Christmas 2006 visiting

Stephanie, Dave and the grandchildren in Australia. It seemed odd to tuck into roast turkey and all the trimmings in a beautiful hotel in Melbourne, whilst outside was sweltering in 35 degrees of heat! After Melbourne, a city we really liked with its Victorian facades and cosmopolitan shops, we stayed with Stephanie in their Army accommodation in Puckapunyal, and barbequed outside most days. We hadn't seen Kasia and Kai for a little while so it was rewarding to see them in their own environment. Although they appeared to us as "little Australians" with their accents and outdoor sports pursuits, they were still fiercely English, supporting England in the cricket Test matches being played whilst we were there!

In 2007 we travelled to Aspen, Colorado to meet up with Donna, Richard and some more of their friends before driving 2,000 miles through New Mexico, Arizona, Nevada and California taking in the wonderful sights of Sante Fe, Grand Canyon, Sedona and Las Vegas – again. We love this cowboy country, epitomised by such towns as Silvertown and Durango in Colorado and Williams in Arizona. The streets are almost exactly as they were in the 1850s and cowboy hats and boots are *de rigeur!*

In 2008 we went to Montreal in Canada and over the border to New Hampshire, Vermont and then to the Adirondaks in New York State to meet up with Donna and Richard and Paul and Lelia where they both have summer homes.

The Adirondaks comprises over six million acres of wonderfully scenic wooded mountains and waterfalls dripping into hundreds of glacial lakes. In summer, many thousands of Americans living in New York City, Philadelphia and Washington drive here to escape the stifling heat – the contrast couldn't be more apparent – the air is sweet and cool – and there's a rugged beauty everywhere you look. There are a staggering 3,000 lakes in total and over 200 miles of hiking trails used by beaver-hatted hunters as well as hikers. The summer homes are built as log cabins, referred to as "camps" and usually adorned with moose's heads and animal skins on the walls and draped over the furniture – there's something very "Davy Crockett" about the place.

The residents delight in explaining their latest sightings of a black bear – they even get quite excited about spotting bear poo close to their camp! I think it gives them a feeling for the pioneering days of hunting and shooting to survive and living an austere way of life. You can rarely get a mobile phone signal, and it's only recently they could receive a television signal! We enjoyed our visit but missed our creature comforts!

During 2008, we were missing the "little Australians" or the "KKs" as we referred to Kasia and Kai, although this was partly offset by the birth of Lewis, a son to Aaron and Jo. Lorraine came up with one of her inspired ideas.

"As much as I miss them, I don't really fancy flying all the way to Australia to see Stephanie, Dave and the KKs. We'd have to stay at least a month to make it worthwhile and I'd miss Lewis. Why don't we meet them halfway, say, somewhere like Los Angeles, and have a family holiday – you know – me, you and *all* the children and grandchildren? We could take a cruise down to the Mexican Riviera – that would be fun!"

"Have you any idea how much that would cost?" I spluttered.

"Come on! You've worked hard. You deserve it!"

As usual, she was right. I could see this would be a memorable trip and who knows what lay ahead in our lives.

It didn't quite work out the way we intended though. First, Aaron and Jo declined. They felt it might be too much hassle taking a one-year-old halfway round the world, which was a fair point. Then Max, who was decidedly up for it, lost his job, so felt he'd be better employed getting another. So, Lorraine and I left the UK on New Year's Eve 2008, bound for Los Angeles to meet up with the "Australians".

The KKs were unbelievably excited to see us and wouldn't stop hugging and kissing Grandma and Grandpa! We set off on the seven-night cruise to Mexico on January 3rd 2009. It was an unqualified success. They were exceptionally well behaved and polite and the cruise suited all of us. There was so much for everyone to do: kid's club for the KKs, entertainment, bars, quizzes and lectures for the adults – no one got bored or fed up with each other and the food, always important to 10 and 11-year-olds, was plentiful and delicious.

We took the kids for a day trip in one of the ports, Mazatalan, and embarked on a tour of the town and the beaches in an open, souped-up golf cart – great fun. They showed us how good they were at swimming and body-boarding in the sea – very impressive indeed!

After a tearful farewell, they went on to visit San Francisco, Grand Canyon and Las Vegas whilst we headed south to see Sharon and Mike in Fallbrook. Donna flew over to visit her son in San Diego and coincided her visit to meet up with us all – we've become such good friends. Unfortunately, Mike had recently had major surgery to remove a brain tumour, but was in good spirits by the time we left – I think he likes the quirkiness of our English accents!

Before catching the flight home from Los Angeles we visited some more friends. One was David Henley! An amazing twist of fate had brought us together. When we visited Lorraine's relatives in Auckland, New Zealand, in early 2007, we checked in to the Auckland Hilton, a superb hotel right on the waterfront.

"I'm sorry, Mr Henley, I have a note here that you and Mrs L Henley cancelled the booking," the receptionist said.

"Don't be silly. We've only just arrived. Why would I cancel?" I responded.

After checking the computer and having a discussion with the manager, she came back and said there'd been an error and checked us in. I thought no more of it until three weeks later, having spent a lazy, sun-soaked week in Fiji on our way back to the UK via Los Angeles, the same thing happened at the check-in desk at Nandi airport.

"I'm sorry, Mr Henley, I've already got you and Mrs L Henley checked in."

"Well, you can't possibly. Here are my cases and these are my tickets. There must be some mistake."

Once again, there was a delay whilst the young lady went behind the scenes to consult her manager. Twenty minutes later, she returned. "No, that's fine. We've sorted it out. Sorry for the delay," she said and handed back my tickets. I hadn't been in the lounge long when there was a tap on my shoulder.

"Are you David Henley?" I turned to see a smiling, smart, slim, grey-haired man, in his early 70s.

"Yes, I am."

"So am I," he said. "And this is my wife, Ludie Henley. We live in Newport Beach, California."

Given the circumstances of our respective travels, this was an amazing coincidence. David and Ludie had been visiting Papua, New Guinea where there was a political uprising resulting in them being unable to leave the island for three weeks. This is why they'd cancelled the Auckland Hilton Hotel booking and had only now been able to get to Fiji to catch the flight home to Los Angeles.

He seemed especially thrilled to meet his namesake and I soon learnt why.

"Do you know there's a David Henley Society in the US? There's even a bridge, a museum and a road named after David Henley in Knoxville, Tennessee," he glowed. He went on to explain that Colonel David Henley was George Washington's right-hand man at the time of the revolution against the British in the 1770s. He was the chief spymaster and head of Indian affairs, a very important role that led to Knoxville honouring him. David and I exchanged email addresses and promised to keep in touch.

About a month or so before leaving on our trip to Los Angeles to meet up with Stephanie and family, my namesake sent me an email saying that if ever we were in California, he'd love us to meet up. I hadn't told him about our trip – it seemed another coincidence.

So, after the cruise, we made our way to Newport Beach, an upscale ocean resort, complete with huge marinas and typical long stretches of beaches as far as one could see. They met us at our hotel and took us back to their home and their daughter's home before dining at the Newport Beach yacht club. We got on so well, especially Ludie and Lorraine, who didn't seem to stop talking from the time we met them at around two o'clock until we left the hotel bar at midnight. During the conversation, yet another coincidence revealed itself.

Lorraine was explaining that we'd met some other American friends we'd known for years on this trip, and casually mentioned that one was the ex-wife of a famous film and TV star, Harvey Korman.

"You don't meant Donna, do you?" Ludie exclaimed.

Lorraine was equally surprised. "You know Donna?"

"She was my best friend. Our kids grew up together. When she moved back east, we lost touch with each other. I haven't seen her for 25 years!"

Ludie just couldn't get over it. Lorraine was so excited, she called Donna when we got to the yacht club and handed over the mobile to Ludie – it was quite an emotional moment! Since then, they've emailed and promised to visit each other.

So much of my retirement time has been spent travelling and I don't regret a single minute. Lorraine often reminds me that our travels are usually remembered by the people we've met, many of whom we're proud to call close friends – it looks as if we've just made two more!

CHAPTER 25
Epilogue

This is the part of my story where the inevitable questions arise:
What would I have changed if I had my life all over again?
Do I have any regrets or disappointments?
Have I fulfilled all my dreams and aspirations?

A combination of the lucky dip into the gene pool and the nurturing of my parents who believed I was capable of achieving anything I wanted from life, set me up with a high level self-esteem. Added to this, my persistent, often obsessive nature, gave me the drive to achieve my goals.

My dad often quoted to me the following poem;
Good, Better, Best,
I will never rest,
Until my Good is Better
And my Better, Best.

The writer remains anonymous but I can't think of a better mantra. Unsurprisingly, it has been passed down to our grandchildren whom I hope will retain the legacy. I've been exceptionally fortunate, too, in being born when I was. I missed the two Great Wars which took so many lives. I wonder how I'd have coped if I was involved. Today the thought of having to kill someone in the line of duty is abhorrent, but in my youth, I believe I'd have just accepted it like many other young men.

My era was blessed with dramatic and exciting cultural, sexual, social and political change and increased prosperity generated by an explosion in property prices. This, despite a couple of recessions that knocked us all back a little.

What about the great musical revolution of the 1950s and 60s? From skiffle to the Beatles via rock 'n' roll – I still can't resist dancing to these nostalgic sounds! The "Swingin' 60s" was famous for its drug culture that somehow passed me by – I knew a few mates who indulged but I wasn't interested. It was so widespread that Jefferson Airplane, a rock group of the time, commented that if you could remember the 60s then you weren't really there!

The innovations and inventions in my lifetime make the Industrial Revolution look pedestrian. I still can't believe we had a man on the moon in 1969. The Internet, email and mobile phones have transformed our lives. We'd never thought it possible to be able to send a message to hundreds or thousands of people simultaneously via email, to see and to speak in real time to your relatives in Australia via the Internet or to call someone in the US via a satellite on your mobile. I'm still impressed by being able to place a card in a machine in a wall, press four digits and collect up to £250 in cash every day if you have the funds!

The science of extracting DNA (a blueprint of every living thing) from body tissue and putting into a readable form, first produced by Dr Alec Jeffries in 1986, has led to the odds of misidentification running into billions to one! As well as paternity issues, it has been used to convict murderers and rapists. Even 25-year-old crimes are now being solved – in some cases leading to correcting wrongful convictions. It's always been one of my fears – being convicted for a crime I didn't commit – I sometimes have nightmares about it. I follow these cases intently.

Although I'd prefer to be in control of my destiny, I believe in letting fate sometimes play its part. In one of my favourite movies, *Sliding Doors*, the heroin, played by Gwyneth Paltrow, has her fate decided by whether she enters a subway train, or whether the sliding doors prevent her boarding. One tiny event changed her life forever.

In my case, how would my life have changed had I been successful in the trial with Watford Football Club when I was 24 years old? If I'd been offered professional terms I'd certainly have signed on. I wasn't, so I redoubled my efforts to qualify as an accountant and to become a success in business.

I often wonder, too, how my life would have been different if I'd gone to university rather than straight to work having left school at 16. I'd never have met Ann, had my daughter, Stephanie or our grandchildren Kai and Kasia.

When Ann and I first got together, I was so young, just 17 when we began our affair, and was incredibly gauche and immature. The fact that she was nine years older than me, was already married and soon to be pregnant with Stephanie and lived the first four years of Stephanie's life with her parents, didn't give us a chance to really establish our relationship. I was determined to make things right, though, and for the best part of 20 years we had a good life together. But it wasn't enough. I regret the pain I caused her when I left.

"What ifs?" happen in every life. Writing this memoir has resulted in a complete and thorough appraisal from *today's* perspective and has led me to conclude that there are very few things I would change about my life. I also have very few regrets or disappointments.

The years 2000-2004 were my worst as far as my health was concerned — I call them my AF years. This is when the effects of atrial fibrillation were at their worst and had the greatest affect on my life.

I've learnt from hearing other people's life stories how incredibly important one's parents are. Our lives are crucially affected by the way they treat us in our formative years. I couldn't have chosen better. I now realise what an enormous amount of debt I owe my parents. They'd be immensely proud of me now even though I didn't make Prime Minister as my mother predicted!

I really regret that when I moved to Hampshire from St Albans, I didn't visit my widowed mother as much as I should and never told her how much I loved her. I recently read *For One More Day* by Mitch Albom which expresses my sentiments entirely. He writes about being able to spend just one more day with his mum after she'd died to say all the things he never said when she was alive — I wish I had that chance.

It will have become obvious to those of you who have stayed with my story this far, how important and vital sport has been and remains in my life. *A Life of Sport and The Sport of Life* is an apt description. Although I regret not having played any of my sports at a higher level, I am deeply grateful to have possessed an average ability which gave me so much pleasure. I still run two or three times a week and can't imagine a Saturday afternoon without watching some sport. Lorraine and I often watch two or three evening soccer matches a week in the season — thank goodness for Sky TV!

There is an extraordinary correlation between business and sport. You won't succeed at either without effort, commitment, and planning. You'll have realised by now that I'm a pretty competitive person, so I was driven to succeed in whatever I attempted. My parents' assertion about my blood group, B Positive, being an instruction for a successful life, was true. Added to this, my positive attitude has helped me through many difficult aspects of my life, not just in business and sports, but also in personal relationships, friendship and health. Also, the disciplines I learned in my early sporting career were exactly what I needed once I entered the business world. I also discovered a further correlation between physical fitness and mental capability. The fitter and stronger I became, the brighter and more confident I felt.

I was fortunate to go to grammar school, firstly in Merthyr in South Wales and then in St Albans in Hertfordshire. This was crucial to my education although I was slow to realise how important it was. So like most people, I regret not studying more. I now realise I made up any gaps by my sheer persistence and drive. A good example was taking my accountancy finals three times before qualifying!

I'm proud of what I achieved in my business career, particularly so for the young people I was able to help develop. All I did was to pass on the baton handed to me by my mentors. They acted as strategic signposts in my career, although it started with Ken Adams Morgan and D A Hopkins at my primary and grammar schools respectively. They shared my parents' vision and saw something in me nobody else saw. In the business world, men like Sid Docree, Dave Lucas, Gordon Harding, Bob Davidson, Terry Milton, Tony Axford, Dave Ruskin and particularly Steve Hayklan, who gave me my very first break at setting up a dealer group, were powerful influencers. They all shared, not just exceptional ability, but a sense of fair play and decency. I wanted to be like them.

Having sold my businesses in 2000 and 2004, I joined the grey-haired world of retirement. I dabbled in a couple of business ventures that didn't take too much time so that I could indulge in my passions of sports, gardening, travelling and lately, writing. When I first retired, I didn't like it. I missed the cut and thrust of business, the thrill of doing deals and pitting my wits against other businessmen. But now, I really appreciate what free time gives me – choice. And everything doesn't have to be done today – tomorrow will be fine.

"You can choose your friends but you can't choose your family!" is a hackneyed, even over-used statement but I wouldn't want to change either. My family isn't big and we don't see each other as much as we'd like, but it's my bedrock. My daughter, Stephanie, Lorraine's boys, Max and Aaron, Aaron's wife, Jo and grandchildren, Kai, Kasia and Lewis, together with Don, Lorraine's first husband and his wife and Lorraine's long-time girlfriend, Brenda, comprise the immediate family. My only other living relative is my cousin Pearl and that's it.

I had two memorable parties when I was 60 and 65. The first was a complete surprise. Lorraine insisted I mustn't arrive at the rugby club until after 8.00 pm on Saturday 2nd November 2002. I thought she may have organised a small party of the rugby guys and their wives but as I entered the clubhouse, a deafening roar went up from 150 family and friends! I was ushered down to the front of the hall in a state of shock. It was a *This is Your Life* evening organised by Lorraine and Rod Ellaway who'd visited my birthplace as part of his research! Alan Kingwell, clutching a huge red folder, acted superbly as MC and introduced many people I hadn't seen for years, many of them telling incriminating tales about me which I'd forgotten!

Some had sent videos from Australia, South Africa and the US. Lelia, resident of New Jersey, went a stage further and turned up in person! What a thrill. Rod produced a montage of old photos supplied by Lorraine and some of my friends from schooldays which he projected onto a huge screen behind me. It was exceptionally emotional, especially when Kai and Kasia, then aged four and five, scuttled in at the end of the evening. It was the most memorable night of my life and I have the red folder to remind me of it.

I didn't want to let my 65th pass ignominiously, so I organised an evening at the rugby club for 120 guests, many of them also attended my 60th. I researched a cabaret act and came up with a superb Elvis Presley impersonator who added in a bit of Tommy Cooper, my all-time favourite comedian. He was outstanding. He got me on stage to join him and the result was hilarious – I never could sing! I was so pleased that many guests said it was the best night we'd ever had at the club.

These two nights were unique in many ways. It's rare that anyone has the chance to share their emotions with *all* their friends and family simultaneously and to be able to tell them what they mean to you.

So what is my life like now? In a word, wonderful! I was once told the secret to happiness:

Love someone,
Have someone who loves you,
Enjoy good health,
And have something to look forward to.

I truly love Lorraine and I believe it's reciprocated — you'll have to ask her! Since the brilliant Professor Morgan's cardiac procedure in 2004, I couldn't feel fitter or stronger. And I've lots to look forward to.

I still get my business kicks by mentoring several local businessmen — something I really enjoy — it makes me feel useful! It's all part of passing on the baton, retaining the legacy. I've been fortunate to have encountered many business issues, especially during recessions, and I have an urge to pass on the lessons I learned.

My ideal winter weekend is watching Winchester or Wales winning the rugby on Saturday, Spurs winning the football on Sunday followed by one of Lorraine's superb roast dinners with Max, Aaron, Jo and baby Lewis. A phone call from Australia, hearing the excited and happy voices of Kai and Kasia would send me to bed entirely contented.

As I'm approaching 67 years old I feel the urgent need of the sun on my back during those drab winter months of January and February. So much so that I've now reached the tipping point, where the warmth of the sun outweighs watching rugby or soccer. I can't believe it, but I can't help it. So in the early months of winter you'll find Lorraine and I somewhere warm with blue skies and turquoise seas. If I can find a TV nearby showing a football or rugby match, it's a bonus!

Our summers are spent either working in the garden, my new passion, or sipping wine on the deck overlooking our lake. On dull or wet days, I've been writing these memoirs which I've thoroughly enjoyed. I'll have to think of something else to write about now – I've got the writing bug!

Have I fulfilled all my dreams and aspirations? I think you can guess my answer!